About King & Queen of the River...

From their birth in the Roaring Twenties, the *Delta King* and *Delta Queen* battled against the odds. As a legendary royal pair, these monarchs of the river ran each night between San Francisco and Sacramento from 1927 to 1940. This rousing true story captures the romance, struggle, and adventure of California's last and most revered paddle-wheel steamers.

The colorful, stirring account chronicles the boats' good and bad years. It takes you behind the scenes for the decision to build the vessels and offers firsthand reports on their launching at Stockton, California. The book then highlights the fun aboard these beloved sternwheelers against the backdrop of Prohibition, waterfront strikes, and the Great Depression. You'll taste the excitement of the last steamboat race in the Golden State, the opening of two of the country's greatest bridges, and a world's fair in the middle of San Francisco Bay.

When World War II ends the two boats' service on the Sacramento River, they join the U.S. Navy, serving on the Bay as hospital ferries, barracks, and troop shuttles. After the war, the twin vessels go their own separate ways. You'll experience the *Queen*'s 7309-mile epic voyage, via the Panama Canal, from the heart of California to the heartland of America—and her later all-out battle to continue passenger service on the Ohio and Mississippi.

You'll t........ of the *King* .... Columbia, ... piracy—and, finally, the boats g...... resurrection at the Old Sacramento waterfront. The book showcases the interesting people whose lives were touched by these celebrated riverboats and brings you detailed maps, schedules, deck plans, and nearly 150 eye-catching photographs, many never before seen in print.

The *Delta King* and *Delta Queen* began as river royalty in an era of bootleg booze, the Charleston, and stock market euphoria. Today, they exist as the sole survivors of a once-proud American tradition, the "night boat." They were also the last steamboats to carry passengers and freight on California waters. This engaging book—covering the vessels' 75 action-packed years—brings you their travels, troubles, and triumphs in a fast, page-turning experience.

You'll find *King & Queen of the River* as captivating and nostalgic as the sound of a steamboat whistle. Fun to read and meticulously researched, it's a fascinating adventure story that also happens to be true.

About the author: Upon taking early retirement from *Sunset Magazine* almost two decades ago, California-born author Stan Garvey went full-time researching the history of the famed *Delta* twins. After searching countless archives, reviewing hundreds of photos, and interviewing former crew members and scores of passengers from the boats' vintage years, he spent four years writing the book. It's the definitive work on the *Delta King* and *Delta Queen*.

KING & QUEEN

of the River

The legendary paddle-wheel
steamboats Delta King
and Delta Queen

STAN GARVEY

**River
Heritage
Press**

P.O.BOX 7441,
MENLO PARK, CA 94026

This edition salutes two boats still making
river history after more than 75 years.

No part of this book may be reproduced in any form without written permission from the publisher, except by a reviewer, who may quote brief portions in a review. Manufactured in the United States of America. Published by River Heritage Press, P.O. Box 7441, Menlo Park, CA 94026-7441. This book is available for gifts, premiums, prizes, or fund-raising at a substantial discount in bulk quantities; for information, contact the publisher.

To order single copies by credit card, call 1 (800) 852-4890.

Publisher's Cataloging in Publication

Garvey, Stan.
    King & queen of the river : the legendary paddle-wheel steamboats Delta King and Delta Queen / Stan Garvey.
    p. cm.
    Includes bibliographical references and index.
    "This edition salutes two boats that have been making river history for more than 75 years."
    LCCN: 2004092735
    ISBN: 0-9642513-5-3

    1. Delta King (Steamboat) 2. Delta Queen (Steamboat)
3. Paddle steamers—United States—History.   I. Title.
II. Title: King and queen of the river

VM461.5.D397G37 2004   386'.32'09794

Cover and book design: Bill Cheney
Editing of text: Sam Connery
Front cover photo: Bill Stritzel collection
Back photo: Sacramento Archives & Museum
Author photo: Mike Russell, San Mateo Times

9 8 7 6 5 4   Fourth printing, revised edition
                Softcover, published June 2004

This book is dedicated to my sister,
Betty Garvey McFerren, whose love affair
with the two legendary steamboats
spans more than half a century . . .
and to those steadfast crew members
who, over the years, faithfully stayed
the course, doing their best to keep
the boats and the tradition alive.

Foreword

The passengers who board the *Delta Queen* for a cruise on the Mississippi or the Ohio and guests who check into the *Delta King* in its role as a hotel in Sacramento can hardly fail to recognize they are entering something historic. Probably few of them, however, recognize what the ships are: the only survivors of what was once an important American institution, the night boat. On Long Island Sound, the Hudson River, Chesapeake Bay, Lake Erie and the California rivers, overnight steamers were an important part of the American transportation system. They typically ran between cities 100 to 200 miles apart, with dinnertime departures and early-morning arrivals. Unless the trip was very short, late-evening departures were avoided because one of the things the operators had to sell—and they did not include it in the ticket price—was a leisurely dinner as the scenery passed by. The trip in a berth on a night boat was typically more comfortable than on a Pullman car, especially because over the short distances the night boats covered, a Pullman usually had to be set out in a yard or spotted at a station for several hours. The noise level around a railroad is high, and the effort to sleep was anything but a relaxing experience.

The night lines scheduled their early arrivals mainly to assure first-morning delivery of their freight. Over the distances they ran, they could equal rail freight speeds, and provide much greater assurance of arrival times. All of this, however, made them easy prey to highway transport. With the spread of hard-surfaced highways in the 1920s, automobiles could cover their routes in a few hours, and trucks could match their assurances of overnight delivery of freight. The night boats were probably a declining industry by 1915, when the LaFollette Seamen's Act hit them with requirements for excessive crews. The most important lines survived the Great Depression, but were badly damaged simultaneously by the stiffening of fireproofing requirements after the *Morro Castle* disaster of 1934 and the spread of unionization after the Wagner Act of 1935. From 1937 to America's entry into World War II, most of the major night lines perished—the Fall River Line, the Cleveland & Buffalo Transit Company, the Hudson River Night Line, and the operation at hand, River Lines. A few companies, notably the Detroit & Cleveland

Navigation Company, made it through the war, but with the end of the Old Bay Line between Baltimore and Norfolk in 1961, the night boat was an extinct institution. Except for the *Delta King* and *Delta Queen*, not a single one of the night boats survived in other services or as a museum piece.

Fortunately, Stan Garvey undertook this project while it was still possible to interview those who rode the two steamers and those who worked on them. The first part of this book is probably the best existing re-creation of life and labor on the night boats. The rest is an account of the highly disparate ways the two vessels survived. I had always presumed the *Delta Queen* was chosen to go on to fame and profit because she was in better condition, but Garvey shows the choice could easily have gone the other way—and nearly did. Indeed, if the Greene Line had anticipated how successful the *Delta Queen* would be, I suspect it would have bought both steamers.

The *Delta King* has been brought back from derelict status, and the *Delta Queen* has survived the efforts to revoke her certificate because of her wooden superstructure, but it would be hasty to conclude that the old steamers will survive indefinitely. It is costly to maintain a vessel as a static facility, and it is not in the nature of ships of any sort to go on forever. We would be well advised to experience both these steamboats while we can.

George W. Hilton

Contents

Introduction

A decade ago, when I began bringing together the pieces for this book, my first reaction was surprise that no one had written the saga of the two sternwheelers before. The story had action, drama, suspense, and even a little comedy—with countless mishaps and near-disasters along the way. But it was also significant history. For here was the story of the world's most famous steamboat, the *Delta Queen,* and her paddle-wheel twin, the *Delta King*—a riverboat that has survived fire, a Canadian landlocking, two sinkings, and a midnight piracy.

Starting in the 1920s, with threads going back to the gold rush, *King & Queen of the River* chronicles the final episode in overnight passenger and freight service on California waters. But the story doesn't stop there. When that phase ended a year before Pearl Harbor, a new experience awaited in the Navy years. Following that interlude, the two boats went their separate ways into the postwar world—each on its own journey of vastly different adventures. The drama has progressed through five decades since World War II and continues today; it is not done yet. Geographically, the action began in California and shifted to other locales, including British Columbia and the Mississippi and Ohio rivers. Appropriately, one of the boats returned to the Golden State.

During their service years in California, the steamers operated in a curious and unique pattern of summer weather, unlike that experienced by any other night boat in the country. Differences in daytime high temperatures between the two destinations were often extreme. If fog blanketed San Francisco, keeping its temperature in the low fifties, while inland at Sacramento thermometers were registering over one hundred, a fifty-degree differential existed between the two cities. Thus you could go aboard at Sacramento where asphalt on city streets was so hot it crackled under automobile tires—and you could wake up the next morning in San Francisco to the sounds of foghorns and water dripping from the boat's railing on the outer deck.

At times in my research, I felt like a detective as I tracked the paths of the two vessels, running into many a blind alley but finding enough breakthroughs to make the effort worthwhile. My research sent me on such interesting and diverse pursuits as seeking out the grave of would-be movie star Dorothy Millette in Sacramento (Chapter 3), scanning the December 1941 passenger list of the S.S. *President Coolidge* for names of Pearl Harbor wounded (Chapter 9), and cruising the Mississippi while listening intently to conversations in the *Delta Queen*'s pilothouse, back in the days when passengers were permitted there (Chapter 20).

At other times, I felt as an archeologist might have felt discovering King Tut's tomb. Although I first became an ardent admirer of the two sternwheelers in the 1950s, I hadn't seen them—both boats had already left California, my home state. Finally, in 1962, I got a close-up look at the *Delta King* and in 1972 took my first cruise on the *Delta Queen*. In more recent times, I spent a great deal of time aboard the *King* during the restoration years at Sacramento and also had the good fortune to take two more trips on the *Queen*.

Adding immeasurably to that feeling of discovery, I found and interviewed former crew members who had worked on the two riverboats on the San Francisco-Sacramento run. I also talked to men who helped build the vessels at Stockton in the 1920s. As far as I know, not one of the stories I collected from these men or the crew has ever seen print before.

In searching for passenger anecdotes to include, I received many happy surprises. But, occasionally, I experienced disappointment when a good story would fall through. For example, I was touched by one woman's recollections about overnight trips she had taken as a small girl on the *King* and *Queen*—how each time the steamer blew its whistle for a drawbridge to open, she would run out on deck in her nightie—how the red and green lights on the bridges reminded her of Christmas trees. Later, however, she remembered that those trips had taken place a few years earlier than she originally thought, before the time of the *King* and *Queen*. Therefore, she had traveled on other craft. It was a captivating story but one for another book and another time.

In a sense, Mark Twain is responsible for the book in your hands. It was my reading of Twain, when I was a boy, that kindled a lifelong fascination with rivers and steamboats. Over the years since then, I collected many photos, clippings, and books having to do with riverboat history, particularly the heritage of California's inland waters. And that, in turn, led to this book.

A personal regret comes from the realization that, while I was born in California and theoretically—as a child in the 1930s—could have traveled on the *Delta King* and *Queen*, I didn't have that pleasure. In fact, I didn't even know they existed until I was a young adult. Unfortunately, that was long after the two paddlewheelers had ceased to operate as a pair between San Francisco and Sacramento. Thus, for this book, I depend on the stories and impressions of others in drawing a picture of those early, unpretentious years of the *King* and *Queen*. Fortunately, I've found former passengers and crew members who have been most helpful and generous in sharing their time and memories.

Many years after the two steamers had retired from commercial service on the Sacramento River and San Francisco Bay, former crew member James E. Riemers praised them as being the very finest. Then he added what might at first seem a cryptic comment but in reality provides a thoughtful view of the boats in their California days. He said, "The *Delta King* and *Delta Queen* were ahead of their time—but too late."

> Stan Garvey
> March 1995

This new revised edition brings the story of the *King* and *Queen* up-to-date, taking it to the end of the century. I suspect that, back in the 1920s and 30s, few maritime observers would have guessed that these boats would survive to see the close of the millennium. But survive, they did—and we're the richer for it. Personally, I'm looking forward to enjoying their charms for years to come.

> S. G.
> April 1999

On the eve of 2002, the 75th anniversary year for the *King* and *Queen,* I'm pleased to offer this new edition that honors these boats and their remarkable lives since their maiden voyages in 1927. After years of admiring them, researching their history, and writing their life stories, I feel a link with the vessels. Also a personal connection: I was born in California the same year they began their nightly service in the Golden State. Now, celebrating their 75 adventurous years, I say: Hurray for the *Delta King* and *Delta Queen,* those irrepressible crown jewels of the river!

> S. G.
> October 2001

Note: The current printing (2004) is an updated version of the 75th Anniversary Edition.

PROLOGUE

A Paddle–Wheel Heritage

Before the California Gold Rush, the Sacramento River flowed clear and pristine from its headwaters near Mount Shasta down the Sacramento Valley and into San Francisco Bay. Known only to American Indians and a few trappers and exploring mariners, the river teemed with fish and wildlife.

Capt. C.A.M. Taber, sailing his vessel from the bay to Sacramento in 1848, described what he saw:

> The sloughs of the main stream were alive with several species of wild ducks. And the wooded banks of the river, as well as the tules [large bul-rushes], were winter home for large bands of deer and elk. Grizzly bears were often seen foraging for acorns in the oak groves near the river.

Three decades later, conservationist John Muir remarked that the forests along the river reminded him of tropical jungles. For many years, the Sacramento retained much of its primitive beauty. By the turn of the century, however, most of the marshland along the lower river had become farmland protected by levees. Yet the Sacramento still had a Huck Finn quality about it. Along its banks stood great cottonwoods, willows, oaks, and sycamores; wild grape and blackberry vines hung to the water's edge.

When steamboats first began plying the river in Gold Rush days, the lush shoreside growth and the clear, moving water presented a striking vista to passengers and crew. But aesthetics had little to do with the emergence and rapid growth of this kind of water travel. The Sacramento and other rivers of the Central Valley simply offered potential avenues of commerce. At a time of mushrooming demand for transportation, riverboats supplied the ready answer.

Few people today, even the California-born, are aware of the large and important part played by river steamers in the state's history. Records show at least 281 of these vessels—sternwheelers and sidewheelers—plied the inland waters of California. The period stretched over a century from the state's first steamboat, just before the discovery of gold in 1848, to the end of the paddle-wheel era in the middle of the 20th century.

The early boats provided transportation to the Forty-Niners on the first leg of their journey from San Francisco to the goldfields. Later on, as the Gold Rush began to fade, riverboats became a lifeline in trade between San Francisco Bay and Sacramento, Stockton, and other valley towns. Going upriver, these boats carried farm implements and fuel, building materials and mining equipment, all the needs of a growing rural economy. On the return trip, they hauled fresh produce and processed foods, grains, and other farm commodities.

Because land transportation was spotty or nonexistent for many years, the passenger trade also continued as an important part of steamboat business. As late as 1869, rail passengers arriving at Sacramento on the new transcontinental railroad had to transfer to river steamers to get to San Francisco, more than a hundred miles away.

Where Did the Boats Come From?

During the Gold Rush, three sources accounted for the presence of riverboats in California.

Some of the larger vessels—former coastwise steamships with side wheels—came under their own power from the East Coast, around South America and to the Pacific and San Francisco. The risk was great. But the money that could be made tempted daredevil captains. So on they came—and many of them made it. Two examples: the *Antelope* and *New World*.

Smaller boats like the *Sitka,* unable to take to the sea, arrived dismantled in the holds or on the decks of sailing vessels. Soon a third source developed, when local shipyards began building steamboats; a prime example was the *Chrysopolis,* built in San Francisco.

Most California-built riverboats had only one smokestack instead of two, as was more common east of the Rockies. And, in later years, they were built with stern wheels rather than side wheels.

When riverboating was at its peak and river level permitted, paddlewheelers traveled 395 river miles from San Francisco to Red Bluff on the Sacramento and 399 river miles from San Francisco to Sycamore Point, near Fresno on the San Joaquin. In winter and spring, steamboats could navigate 600 miles north and south in the heart of California without ever touching salt water. In spite of their slow pace, 3 to 10 miles per hour, they covered substantial distances.

In its early days, steamboating in California had its dark side. In his book, *Paddle-Wheel Days in California,* Jerry MacMullen says:

> It was a wild, dizzy, hell-roaring period, marked by a carefree disregard of danger. . . . A river captain, in many cases, owned his own vessel and ran it until it wore out, caught fire, rammed another or got rammed by it, blew up, or was snagged. With the shoestring independents, anything approaching a normal repair schedule was unheard of.

Yet, typically, the boats were advertised as "the finest steamer on the river . . . just completely overhauled and absolutely safe." Riverboats crowded waterfront space at Sacramento so tightly they often had to dock upstream or downstream from their intended landing. Competition brought price cutting. Passenger fares between San Francisco and Sacramento dropped to a dollar, then to fifty cents, then—briefly in the 1850s—to only a dime.

Despite the rough and tumble competition, the era possessed a certain charm. MacMullen describes it this way:

> By day and by night those steamers made the run from the broad expanse of San Francisco Bay, through narrow Carquinez [Strait], and on past the myriad islands of the [Sacramento-San Joaquin] Delta . . . to where the rivers wind away from the sea, back toward the distant hills. Dazzling summer sun picked out their white paintwork and silhouetted them, cameo-clear, against the willows and cottonwoods which lined the banks, the varying shades of green accented by dark blobs of mistletoe clinging to the branches above the slowly moving stream. Then cabin and pilot-house windows were dropped, giving to crews and passengers the luxury of a breeze as they watched the heat waves shimmering above the broad, yellow stretches of valley land.
>
> Later would come the rains of winter, when the steamers struggled valiantly against the surge of high water from the mountains and canyons sweeping irresistibly on to the sea. And there were days and nights of fog—a foggy night with a full moon was the worst—when the

pilots had to guess just when they were opposite the cottonwood with a branch broken off on its west side that lined up with a little ruined adobe house, at the precise moment for giving her three spokes of the wheel for the next turn.

MacMullen tells about the great diversity of people encountered on board these boats in the 19th century—"prospectors, Chinese, empire-builders, gunmen, tinhorns and trollops; rural blades bound for the delights of the City, Kanakas [Hawaiians], bindle stiffs, merchants, bankers, Filipino farmhands; turbaned Hindus on their way to the rice fields . . ." He continues:

> With their growing pains out of the way, the riverboats provided dependable transportation at attractive rates, both for business purposes and for the relaxation of the jaded and weary. They catered to an age when people had time to live—time to stand in the lee of the texas [top deck of a steamboat] on a sparkling winter night and watch the stars, so bright they seemed to rest just above the murky skeleton of the hogging frame and the crown of the tall smokestack, and there was no sound but the soft chunking of paddle wheels . . . And it was remarkable how even that slight sound would carry across the water on a still night . . .
>
> And there were nights when the moon would come, huge and golden, up from behind distant mountains, lighting up the fields and throwing inky-black shadows from the trees along the banks—a twinkling light in a farmhouse window, level with the deck on which you stood; cattle standing motionless in the fields; the low squawk of some night bird . . .

Steamboating in California began inauspiciously in the summer of 1847 when a Russian sailing vessel arrived on San Francisco Bay and unloaded the *Sitka*, a small disassembled paddlewheeler from Alaska. The little steamer, only 37 feet long and nine feet wide, was reassembled and delivered to its new owner, William A. Leidesdorff, who had bought it from the Russian-American Fur Company. In late November, after using the vessel on the bay, he decided to attempt a voyage of more than a hundred miles upriver to Sacramento. The *Sitka* made it, but it took her six days and seven hours, perhaps setting some kind of dubious speed record for steamboats.

Less than two months later, in January 1848, James Marshall discovered gold on the American River in the foothills east of Sacramento. That discovery set off

The Chrysopolis, *finest of California's riverboats in the 19th century, won the hearts of many a passenger and crew member. Converted into a double-ender ferryboat named the* Oakland *in 1875, this relic of the past provided ferry service on San Francisco Bay until 1940.*

Boats Before the King and Queen

Throughout the riverboat period, California had a number of steamers famous in their time. Here are a few:

CHRYSOPOLIS: In the 19th century, probably the most well known and popular steamboat was the *Chrysopolis*. Built in 1860 in San Francisco, this sleek, fast side-wheeler was almost as long as the *Delta King* and *Delta Queen* (to be built in the following century) but much narrower. In 1861 the *Chrysopolis* set a record for steamboats that still stands, traveling from Sacramento to San Francisco in 5 hours and 19 minutes—a speed of almost 23 miles an hour. For comparison, the *King* and *Queen* took 11 hours for the same trip, traveling about 10 to 11 miles per hour (speed was not emphasized with the two *Delta* boats).

Nothing was spared in constructing the *Chrysopolis,* the epitome of Victorian elegance. The finest materials and work-manship went into building what river historian Richard E. Brown calls "the Sacramento River's luxury liner of 1860, comparable to what the *Delta King* and

Delta Queen would be in the next century." Oddly enough, in later years the three boats shared a relationship. At the end of her river career, the *Chrysopolis* was converted into a San Francisco Bay ferry and renamed the *Oakland*. Brown notes that, "In her role as ferryboat, the *Oakland* often 'rubbed noses' with the *King* and *Queen* on the San Francisco waterfront—luxury vessels of different eras crossing each other's wakes."

ANTELOPE: The *Antelope,* another speedy sidewheeler of the early era, made a name for herself in several ways. Built on the East Coast in 1847, she operated as a Long Island excursion steamer until 1850, when she braved the trip around South America to get to the lucrative Gold Rush trade. Because she carried gold dust and bullion from Sacramento to San Francisco for Wells Fargo, the *Antelope* became known as the "Gold Boat." She was also called the "Lucky Boat," since she never experienced any fires or explosions. The *Antelope*'s most famous moment came in 1860, when she carried the first Pony

Express mail between San Francisco and Sacramento.

NEW WORLD: Another fast steamer of that period, the *New World* was pirated from the East Coast immediately after her launching in 1850. Because of unpaid bills from construction of the boat, creditors attached the sidewheeler and sent deputies aboard at its New York dock. On a ruse, Capt. Ned Wakeman sneaked the boat out and headed for the open sea, leaving the lawmen on a nearby mudflat. Three months later, after an adventurous trip around South America, the *New World* arrived in San Francisco.

LATER BOATS: With the exception of the *Chrysopolis* (remodeled as a ferryboat), the above steamers were gone by the time of the *Delta King* and *Queen.* But a few riverboats of another generation still operated alongside the *King* and *Queen* in the 1920s and 1930s. Some ran from San Francisco to Sacramento, while others ran the Stockton route. About half were built in the 19th century, half in the early years of the 20th century. Although they all performed important duties, some may be remembered best for roles other than their workaday jobs. For example:

MOVIE STARS: Starring with Will Rogers in the 1935 movie *Steamboat Round the Bend*, six California riverboats distinguished themselves disguised as Mississippi River steamers. They included the *Leader, Port of Stockton* (ex-*Capital City*), *T.C. Walker, Pride of the River, Capt. Weber,* and *Cherokee.*

LANDLOCKED: Four steamboats earned a place in history by ending their careers high and dry in the Delta. The *J.D. Peters, Reform, Onisbo,* and *Navajo* teamed up to save Mandeville Island after a levee break in 1938. They were floated in to block the opening in the broken levee.

Then the *J.D. Peters,* the only one still with power, was fired up and pushed the water off the submerged island with her paddle wheel. The four ended up land-locked as bunkhouses for farmhands. Two other sternwheelers, the *Isleton* and the *Dauntless,* had the unique distinction in the 1930s of being converted from steam to diesel power and from paddle wheel to twin-screw propulsion.

PADDLE-WHEEL PAIRING: The *King* and *Queen* were not the first steamboats on the San Francisco-Sacramento run to work in pairs. Richard E. Brown points out two early running mates: the *Chrysopolis* and the *Yosemite* (built in 1860 and 1862 respectively). He also cites the *Apache* paired with the *Modoc* (both built 1880), *Pride of the River* (1878) with the *Isleton* (1902), and the *Navajo* (1909) with the *Seminole* (1911). Next came the two vessels described below.

NOTED PREDECESSORS: An important place in history must be reserved for the California Transportation Company steamers that preceded the *Delta King* and *Queen* on their run: the *Capital City* (1910) and the *Fort Sutter* (1912). Although not quite as large or luxurious as the *Deltas*, these vessels did offer the latest amenities, including hot and cold running water in every stateroom. Probably their biggest claim to fame is the precedent they set for the *King* and *Queen.* Their excellent "bloodlines" were passed along to the new boats, influencing design.

After being replaced on the Sacramento in 1927, the *Fort Sutter* and *Capital City* (renamed the *Port of Stockton*) moved to the San Joaquin River for the San Francisco-Stockton run. Later these sternwheelers served as back-up vessels for the *Delta* boats.

a chain of events that would affect the lives of hundreds of thousands of people, change the face of California, and provide the basis for a robust riverboat trade. By late spring of 1849 San Francisco lay nearly deserted. Gold fever had struck en masse.

Most of those who left the bay started their journeys to the gold fields on some kind of water transportation. But while the earliest trips were made on vessels powered by wind, not steam, it wasn't long until the first regularly-scheduled steamboat run from San Francisco to Sacramento was established. That honor came to the sidewheeler *Sacramento* in September 1849. One year later, California came into the Union as the 31st state. By the end of 1850, twenty-eight steamers cruised the Sacramento and Feather rivers. Other rivers also became waterways of commerce—the San Joaquin, American, Tuolumne, Mokelumne, and Stanislaus.

Steamboating continued to grow in the decades following the discovery of gold. Many transportation companies formed—some large, some small. One of the smaller ones, which later would become a leading name in the business, got its start in the 1850s when Captains Nels Anderson and Andrew Nelson began handling freight on the river. Two decades later, in 1875, the partners incorporated as the California Transportation Company. The C.T. Co. would come to play a key role in river commerce, operating one of the more prominent and long-serving fleets of river steamers.

Management of the company eventually passed to Anderson's son, Alfred E. Anderson (known as A.E. Anderson, often called Capt. Anderson). As company president, he became a major presence on the river. He expanded his firm's passenger and freight operations to include service between San Francisco, Stockton, and Sacramento. Later, in the 1920s, he would become the guiding force behind the building of the luxury steamers *Delta King* and *Delta Queen*.

Anderson faced an early challenge from the grim legacy left by hydraulic mining. Beginning soon after the discovery of gold and continuing for thirty years, this type of mining devastated the California foothills and caused floods in the valley. Miners used powerful jets of water to blast away soil and gravel, destroying entire hillsides. Mud and debris washed down the tributaries into the Sacramento River, making its streambed rise. This not only created flooding but added to the woes of steamboat navigation. The river shoaled—it was transformed from a clear, deep waterway into a shallow, muddy stream. Although hydraulic mining was virtually outlawed in the 1880s, navigation remained difficult and river commerce declined. Railroad competition for the freight dollar just made matters worse.

Capital City *and* Fort Sutter *developed the San Francisco-Sacramento passenger traffic inherited by* Delta King *and* Delta Queen. *While the older vessels were first to display certain design features later used on the more glamorous Delta boats, these pass-along features did not include wooden hulls, the exterior structural bracing, or open paddle wheels pictured here.*

Early in the 20th century, at a low point for inland water transportation in California, A.E. Anderson organized a successful movement to restore the river. He made numerous trips to Washington, D.C., and to the state capital to lobby for navigational improvements, which included dredging, placing wing dams, and creating new channels. As a result, Anderson became the most respected figure in California river transportation; his reputation grew as a man of integrity and action.

At a 1914 get-together on Sherman Island in the Delta, the river community honored Anderson for his hard work, persistence, and leadership in getting the state legislature and Congress to fund the project. Those attending the gathering proclaimed him "King of the River."

Perhaps that honorary, royal title explains the choice of names for the company's two new sternwheelers a decade later. In any case, by the early 1920s, Capt. Anderson would be confronted with the major decision of his life. At a time when many people thought river transportation was on the decline, he would decide to put his company's financial resources on the line to construct two of the biggest, fanciest, and most costly riverboats ever built—the *Delta King* and *Delta Queen*.

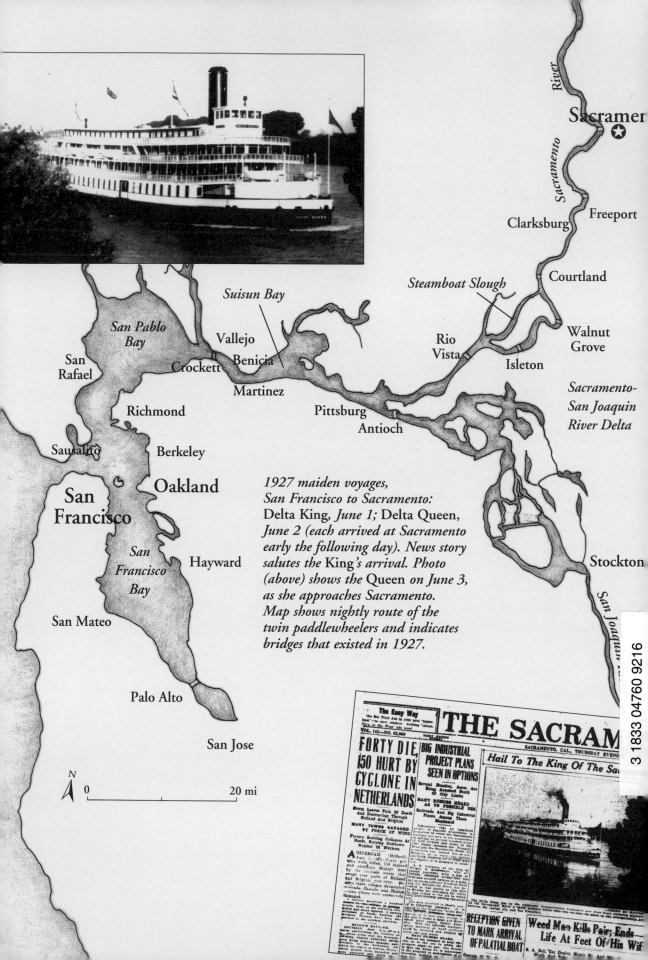

Sacramen[to]

River

Sacramento

Clarksburg
Freeport

Steamboat Slough
Courtland

Suisun Bay

Vallejo
Benicia
Crockett

Rio
Vista
Walnut
Grove

San Pablo
Bay

San
Rafael

Martinez

Isleton

Sacramento-
San Joaquin
River Delta

Richmond

Pittsburg
Antioch

Sausalito

Berkeley

Oakland

San
Francisco

1927 maiden voyages,
San Francisco to Sacramento:
Delta King, *June 1;* Delta Queen,
*June 2 (each arrived at Sacramento
early the following day). News story
salutes the* King's *arrival. Photo
(above) shows the* Queen *on June 3,
as she approaches Sacramento.
Map shows nightly route of the
twin paddlewheelers and indicates
bridges that existed in 1927.*

San
Francisco
Bay

Hayward

Stockton

San Joaquin

San Mateo

Palo Alto

San Jose

N   0   20 mi

The Easy Way

THE SACRAM[ENTO]

VOL. 141—NO. 22,969   SACRAMENTO, CAL, THURSDAY EVEN[ING]

**FORTY DIE,
150 HURT BY
CYCLONE IN
NETHERLANDS**

**BIG INDUSTRIAL
PROJECT PLANS
SEEN IN OPTIONS**

Hail To The King Of The Sa[cramento]

**RECEPTION GIVEN
TO MARK ARRIVAL
OF PALATIAL BOAT**

**Weed Man Kills Pair; Ends
Life At Feet Of His Wif[e]**

1

Sacramento, Here We Come!

San Francisco, Wednesday, June 1, 1927: Today, history is being made. It's the beginning of two memorable days and nights that will earn a permanent place in the colorful lore of American steamboating. Let's imagine you're there to witness the first of two historic maiden voyages.

Like many San Francisco days in the late spring, June 1 dawns with coastal fog shrouding the hills and bay. By afternoon, the skies clear. The weather forecast of "fair and mild with moderate westerly winds" promises what appears to be just another typical day for the city by the Golden Gate. But by early evening, a grand adventure will have begun.

Two new riverboats, the finest ever built, lie on the waterfront awaiting their inaugural trips to Sacramento. They're identical twins—the *Delta King* and the *Delta Queen*. Once entered into service, they'll alternate in their nightly runs between the two cities. The *King* will go first, leaving the dock at 6:30 this evening. Tomorrow night, the *Queen* departs, completing the debut of the royal pair.

It's now late afternoon. The *King* sits on the south side of Pier 3, near the Ferry Building, bow nosed up to the head of the slip. At wharf level on the starboard side, dockworkers are loading cargo for Sacramento onto the freight deck.

With baggage in hand, you've just made your way along the busy waterfront to Pier 3, the passenger and freight terminal of The California Transportation Company. You enter the big front door. Immediately, you feel excitement and anticipation in the air. An electric energy is coming not only

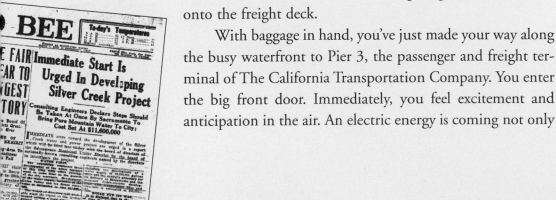

from those inside the building but also from the crowd gathering on the pier next to the bow of the *Delta King.*

After a short wait in line, you get to the ticket window and buy tickets, reserve a stateroom, and check your bags. You take a seat in the large waiting room and listen for the call to board. An hour before departure, passengers will leave the building through a side door and climb the gangplank to the Saloon Deck, which is the first passenger deck. It's just above where the freight is being stowed.

At last, the purser's call rings out. You're caught in a rush of passengers, eager for their initial close-up view. Your first impression of the new steamboat is its great size. Stretching out alongside Pier 3 almost as long as a football field, the boat stands four decks high. Name boards on the front and sides of the towering pilot-house proclaim "Delta King."

As you start up the gangplank on the *King*'s port side, you become aware of the vessel's tongue-and-groove siding painted a glossy white, the colorful stained-glass panels above the windows, and the rich dark wood of the deck railing, window trims, outside benches and doors. When you reach the top, elbow to elbow with other smartly-dressed passengers, you catch your reflection in the plate-glass windows and polished brass.

Once on board you hesitate, tempted to stop on the outer deck for a moment and join a high-spirited group calling and waving to friends and family on the dock below. It's like a gala party. Yet you're eager to explore the inside.

Curiosity wins out. You walk through the double doors and enter the lobby. Here is a further taste of the festive atmosphere aboard the *Delta King*, as officers, crew, and wide-eyed passengers prepare to depart on the boat's first trip from San Francisco to Sacramento.

The grand staircase—with its ornate bronze filigree and its large, curving Honduran-mahogany handrails flaring out into the lobby—seems to beckon you to the deck above. This elegant centerpiece, identical on both the *King* and *Queen*, years later would inspire these words of praise: "The lady passengers could really peacock down that staircase in their evening dresses for the Captain's dinner."*

Turning away from the grand staircase, you notice the Old English oak paneling with its rich mahogany trim, the graceful wicker chairs, the gleaming brass chandeliers. The scents of fresh paint, varnish, new upholstery, and Oregon cedar intermingle—everything smells new.

* Tom Greene in *The Saga of the Delta Queen* by Frederick Way, Jr.

As you face the stern, to the right is the purser's office, where you stop to pick up a stateroom key. Across the lobby, a counter offers candy, tobacco, and magazines for a nickel or a dime; next to it is the barber shop. Behind the lobby, a spacious dining room displays fresh flowers on linen-covered tables and mahogany chairs with seats upholstered in soft brown morocco leather. Big windows, port and starboard, assure passengers a full view of the bay or river while dining.

Walking aft through the dining room and into the social hall near the stern, you're attracted by the richness of the hall's furnishings: comfortable overstuffed leather chairs, a grand piano and—overhead—two large curved skylights of stained glass. Under the skylights, imported tapestries grace the walls. A friendly crewman in trim navy-blue uniform and white cap tells you that upholstery, drapes, and tapestries are all the personal selection of A.E. Anderson, president and majority stockholder of The California Transportation Company.

In addition to staterooms that open off the social hall, the boat has passenger cabins on the next two levels above, the Observation and Texas decks. Heading toward your stateroom, you climb the stairs to the Observation Deck, sometimes called the Boat Deck. Your room, priced at $4, is one of the more expensive. Located near the stern, it has twin beds and a private bath floored with small white hexagonal tiles. The choices offered had included double, single, twin beds, or double berths in cabins with or without private bath. Prices ranged from $1 to $5. Fare and accommodations were sold separately, thus allowing passengers to buy a ticket for the trip without paying for a cabin (they could sleep on a bench or chair). Fare was $1.80 one way, $3 round trip. You bought round trip.

Suddenly, you're aware of a low-pitched moan that builds until it seems to vibrate the very deck you're standing on—the *Delta King*'s steam whistle is announcing the maiden voyage about to begin. You rush for the outer deck to catch the activity and excitement of departure.

A gentle sloshing noise comes from the paddle wheel, already turning under its spray cover. Capt. George Goodell shouts commands through a megaphone to his deckhands, as they retrieve the mooring lines. Within seconds, the *King* begins to move astern and away from the dock. Shortly, the boat clears the end of the pier.

With a hard turn of the rudders, the huge vessel swings around until its bow points north. For a moment, the *Delta King* rocks gently on the bay. Up in the pilothouse, Capt. Goodell signals the engine room "slow ahead," and the paddle wheel begins to push the vessel forward, ever so slowly at first, then faster. A cheer rings out from passengers lining the outer decks. You're on your way to

Sacramento, more than a hundred miles inland and a memorable night's journey away.

Walking to the stern, you see the rolling wake of the paddle wheel. Out beyond the wake, the Ferry Building, Pier 3, and the San Francisco skyline are receding in the distance. To the west, a low sun's reflection on the water by Alcatraz Island dazzles the eye. You feel a fresh, cool breeze from the Golden Gate. Wisps of fog hug the Marin County shore.

The slight vibration and rhythmic splashing of the paddle wheel seem reassuring, though occasionally spray from the wheel blows almost to the first passenger deck. In spite of a small chop on the bay, the ride is satin smooth. Moving away from the stern, you're impressed by the quiet, the tranquility.

Social hall exhibited fine imported tapestries (top) framed by curved skylights of stained glass. Grand staircase provided the boats with an ornate centerpiece.

Off the port side, the ferryboat *Eureka* is heading for San Francisco on her short run from Sausalito. Angel Island comes into view, and Mount Tamalpais looms to the west. The view is dramatic. But it's beginning to get cold out on deck. After passing Red Rock and The Brothers—three minuscule islands in the bay—you decide to go inside where it's warm and dinner awaits. It's nearly 7:30, and you're getting hungry.

The chief steward greets you and your party at the entrance to the dining room and leads the way to your table, next to a large window on the port side. He presents a menu that features a five-course table d'hote dinner for 75 cents. Because Prohibition* is in effect, no alcoholic beverages are offered. But it appears

---

* Prohibition, the 18th Amendment, began in January 1920 and was repealed by the 21st Amendment, which took effect in December 1933.

that some diners have brought their own. Filipino stewards in crisp white jackets are busy waiting table. The aroma of freshly-prepared food whets your appetite, and soon you order from a varied menu that includes pork chops, chicken, ham, and roast beef.

While awaiting the first course, you observe a group of *Delta King* officers, in their neat uniforms, eating at the captain's table in the center of the room. They chat and occasionally laugh, but you're not close enough to catch their conversation. Your attention turns to the scene outside the window. The sun has just set. In the west, the sky is bright with golden tones that contrast with the broad expanse of San Pablo Bay's gray-blue surface and the darker indigo hills in the distance.

You're more than satisfied with the delicious food and impeccable service. After dinner, crew members move tables and chairs to the sides of the dining room to make room for dancing. A four-piece band starts to play. The floor fills with dancers doing the two-step, waltz, fox trot, and Charleston.

Before bedtime, you can't resist walking the decks for a few minutes. The air is fresh; the stars are bright. The *Delta King* has already passed the newly-built Carquinez Bridge and the towns of Vallejo, Crockett, Martinez, and Benicia. The boat now cruises the upper reaches of Suisun Bay and soon will be steaming on the Sacramento River. Off to starboard, the lights of Pittsburg sparkle. Antioch glows in the distance.

In your cabin you're barely conscious of the paddle wheel's soft pulsations; it's only a matter of minutes until you're lulled to sleep between crisp new sheets. About midnight, you're awakened briefly by the steamboat's whistle signaling the Rio Vista drawbridge to open. Although the *King* passes four more such bridges—at Isleton, Walnut Grove, Courtland, and Freeport—you're not aware of hearing the whistle for any of them. You're sleeping too soundly.

Seemingly just minutes later, you blink your eyes at the soft daylight filtering into your cabin from around the window shade. There's no feeling of movement. A peek outside confirms your suspicion—the *Delta King* has already docked at the M Street wharf in Sacramento. It's morning on Thursday, June 2. The skies are blue; the air is balmy. After a leisurely breakfast of ham and eggs, pancakes, and sliced oranges in the dining room, you leave the boat for a visit with friends in Sacramento.

Meanwhile, on board the vessel, officers and crew are getting ready for a public open house in the afternoon. Everything must be shipshape for the celebration honoring the *King*'s inaugural cruise.

Uptown at the Senator Hotel preparations are under way for a noon luncheon and reception for Capt. A.E. Anderson, who, as company president, has made the voyage. When the hour arrives, Mayor Al Goddard of Sacramento and area Rotarians welcome Anderson and offer their tributes. The mayor expresses the city's appreciation for the two new sternwheelers. Capt. Anderson thanks his hosts for their hospitality and describes the amenities offered by his vessels. He invites all to board the *King* and see for themselves in the afternoon. The luncheon program ends with music and dancing performed by artists from the Senator and Hippodrome theaters and the company of *The Vagabond King,* which is playing in town. As Anderson leaves the hotel, he is serenaded by the Sacramento Boys' Band, which then leads a procession down K and across to M Street, a dozen blocks to the wharf.

For a few minutes the luncheon guests—including the mayor, officers from the Army Corps of Engineers, and a number of other dignitaries—have the *King* to themselves. They walk the decks, inspecting the vessel they've been told offers the most modern river transportation in the world. Then the open house begins, and the public comes aboard. Young and old, families with children, people of all descriptions swarm over the boat. They tour the glistening craft, uttering countless words of delight and praise. Music and light refreshments add a festive air. By the end of the warm afternoon, 3,000 guests have boarded the new sternwheeler.

In the evening, area residents see a large photo of the *Delta King* front-page center in the *Sacramento Bee* and, over the picture, a three-column headline that reads: "Hail to the King of the Sacramento." The accompanying news story is headlined "Reception Given to Mark Arrival of Palatial Boat," and it tells of the luncheon and the afternoon open house. It says the *King* leaves on the first return trip to San Francisco this evening and will pass the upbound *Queen* somewhere on the river tonight. The story also reports, "The *Delta Queen* will dock at Sacramento tomorrow morning, and the same sort of public reception given the *King* today will be held on the *Delta Queen* tomorrow afternoon."

Within a few days, nearly everyone in Sacramento knows about the two new steamboats. The city's newspapers run stories about them on June 2, 3, and 4. But in San Francisco, not one of the four big dailies covers the inaugural trips. Possibly the follow-up stories on Charles Lindbergh's transatlantic flight manage to crowd such news off the pages of that city's papers. His story, after all, is symbolic of a new day, while the *King* and *Queen* represent an older era. Or perhaps it's just that

CALIFORNIA TRANSPORTATION COMPANY

Through the Heart of California

COMFORT and LUXURY AFLOAT

C.T.Co.

**SAN FRANCISCO
SACRAMENTO
STOCKTON**

THE DELTA ROUTE

CALIFORNIA TRANSPORTATION COMPANY

TIME TABLE

SAN FRANCISCO — SACRAMENTO
Fare $1.80 — Round Trip $3.00

Steamers De Luxe
"Delta King"   "Delta Queen"

DAILY

Leave	*(Except Sunday)*	Arrive	
San Francisco..6:30 P.M.		Sacramento....5:30 A.M.
Sacramento....6:30 P.M.		San Francisco..5:30 A.M.

No Stops En Route

DINING ROOM SERVICE
Table d'Hote and A'La Carte

Dinner 6:30 to 8:30 P.M. — Breakfast 6:00 to 9:00 A.M.

Staterooms are air cooled in summer
and warmed in winter.

Have Hot and Cold Running Water

Suites of Two and Three Rooms with Bath or Shower
Attractive for Automobile Parties

These steamers Connect at Sacramento with
SACRAMENTO-NORTHERN RAILWAY
FOR
MARYSVILLE, YUBA CITY, OROVILLE, CHICO,
COLUSA, WOODLAND AND WAY STATIONS
Also Connect With
AUTO STAGE LINES FOR GRASS VALLEY,
NEVADA CITY, LAKE TAHOE RESORTS

Passenger Steamers
"Pride of the River"
"Isleton"

SAN FRANCISCO — SACRAMENTO
AND
RIO VISTA, ISLETON, RYDE, WALNUT GROVE,
COURTLAND AND WAY LANDINGS

Leave	Arrive
San Francisco..6:00 P.M.	Sacramento....7:00 A.M.
Sacramento....5:00 P.M.	San Francisco..6:00 A.M.

C.T. Co. timetable: front cover (left) promised "comfort and luxury afloat," while schedule (right) showed arrivals, departures, dining service, and connections. Inside, photos of amenities enticed passengers.

"DELTA KING" STEAMERS DE LUXE "D

Observation Room on Boat Deck

Nearing Sacramento

Main Lobby on Saloon Deck

Looking Into Dining Roo

AT YOUR SERVICE

Leaving SAN FRANCISCO 6:30 P.M.   *Leaving* SACRAMENTO 6:30 P.M.

SPECIAL ADVANTAGES FOR AUTOMOBILE PARTIES

Main Saloons and Staterooms are cooled with washed air in summer and warmed in winter. Hot and cold running water in every stateroom. Staterooms are single or en suites of two and three rooms with twin beds or double bed with or without private bath or shower. Dining room service Table d'Hote and a la Carte. A call bell in every stateroom for convenience o always in attendance to assist passengers on and off the boat with their baggage. When going beyond Sacramento put your automobile aboard; have a r and an early start from Sacramento.

"Boys in white coats are always in attendance," says the brochure. "Washed air in summer"

LTA QUEEN"

Suite with Double Bed and Shower

Twin Beds and Bath

A Nook in the Social Hall on Saloon Deck

connects with Purser's office and boys in white coats are
ght's sleep, get a six o'clock breakfast aboard the boat

refers to the evaporative cooling system.

riverboats don't seem important to a city accustomed to ocean-going ships coming and going every day.

In late afternoon of June 2, just 12 hours after arriving in Sacramento, you head back to the M Street wharf and reboard the *Delta King*. As scheduled, at 6:30 p.m., a small tugboat pulls the steamer's bow around until it's pointed downstream. With a blast of its whistle and the gentle splash of its paddle wheel, the craft begins the return trip to San Francisco. Again the *King* carries a jubilant crowd.

At that same moment, the mirror image of the *King*'s departure from Sacramento is taking place in San Francisco. The *Delta Queen* backs away from Pier 3 and heads north. She has started *her* maiden voyage.

Yesterday on the *King* you bundled up to protect against chilly gusts from the bay. Tonight, going downstream, it's the same boat but a different experience. Mainly, it's the contrast of the Sacramento Valley's warm dry air with the cool marine climate of San Francisco. But it's also the new visual sensations of lush shoreline and smooth flowing water.

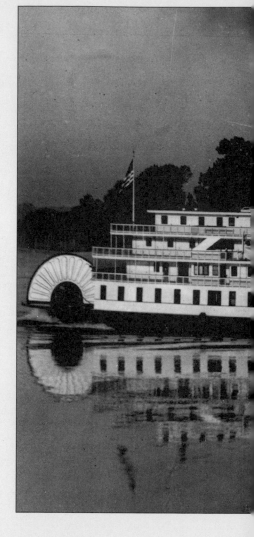

On the outer deck, you feel the calm of a late-spring evening in the valley and the warmth of a sun low in the western sky. People on shore seem almost close enough to reach out and touch. They stand and watch; many wave. You return their waves. As the *King* travels downriver at 10 miles per hour, the gentle breeze is refreshing. You're mesmerized by the passing scene and the rhythmic sound of the paddle wheel. Now and then, you detect the unmistakable smell of the river—the scent of dampness, mud, and tules.

Riverbank greenery presents a captivating vista. Huge cottonwoods, along with smaller willows and an occasional oak, black locust, or sycamore, rise above you. Wild grape and blackberry vines hang from the trees and touch the water. Here and there, openings through the trees reveal orchards and broad fields of

The glistening white superstructure of the Delta King *reflects on the glassy-smooth surface of the Sacramento River.*

farmland. Off to the southwest in the gray distance, 3,849-foot Mount Diablo, the area's most prominent peak, comes into view.

At sunset, just above Clarksburg, the *King* rounds a bend and, for a moment, heads due west. Here, the vessel cruises directly into a wide luminous sky bright with orange, red, and lavender. The breathtaking scene brings a pause in conversations. Now, cars on the levee roads are beginning to turn on their headlights. In the gathering darkness, an occasional car slows down and briefly holds even with the boat. To those ashore, the large paddlewheeler, steaming down the river with lights ablaze, is a majestic sight.

The *Delta King* continues downriver while the *Delta Queen* approaches from San Francisco Bay. As midnight nears, you decide to stay up, anticipating the historic first passing of the twin steamers. While waiting for a glimpse of the other craft in the cool night air of the outer deck, you join others in singing old favorites: "Clementine," "There's a Long, Long Trail," and "I've Been Workin' on the Railroad."

All at once, you hear a shout: "She's coming—up there ahead! See the lights!"

Up in their pilothouses, Capt. George Goodell on the *King* and Capt. John Stephenson on the *Queen* each prepare to salute the other boat with a blast from the whistle. When the two steamboats come within a few hundred yards of one another, just below Rio Vista, their whistles cut loose. The river and countryside echo with deep resonant tones, returning the sound from the boat's own whistle mingled with reverberations from the blast of the other vessel.

Then, near silence. The *Delta King* and the *Delta Queen* pass each other and continue on their way into the blackness of the night, initiating a new chapter of riverboat lore.

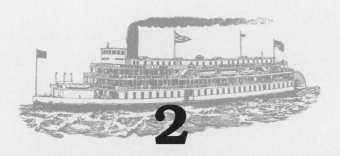

2

The King and Queen Are Born

Although the maiden voyages of the *Delta King* and *Delta Queen* brought joy and celebration, the decision to build the new steamboats had not come without controversy. A look back now, behind the scenes at the California Transportation Company, and a glance at Northern California's bay and river transportation in the early 1920s will provide the setting.

Full of color and excitement, the San Francisco waterfront teemed with activity 24 hours a day. Steamships, ferries, and riverboats crowded the piers; trolleys, cars, trucks, and people crisscrossed the Embarcadero, the city's wide bayside boulevard. Writing in the *San Francisco Chronicle* seven decades later, columnist Herb Caen waxed nostalgic about the days when his city was the leading seaport on the Pacific Coast:

> . . . a hustle-bustling waterfront that operated all night, ships from the seven seas being unloaded under great spotlights, cranes swinging, cargo nets rising and dropping, stevedores and longshoremen sweating and shouting, the toy trains of the Belt Line railroad shuttling back and forth. The tugs nosed around like hungry terriers, trucks rumbled in and out of the nearby produce district at 4 a.m., and at dawn you could have a cup of java in an all-night dump with sawdust on the floor.

Deep inland more than a hundred miles to the northeast—at the other end of the bay and river route—lay the busy Sacramento waterfront. As the capital city's nautical link to San Francisco and the Pacific, it pulsated with its own rhythms. Paddle-wheel steamers splashed their way to and from wharves along the

Sacramento River next to the M Street Bridge, while fast electric trains clattered across. Riverboats, with barges in tow, headed upriver for destinations as far north as Colusa, 85 river miles above Sacramento. Never-ending truck traffic loaded and unloaded at riverfront warehouses. Steam locomotives hauled their loads north along Front Street toward the huge Southern Pacific rail yards.

Any evening except Sunday, you could climb aboard a river steamer at Sacramento or San Francisco for an overnight trip to the other city. The *Fort Sutter* and the *Capital City,* nearly identical sternwheelers, worked as a pair from opposite directions. On a given night, one gave upstream service, the other downstream service (just as the *King* and *Queen* would do in later years). They offered the finest meals and accommodations on the river and carried freight as well. True, passenger traffic had decreased from the previous decade, but these two steamboats owned by the California Transportation Company were still popular. According to C.T. Co. historian Bill Stritzel, the boats continued to earn yearly profits.

By the early 1920s, however, the company had begun talk of building two new riverboats to replace the older pair. The new craft would be larger and more luxurious than anything ever seen on the Sacramento or on any river in the United States. Since the existing boats still performed well, one might wonder why the company would consider embarking on such a major undertaking. A.E. Anderson, the C.T. Co. president and majority stockholder, reasoned that to keep old customers and attract new ones, the company needed to provide modern first-class accommodations. He also wanted extra freight capacity for peak cargo periods.

The *Fort Sutter* and *Capital City* had built a large following of regular passengers over the years. For weekend and vacation, the overnight San Francisco-Sacramento run continued as a favorite of families, couples, and single people. The vessels also attracted businessmen who, after two good meals and a restful night's sleep, could arrive in early morning at their destination city to handle a day's business. Capt. Anderson hoped that two new deluxe riverboats would continue the tradition and build upon the success of the existing boats.

Some people, however, differed with his reasoning. Jim Burns, outspoken Port Engineer for the C.T. Co., was one. He pointed out that the two vessels currently in use were still profitable and in good condition—that building two expensive new boats would be a risky venture. His son, John, recalls the anguish his father experienced before the company made its decision to build the new craft. "My dad took this very seriously. He had real misgivings."

Over the years, Jim Burns had come to know men of finance in San

Francisco, including A.P. Giannini, founder of the Bank of Italy, which later became Bank of America. From what Burns learned from these people—and from observing the growing number of cars and trucks and the plans for new highways—he could hardly be optimistic. While Burns knew the C.T. Co. was in a position to finance two expensive new steamers, he was concerned that construction might require bank financing as well as company funds. He thought that taking on such an enormous project would dangerously reduce the firm's capital and might even jeopardize its existence.

Jim Burns presented his case to Anderson and the C.T. Co. board of directors. They listened. But the tide was running against him. He couldn't stem their enthusiasm for building two of the finest steamboats ever seen on the country's inland waterways. To them it was more than a matter of wanting larger boats with more capacity; clearly, owning such grand boats would bring even greater prestige.

If all went well, the vessels would increase passenger business while adding greater freight-carrying capacity. According to Bill Stritzel, freight was the true profit center for the company. In any case, Capt. Anderson was determined to build the two boats. Encouraged by earlier successes in business and government dealings, he had confidence he could handle any challenge. In the early 1920s, Anderson couldn't foresee the Great Depression coming at the end of the decade. Right up to the stock market crash in 1929, many businessmen and economists still didn't see its approach. Anderson's company wasn't alone. A number of coastal and river steamship lines in this country were also building overnight vessels.

And so the die was cast. Although Jim Burns had opposed the decision, once it was made he put all his energy into the new venture. Between 1924 and 1927, he spent most of his time at the shipyard in Stockton, California, where the boats were built. The yard, located on the San Joaquin River, was owned by the California Navigation and Improvement Company, a firm controlled by C.T. Co. Serving there as Superintendent of Hulls and Machinery, Burns directed the complex boat-building operation (for the steel hulls, it could be called assembly). Anderson remained at Pier 3, the company's headquarters in San Francisco, but he made frequent trips to Stockton to keep track of progress.

The new steamboats would be identical and named for the route they were to run each night. For years the company had promoted its Sacramento River boats as running the "Delta Route." This referred to the upper part of their journey, where the vessels passed through the northwest portion of the Sacramento-San Joaquin River Delta—that maze of countless islands and a thousand miles of waterways at the confluence of the two rivers. So it seemed natural to name the new sternwheelers the *Delta King* and the *Delta Queen*.

Plans called for four decks of wooden superstructure, the same number as the *Fort Sutter* and *Capital City*. But the *King* and *Queen* were to be the first California riverboats built with steel hulls. The top three decks of oak, mahogany, teak, and Oregon cedar would be passenger decks. The first or main deck would be for freight and autos, with engine room near the stern. The boat's hold, a lower level not considered a deck, would be below the freight deck within the hull, mostly above but partly below the waterline. This space would house boilers, machinery, economy quarters for men, the galley, and crew quarters for stewards and deck-hands (officers' cabins were forward on the top deck).

Launching ways, on which the *King* and *Queen* were built, had room for only one vessel at a time. Work started first on the *Delta King* with the "laying of the keel" on December 28, 1924. Crews then began work on the steel skeleton of the hull. Galvanized-steel hull plates had been fabricated in Scotland and bolted together there to ensure proper size and fit. Then plates had been carefully num-

---

A President's Attention to Detail

As president of the C.T. Co., Capt. A.E. Anderson displayed a keen interest in the day-to-day operations of his company. So it came as no surprise that he went to great lengths to make his new steamboats the finest. In the early 1920s, he and his Port Engineer, Jim Burns, made several trips to Scotland to study methods of hull and superstructure construction.

They consulted with marine architects at the shipyard of William Denny & Brothers, Ltd., in Dumbarton, Scotland, and contracted with that firm for steel hull-plate and machinery manufacture. It was at Denny's that Burns, as a young man, had carried out his apprenticeship in iron-ship building.

Capt. Anderson also visited France to find tapestries for the boats' social halls. When construction began, he watched every detail of their building and even

corresponded with suppliers about materials and quotes. From his San Francisco office at Pier 3, Anderson sent a steady stream of letters and memos to Jim Burns, who spent most of his time at Stockton during the construction. A letter Anderson wrote in September of 1926 is illustrative: In this one communication, he discussed an array of technical items—porthole rings, fire hoses, sewage tanks, compressors, and spring lines—and referred to three suppliers and one craftsman.

Once or twice a week, Capt. Anderson went to Stockton to check progress and inspect workmanship. Reportedly, from trip to trip he changed his mind about the way he wanted the boats finished. A story is told that the foreman instructed carpenters to drive nails only halfway in, pending Anderson's final approval of the job.

Four Decks of Superstructure/Seven Compartments of Hull:

FREIGHT DECK (main deck): Cargo and autos forward; engine room aft. A bow house far forward on open deck.

SALOON DECK (first passenger deck): Purser's office, dining room, barber shop, and lounge forward; social hall and staterooms aft.

OBSERVATION DECK (also called Boat Deck): Lounge forward, with cocktail bar after Prohibition repealed; passenger cabins aft. Six lifeboats on outer deck.

TEXAS DECK: Pilothouse and officers' quarters forward; passenger cabins aft.

Tillers operating the four steel rudders were controlled from the pilothouse.

Galley, where food for passengers and crew was prepared. Stewards and deckhands ate here. Had dumbwaiter to dining room two decks above.

Two watertube marine boilers for the steam engine, equipped with four burners each.

Chain locker and steam engine for windlass and capstan.

Machinery, pumps, heating and cooling equipment, water storage.

Crew quarters for stewards and deckhands.

Quarters for men passengers only; 42 berths without frills for 50¢ each.

Note: For further vessel specifications and construction details, please see pages 257–61.

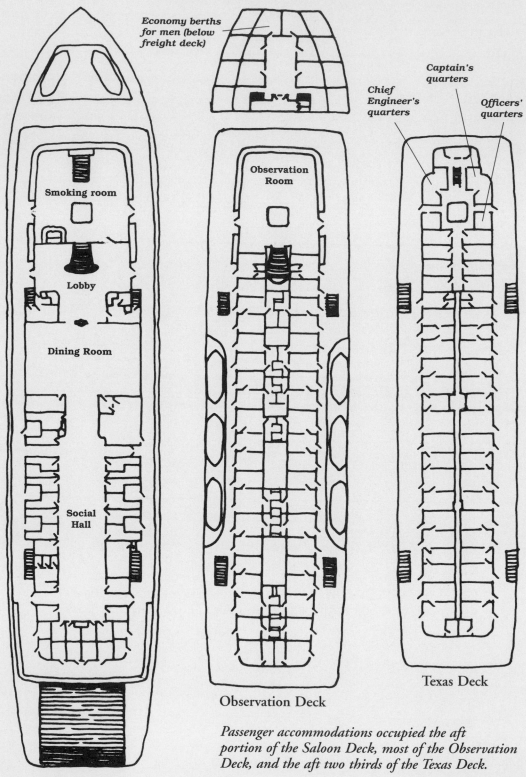

Economy berths
for men (below
freight deck)

Chief
Engineer's
quarters

Captain's
quarters

Officers'
quarters

Smoking room

Observation
Room

Lobby

Dining Room

Social
Hall

Texas Deck

Saloon Deck

Observation Deck

*Passenger accommodations occupied the aft
portion of the Saloon Deck, most of the Observation
Deck, and the aft two thirds of the Texas Deck.*

bered, disassembled, and shipped to Stockton where workmen put them together "by the numbers" and joined them permanently with rivets. (For specifications and construction details, see Appendix.)

When the steel hull was finished, carpenters took over and built the freight deck of ironbark, a hardwood imported from Siam. With the completion of this first deck in early May 1925, the shipyard was ready to launch the *Delta King*— without additional superstructure. Anderson and Burns had decided to put this embryonic vessel in the water to make room for the *Queen* on the launching ways. The *King's* remaining three upper decks would be constructed after launching.

Excitement filled the air on Monday morning, May 9, as the first of the two "million dollar boats"—incomplete and nonoperational—was readied for launching. A crowd gathered on the Stockton Channel. Men who had worked on the vessel stood next to the ways along with Anderson, Burns, dignitaries, newspaper reporters, and local citizens. The *King* would go sideways into the water, customary procedure for flat-bottom boats built on banks of narrow rivers.

It took half an hour to remove the blocking. Then a signal rang out—the boat was released. Sliding down the greased ways, the vessel splashed into the water, rocked for a few seconds, and then settled alongside the dock. A perfect launch.

That afternoon the *Stockton Record* covered the event:

DELTA KING GRACEFULLY SLIDES FROM WAYS AT LAUNCHING TODAY
Superstructure Work to be Complete by End of Year
Delta Queen Work Starts

The largest river steamer ever built in Stockton, the Delta King, is gently floating on the waters of the Stockton channel after a perfect launching this morning at 8 o'clock. Captain A.E. Anderson, president of the California Transportation Company of San Francisco, discussed the successful launching of the hull. In a voice trembling with emotion, he pointed out the "skin" of the craft and said: "Look, there is the 'skin' of the ship and not a single weep."

Proudly he walked from watertight compartment to watertight compartment, from starboard to port, from bow to stern . . . pointing with pride . . . not a drop of moisture was to be seen anywhere.

"I was on board the *Delta King* when it went down the ways," says Ernie Goen, former Stockton shipyard worker. During construction, his job was to gather all material needed for the following day and have it ready for the shipyard crane

Early construction photo taken at Stockton in 1925 shows steel
components from Denny's shipyard in Scotland marked with "P"
for port and "S" for starboard along with a number indicating
position. "Made in Scotland" was true for these parts but not
true for wooden superstructures, which were built at Stockton.

The Delta King was launched first. With framing
complete only on the freight deck, the King splashes
into Stockton Channel on May 9, 1925.

Fall 1925: above left, the King's *superstructure is well under way, while the* Queen, *at right, is still in an early stage.*

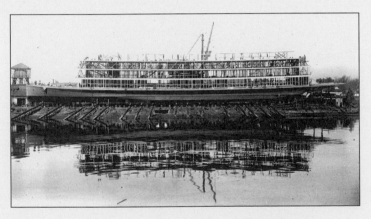

Two days before the big event, Delta Queen *sits on the launching ways.*

On December 12, 1925, the Queen *slides into the water. Unlike the* King, *she had framing on all decks before launch. Since the ways had room for only one vessel at a time, the* King's *early launch allowed work to begin on the* Queen.

to pick up. But on launching day, Goen played a different role: he was assigned to ride the *King* down into the channel (and to do it again later on the *Queen*). He said, "It was kinda exciting, but I was in the hold and couldn't really see much. Once she was in the water, I had to crawl through the hull, looking for leaks. Didn't find one. But I can tell you, it wasn't no picnic."

Ed Jackson, a friend of Goen's since childhood, worked as an apprentice machinist and draftsman at the Stockton Iron Works, next to the shipyard. He made blueprints of the plans sent from Scotland and delivered them to Burns and the foremen at various points on the construction site. Jackson's most vivid memory: "There were a jillion fellas all riveting at once—the noise was deafening!"

Lee J. Sorenson, in his early teens at the time, recalls the launch of both stern-wheelers. He says, "It was quite an event for us kids. The waves from the launching were over six feet high, bouncing back and forth between the ship and concrete retaining walls on the opposite side of the river."

With the *King* in the water, work could begin on the *Delta Queen;* her "keel was laid" on May 18. Since no other vessel waited to use the launching ways and since the *King* occupied most of the space at the fitting-out dock, the *Queen* remained on the ways for seven months, long enough for workmen to complete her steel hull and for carpenters to build a wooden framework for her superstructure four decks high.

When her turn came for launching, the *Queen* looked more like a real steamboat—more regal than the *King* had looked in its debut. She showed a faint outline of the beautiful craft she was destined to be. But, as the *King* had been first born, the *Queen*'s launching didn't attract quite the same attention from local observers and the press. Nevertheless, it was a big day when the second "million dollar boat" came off the ways at 3:40 on Saturday afternoon, December 12, 1925. Historical footnote: The *Queen* was the last river steamer to be launched on those ways, which are still visible today at low tide.

On the following Monday, the *Stockton Record* ran the headline: "DELTA QUEEN LAUNCHING IS ALL SUCCESS" with a news story that said: "Following an inspection of the boat after the launching, Capt. Anderson declared not a 'weep or tear' of water leaked around any of the thousand rivets. He highly praised his workmen."

Almost a year later, in November 1926, Burns got steam up for a test of the *Delta King*'s boilers. But as late as January 1927, the C.T. Co. was still calling for bids on finishing work for the two vessels. The operation dragged on into the

Shipyard workers pose for a portrait with the boats they built. At this time, the two "million dollar steamboats" are floating on the Stockton Channel, complete and ready for service. The Queen *is on left, the* King *on right.*

Stockton Daily Evening Record

STOCKTON, SAN JOAQUIN COUNTY, CALIFORNIA— FRIDAY, MAY 20, 1927

Stockton-Made Million Dollar Palatial Steamers Dedicated

Peerless in World Annals of Inland Waterways

ALL SECTIONS OF STATE SHARE IN DEDICATION HERE

Tributes Paid Capt. Anderson, Builder of Peerless Steamers

Speakers at Luncheon Session Predict Big Things for Stockton

CENTRAL CHURCH ORGAN WRECKED BEYOND REPAIR

Pipes Kicked In and Instrument Is Otherwise Mutilated

Work of Boy With Fancied Grievance Is the Theory Investigators

Monarchs of the Waters — By Yardley

The Delta King and the Delta Queen Will Play a Big Part in Development of Delta

HATS OFF TO HIM

Palatial Steamers Finest Craft Afloat in Inland Waters of All the World

Red Cross Has Important Mail for Veterans

Prison Terms for Local Offenders Are Reported

GUEST TICKET
Honoring
CAPTAIN A. E. ANDERSON
On the Occasion of Completion of Boats,
DELTA KING and DELTA QUEEN

Luncheon 12:15 Noon
MAY 20th 1927

MASONIC TEMPLE

THE CALIFORNIA TRANSPORTATION COMPANY

Cordially Invites Friends and Patrons to Inspect the new Steamers

"DELTA KING" and "DELTA QUEEN"

at Company's Shipyard, Foot of Harrison Street

Friday, May 20, 1927, from 2:30 P. M. to 5:00 P. M.

These vessels, sister ships—1823 tons—have been constructed and furnished completely at Company's shipyard, Stockton.

President A. E. Anderson, assisted by Messrs. C. D. Clarke, Vice President; A. A. Bowman, Traffic Manager; A. E. Pryor, Stockton Agent; J. E. Crew, Sacramento Agent, and James Burns, Superintendent Hulls and Machinery, will be pleased to welcome our friends and patrons on this occasion.

Big day at Stockton, May 20, 1927: Local paper reports on festivities; dignitaries receive tickets for VIP luncheon; Stockton Record cartoon expresses high hopes; and newspaper ad announces the public open house. Optimism and excitement prevail.

spring. Newspapers reported company plans to put the boats into service by late April. Although the C.T. Co. wasn't able to meet that schedule, on April 24 the *King* took a trial run. The next day, the Stockton paper reported:

> The Delta King . . . was taken out on a trial run yesterday afternoon, returning . . . about 9 o'clock last night. The trip was entirely successful—this being indicated, upon the craft's return, by the long and triumphant blast of the boat's whistle.

Construction of the two vessels ended up taking more time and money than expected, and the company had to borrow heavily. The financial squeeze on the C.T. Co. was made worse by its acquisition of the California Navigation and Improvement Company just before the boats were finished. At the end of the construction period, the company issued $650,000 in bonds and $750,000 in stock to pay off its indebtedness.

The dollars-and-cents cost for each boat is often shown as $875,000. But when other expenses are taken into account, for such things as furniture, carpeting, bedding, galley equipment, and other furnishings, the term "million dollar boat" is quite apt. A million dollars was big money in 1927—it represented a new high for the cost of a riverboat. And the C.T. Co. had built two of them! For perspective, consider that a smaller but very respectable steamboat had been built on the Ohio River just a few years earlier for $65,000.

On Friday, May 20, to celebrate completion of the *Delta King* and *Queen,* the Stockton Chamber of Commerce gave a luncheon with Capt. Anderson as guest of honor. The affair was attended by dignitaries from all over Northern California, including Congressman Charles F. Curry and representatives from the governor's office. Following the luncheon, the C.T.

Disquieting omen for Delta *boats: The Carquinez Bridge between Vallejo and Crockett opens on May 21, 1927, the same day the* King *leaves Stockton for San Francisco. Bridge portends highway competition to come.*

Co. held a dedication ceremony and open house on the twin boats, where guests enjoyed refreshments and dancing to the music of two orchestras.

Now the *King* and *Queen* were almost ready to replace the veteran steamers *Fort Sutter* and *Capital City*. Soon they would begin their new lives on the Sacramento River and on San Francisco, San Pablo, and Suisun bays. On Saturday morning, the *King* left Stockton and headed for San Francisco, arriving there in about eight hours.

On that same day—May 21—two other events took place that spoke of changes coming in the transportation habits of this country and the world. Charles A. Lindbergh completed his transatlantic flight and landed in Paris. And, in California, of more immediate concern was the opening of the new Carquinez Bridge between Vallejo and Crockett, forming a highway link between the Bay Area and Sacramento. It opened officially when President Calvin Coolidge pressed a button in Washington, D.C. As the *King* passed under that bridge on the way to San Francisco, cars and trucks sped across for the first time. To those on the boat who glanced up and observed the traffic flowing high above them, competition for the passenger and freight dollar was clearly evident.

Three days later, the *Queen* departed Stockton for the bay. Ellis Collins, a long-time Delta resident, says he was on board with his uncle, Capt. John Stephenson, "when they 'set the compass' on San Francisco Bay." He recalls, "They used a master compass to adjust the newly-installed compass on the *Queen*. Otherwise, metal in the boat would have caused erroneous readings."

On May 24 the *Record* described the *Queen*'s departure from Stockton:

DELTA QUEEN IS GIVEN FAREWELL

Bidding farewell and good luck to the new river steamer Delta Queen, boats and factories on Stockton channel this morning tied down their whistles as the boat steamed away from the shipyards of the California Transportation Company and proceeded on its first trip to San Francisco. The two "million dollar boats" will undergo a series of tests on San Francisco Bay before being placed in service.

The *Delta King* and *Delta Queen* completed their test runs and prepared for their maiden voyages. Although no one knew it at the time, the two paddle-wheelers were also preparing for a unique place in the history of inland water travel. When the twin vessels began their nightly cruises, they would be inaugurating the last steamboat service for passengers and freight on California rivers.

3

Voyages in the Dark

In spite of gale-force winds, torrential downpours, and dense fog, the *Delta King* and *Delta Queen* never cancelled a trip or stopped to tie up en route between San Francisco and Sacramento. When you consider that these C.T. Co. steamboats ran every night of the year regardless of weather and visibility, you can appreciate their safety record.

In their more than 13 years of commercial service (including 14 summer seasons), each made almost 4,500 voyages on bay and river for a total of nearly 9,000 trips in all. That represents roughly a million miles of water travel, comparable in distance to four trips to the moon. And they did it all by steam and paddle wheel—all without radar, depth finders, or other sophisticated navigational aids—and all without a serious accident.

But what were the hazards of navigation for the *King* and *Queen?* Most deadly of all was the danger of collision with a bridge or another vessel. Of lesser consequence, but more likely to happen, was risk of running aground on shoals or wing dams in the river.

Had these boats run in the daytime, the pilot's job would have been considerably easier. But because of their night schedule, the *King* and *Queen* were destined to navigate most of their time in the dark with visibility at its worst. On a clear night when the moon was bright and visibility good, the pilot's job was relatively easy. Other times, in pitch-black darkness with only the stars or cloudy skies overhead, his work became harder. But the real test came on those nights when dense tule fog (named after a local bulrush) blanketed the area. In his book *Paddle-Wheel Days in California*, Jerry MacMullen describes this phenomenon:

It is in the Delta country, and along certain stretches of the Sacramento, that the tule fog reaches its highest stage of perfection. Since the beginning of time it has had nothing to do but devote itself to the task of becoming a good, rousing, thoroughgoing fog—and it certainly has learned to do a workmanlike job. . . . River seamanship is an art in itself, and any of the salt-water brethren who are inclined to look down their noses at river pilots are invited to try it themselves sometime, preferably with a vessel of no great value. The river pilot must know all the answers, and know them right now.

In dense fog, the skippers of the *King* and *Queen* couldn't see the water in front of their boats or even their own crafts' bows. So they had to rely on devices other than their eyes. A navigational chart, sometimes called the Pathfinder,

proved indispensable. This was a scroll stretched between two reels; as the miles passed, the pilot turned a crank to move it accordingly. A red light, shining up through the paper, illuminated the chart without interfering with the pilot's night vision.

The chart showed every compass course—and the number of seconds to be spent on each course—for the entire trip. Between San Francisco and Sacramento the chart gave 318 separate courses or compass headings. A heading might last 30 seconds, a minute, or longer. The pilot also had to adjust for the particular stage of tides in the bay and speed of current in the river, factors that could vary widely from day to day and even hour to hour. In addition, he drew from his own experience and made full use of his senses: a brief glimpse of shoreline, the dim glow of lights in the fog, the sound of foghorns, or echoes from the shore.

Pilots used the moving chart on every trip in good weather as well as bad, so it became second nature to them. On the bay, the chart was usually enough; changes of course were based on compass reading, knowledge of wind and tide, and elapsed time. But on the upper portion of the trip, the chart had its limitations. The river there was often shallow and always narrow, and variation in speed of the current from low water to flood level was extreme. There was no margin for error,

Delta King *and* **Delta Queen** *were night boats. Thus photography of the vessels cruising bay and river was limited to the time of year when long days allowed picture-taking close to arrival and departure time or when they took infrequent day trips.*

Early advertisement for Sacramento area residents. Similar ads ran in San Francisco promoting travel to capital city. In beginning, boats operated six days and laid over on Sunday (as noted above). Later, in 1930s, they worked seven days a week.

and pilots needed something more.

Long before the *Delta* twins cruised the river, steamboat captains discovered a primitive kind of "radar" enabling them to navigate in fog; they used echoes from their boats' whistles. They found that a quick blast followed by the returning echo (from house, barn, trees, or riverbank) would tell them where they were and how close they were to shore. The time the echo took to return to the boat and the direction from which it came revealed their position. But as an added precaution in foggy weather, often someone stood watch on the bow. By the time of the *King* and *Queen,* pilots bounced their whistles not only off well-known landmarks but also off specially-built "echo boards" along the river.

To hear better on foggy nights, pilots kept the side windows open and demanded absolute quiet in the pilothouse. Eldridge "Jim" Bowie, the *Delta Queen*'s last purser in California, describes his visit to that tense center of navigation: "They blew a very short whistle that bounced back almost simultaneously. To the casual observer, it sounded like all one blast. I had to sneak up the stairs in the darkness to get there and keep my mouth shut—then quietly return to my office. Tule fogs made you stop and think; occasionally the *Queen* got so close to the riverbank that she caught leaves and branches on her decks." "Sometimes," says former freight-clerk Herb Rummel, "branches or snags would break windows on the freight deck."

Consider the following worst-case scenario, in terms of weather and water conditions, for a *Delta King* or *Delta Queen* pilot to deal with: The boat is headed downstream with a full load of passengers and a heavy load of freight (about 800 tons). It's winter and the Sacramento River is running full. This means the current is fast—7 or 8 miles an hour (this is years before Shasta, Oroville, and Folsom dams helped control the flow). Driftwood, debris, and even an occasional uprooted tree float down the river. The heavy rains have ceased, but now a dense tule fog settles over the river, reducing visibility to zero. The speed of the river itself would be fast enough, but to maintain steerage, the vessel must provide its own forward motion in the water. This adds another 6 or 7 miles per hour. So the boat is moving downstream faster in relation to the shore than the captain would like if he had a choice (which he doesn't). Even if the pilot needed to, there's no way he could stop the boat quickly. Downriver, during the next few hours, five drawbridges must open—and open on time—to avoid the possibility of a disastrous, splintering wreck. It was not a situation to be taken lightly.

Passengers on the *King* and *Queen* generally weren't aware of these hazards or of the tensions in the pilothouse. It's just as well—otherwise, they could scarcely have been relaxed enough to enjoy their trip. Crew members, however, were aware of what was going on. Former freight-clerk Gordon Ridley says, "It could be pretty scary, because you're thinking, 'Will the bridges open in time?'" Discussing his first experiences with tule fogs as a crewman, he continues, "You, the onlooker, didn't know where you were going; you were putting your trust in somebody else. The first few times we went through fog and I looked out and couldn't see anything, I thought, 'How can they steer this darn boat, how can they even take it out?' Yet we made all the bends—made all the bridges."

Both the *King* and *Queen* had a searchlight atop the pilothouse, but it was used only for docking in the dark, for emergencies, and to pick out another boat or other object on the water—not for navigation. And it was worthless in fog. Even without fog, pilots found out long ago they could see more without the help of a light. It's surprising how much you can see even on a pitch-black moonless night, once your eyes adjust to the dark.

On a foggy November evening in the early 1930s, luck nearly ran out for one of the *Delta* boats. Dewitt Hightower, pilot on the *Delta King* that night, recalls his experience in an interview conducted by Denny S. Anspach, M.D.:

We'd had fog all night. The *Queen* was coming upriver with a strong flood tide, and she had about 700 tons of cargo. We were going down with 700-800 tons of rice and canned goods. Usually, the boats would pass below Rio Vista, around Three Mile Slough. We'd already left the Rio Vista dock—I was at the wheel, and Capt. Atthowe was with me in the pilothouse. We were sounding our fog signal and expected to hear the *Queen* shortly. But it was some time before we heard her. It was about midnight, and she was blowing four whistles—which meant she was in trouble!

We followed those signals in the fog and hauled over to the south shore at Sherman Island. There we spotted the *Queen*; she'd grounded herself in an inlet at the lower end of the island which was mostly tules and had been filled in with rock. We were still in deep water, so we put a line on her and tried to pull her from the stern. But the tide had started to recede—she wouldn't budge.

Capt. Peterson on the *Queen* called out with his megaphone—he wanted us to come alongside and see if we could lighten his freight load enough to refloat the boat. But we already had 700-800 tons of cargo aboard. Capt. Atthowe said, "No, I'd only get myself stuck." So we went on downriver a ways until we could get to a telephone [no radios on board the boats in those days]. We reported the problem and then continued to San Francisco.

Passengers on the *Queen* had a choice of staying on board until she was refloated or of being transported by car to Rio Vista or Sacramento. Most chose to stay aboard and arrive late. Next morning most of the cargo was unloaded onto barges to lighten the vessel; then she backed away from the island with the help of tugboats at high tide. The *Queen* arrived at Sacramento about 7 p.m. [over 12 hours late], then turned around and left for San Francisco about midnight [only about six hours late]. So she never actually lost a trip. But, due to Coast Guard regulations, she had to go into drydock for inspection when she got back to the Bay Area.

Ray Fisher, assistant freight-clerk the night of the incident, rode on the boat that went aground but recalls the incident somewhat differently. He remembers it was the *King,* not the *Queen,* that went aground. He says it hung up on the rocks of a wing dam in the Middle Ground, downriver from Sherman Island:

It was about 10:30 or 11—I was busy rating bills of lading and typing up freight bills with Ben Shelton. All of a sudden the vessel sort of slowed down and shuddered. Then it seemed as if it was climbing. We looked at each other with surprise. Charlie Jessen, the purser, was the first to speak, "What the hell was that!" The deck appeared to tilt back toward the stern. I put a typewriter-ribbon reel on the floor to check it out—and sure enough, it rolled astern. Then we heard voices out on the various decks. People were coming out and wondering what had happened. A searchlight was playing in the fog, but you really couldn't see anything.

The *Delta* boats had mail contracts, so a launch was sent down the next day to take the U.S. mail, along with Fisher as official custodian, to Rio Vista. From there, he took the mail to Sacramento by car. He reports that later the crew enjoyed a few laughs at the expense of Capt. Peterson. "All in the spirit of good fun," according to Fisher.

Because of the high silt content of the river in the rainy season, sandbars could form in the river within 24 hours and cause navigational headaches, problems that usually turned out to be more nuisance than hazard. And, because of the rapid buildup of shoals in the river, charts didn't help much in avoiding them. So,

In San Francisco, the King and Queen docked at Pier 3, near Ferry Building with its spire and clock tower. Freight went through the big door, passengers through the smaller door to right. Below, Pier 3 as seen from bay side. Waiting room was to left of docked boat's bow.

At Sacramento, the King and Queen docked at the M Street wharf, just downstream from the bridge over the Sacramento River. You can see old bridge's girders in the photo at right, behind the boat leaving for San Francisco. Tower Bridge (top photo) replaced the old structure in 1935. Bottom photo shows freight trucks and steam engine at Sacramento terminal, passenger office and waiting room at right.

in spite of the shallow draft of the *King* and *Queen* (about six to eight feet depending on load), pilots had to swing wide in the bends, hoping to find enough water. Dredges worked the year round trying to keep the channels open.

"Sometimes," according to Herb Rummel, "the *King* and *Queen* would run into a silt barrier that wasn't there the day before. If the vessel couldn't push over the bar, then we'd have to back off and look for a deeper channel in the river." "To get off a sandbar," Eldridge Bowie reports, "we used the paddle wheel in reverse, rocking the boat back and forth by turning the rudders until the boat would slide back off the bar."

Gordon Ridley recalls a story told to him when he first came on the job: "The steamer was going upriver late one night in the fog, and eventually they wondered why they didn't get to Sacramento. They said, 'It's 5:30 and we should be there by now.' When it got light, they found they'd been stuck all night on a sandbar. The bow of the boat was free—the stern was free—just the middle was caught. So the boat pivoted right and left, but it hadn't moved a foot." A tall story for the new man on the boat.

While not as potentially dangerous as fog, heavy winds could also cause problems for a river pilot. Capt. Robert Atthowe, San Francisco bar pilot, remembers his grandfather William J. Atthowe, who was captain of the *King* in the 1930s, telling him how tricky navigation in the wind could be: "The boats were high and would catch the wind. And being flat-bottomed, sometimes they were almost unmanageable in a strong wind." Former crew members of the *King* and *Queen* usually mention two locations where the wind blew the hardest: the bay opposite the Golden Gate and the river at Rio Vista, particularly the latter. That this stretch of river has become a mecca for windsurfers in recent years comes as no surprise to those who steamed by it in their days on the San Francisco-Sacramento run.

Ray Fisher recalls being awakened occasionally in the early morning as his San Francisco-bound boat would begin shaking just off Alcatraz Island "when the vessel started to buck with a strong tide running." The roughest water is created when a strong onshore wind fights against an outgoing tide. This combination causes major swells, troughs, and whitecaps. At Rio Vista the same principle applies. But there, a heavy river current—coming downstream at the same time the tide is going out—can add to the speed of the flow and further accentuate the roughening effect of the wind. Gordon Ridley recalls a few times when the wind blew so fiercely at Rio Vista that the *King* and *Queen* couldn't make their scheduled landing (this stop was made only for a brief period in the early 30s).

True, the *King* and *Queen* had no major accidents and hence no passenger fatalities or injuries due to accidents. But there were occasions when passengers went overboard—sometimes for reasons of their own and sometimes with little or no ill effect. Ray Fisher tells about a wedding party one night at Rio Vista, when his boat had stopped to pick up a young bride and groom beginning their honeymoon: "Some guy runs out there—he has a jug of wine in his hand. I think he fell through a hole in the dock or ran off the end of it. The cry went out, 'Man overboard!' We had searchlights on the water and got him out in just a few minutes. No sooner did we get him out than he starts to run out on the dock again—his friends had to restrain him." No lasting damage; just a little added excitement for the midnight stop at Rio Vista.

A mysterious episode in 1932 proved to be a different matter. On September 6, would-be movie star Dorothy Millette boarded the *Delta King* at San Francisco. When the boat arrived the next morning in Sacramento, she was missing. Crew members found her clothing and personal effects still on the boat, and it was assumed she had committed suicide by jumping overboard. A week later her body was discovered in Georgiana Slough, just off the river near Walnut Grove. The whole affair might have taken its place as a minor footnote to Sacramento river history had it not been for Millette's connection to Paul Bern, top MGM producer, and Jean Harlow, the studio's new superstar.

Harlow and Bern had gotten married in July 1932. Just two months later, on September 5, Bern was found shot to death in his Beverly Hills home. The next day Millette boarded the *Delta King*, went overboard, and drowned. Although the two deaths took place five hundred miles apart, it's possible they were related.

Years before, Bern and Millette had lived together in New York. As an unwed couple, they violated society's standards. When she became increasingly erratic, he put her in a sanitarium and came west. Later, as a famous producer, he still paid her bills in the East. For a decade, she begged to join him in Hollywood. He rebuffed her pleas. Cognizant of the moral climate of the times, Bern took great pains to keep the affair a secret. He feared a scandal might destroy both his career and Harlow's—and even bring MGM down with them.

Several books have been written offering theories on Bern's death, which was listed officially as suicide. Some allege that Millette killed him—that listing his death as suicide was a cover-up to avoid a scandal. Others maintain that it was, in fact, a suicide.

As for the puzzle of Millette's demise and her trip on the *Delta King*, a book called *Deadly Illusions* by Samuel Marx and Joyce Vanderveen touches on the subject. It says that ticket agents, stewards, and even passengers who had been on the boat were questioned. Indeed, some had observed a distraught woman on the voyage upriver. At the inquest, L.I. McKim, general passenger agent in Sacramento, said the stub of her room ticket and the return portion of her round-trip ticket were found in her purse. Steward A.P. Cantor testified that just before leaving the pier in San Francisco, Millette rang the bell for room service and requested a Bromo-Seltzer—"she was acting nervous and worried." Waiter Lorenzo O'Hero reported that she passed up the regular dinner menu, saying, "Give me spaghetti and ice cream—that's all I want." Henry Garrick, a passenger who got off at Rio Vista, recalled "a very beautiful woman with pretty hair and eyes. She seemed to be all alone and quite nervous, kept walking around the decks, didn't seem to notice anyone—she had her eyes way off in the distance."

While all these witnesses had observed her, none made any startling disclosures or offered new evidence. Why did she choose to ride the *King,* and why did she buy a round-trip ticket? Did she jump or fall off the steamboat—or was she pushed? We may never know.

If you believe in ghosts, by all rights the *Delta King* should be haunted by the ghost of Dorothy Millette. Steven K. Boyd, who served as night watchman during the vessel's restoration at Sacramento in the 1980s, won't argue with that possibility. He says he saw the form of a woman on an upper deck one dark night, but he passed it off as an associate of the owner visiting the boat. Next day it was discovered that neither the owner, the associate, nor anyone else had gone aboard that night.

Speaking from personal experience during the *King's* restoration years, I found the big old vessel a bit spooky in the middle of the night when empty and without lights. Especially with no one else aboard. Having spent many a night lying on the deck in sleeping bag amid sawdust and lumber, I heard a cacophony of odd noises. When the wind blew, windows rattled and the superstructure produced an assortment of creaks and groans. But no apparitions appeared. At least, not while I was awake.

4

Life on Board the Delta Twins

New crew members on the *Delta King* and *Delta Queen* often had to endure playful initiation rites. According to former freight-clerk Herb Rummel, "When you first come to work, the crew pulls all these fancy little gizmos on you, like giving you a pail and funnel and telling you to measure all the oil that comes on board."

Rummel describes one of the more elaborate jokes played on him: "Because the purser's office has keys to all the staterooms, I saw nothing unusual when *Delta King* purser Buck Neiger asked me to go find the keelson key. He says, 'Herb, you better go up to the wheelhouse and see if Capt. Atthowe has it.' I knocked on the door and said, 'Captain, do you have the keelson key?' 'No,' he says, looking all around and opening drawers, 'I think I gave it to Chief Ely. You go down below—I'm sure he's got it.' So I went down to the engineer's office and repeated my question, only to be told I'd better go up and see Williams, the steward, who said he didn't have it either. Finally, I returned to the purser's office. Buck laughed and confided that there was no such thing as a keelson key on the *King*." [The keelson is part of a boat's keel structure.] Rummel concludes, "When they pulled things like that on you, you knew you were accepted."

On occasion, crew members played little jokes on the passengers, too. They found it fun to mislead people in harmless ways. A favorite trick was to appear worried that the smokestack was going to hit the railroad bridge at Benicia. According to Rummel, "If you stood aft, topside, and watched as the *King* approached the bridge, you'd swear the funnel was too tall to go under. Actually, even at high tide, the clearance was at least eight feet—but it sure didn't appear that way. You held your breath as the boat went under. The passengers, especially the ladies, used to scream. We had a lot of fun with that, especially if a good crowd was on board." Former passenger Carl Balch recalls being told that the crew was going to "take the chimney down" going under the bridge. "But the boat just kept right on going—it looked as if we would hit the bridge for sure!"

Former freight-clerk Gordon Ridley tells of his amusement in taking passengers for a tour of the boat: "Down on the deck near the engine room was a big tank of water that was filled through an opening in the bottom of the ship. It was bay or river water and was used only for flushing toilets. We'd take people down there and let them step up on a stool so they could look down into the tank. Usually, fish were in it; the movement of the boat had created a suction, drawing them up with the water. Most were striped bass about 10 to 12 inches long. Once in a while we'd find a big one that was a couple of feet long; that was real scary, because he'd be thrashing around. Of course, the minute the boat slowed down, the fish would go back down into the river or bay unharmed. Anyway, we had fun with the passengers—we told them that was where we kept our supply of fresh fish."

*Captains above:
W.J. Atthowe (top)
and W.L. Cooley*

All playfulness aside, crew members of the *Delta King* and *Queen* worked hard and often long hours as well. On their nightly runs between San Francisco and Sacramento, piloting was divided into two six-hour shifts—one pilot from 6 p.m. to midnight, the other from midnight on. But, as a safety factor, two men were in the pilothouse at all times: a pilot and the captain or a pilot and the first mate.

At Sacramento, the steamers remained at the dock all day. But in San Francisco, after docking at Pier 3, they spent part of their day "peddling," a term meaning pickup and delivery of large shipments around the bay. After passengers had eaten breakfast and disembarked—and smaller shipments called less-than-carload lots were unloaded onto the pier—the boats traveled to other docks on the San Francisco waterfront. On these short trips they delivered the carload shipments they'd brought down from Sacramento, and they picked up any large shipments for that evening's run upriver.

Capt. William L. Cooley in pilothouse of Delta Queen *and Capt. William J. Atthowe on* Delta King: *This is one of those rare occasions when the two boats were together. These two captains commanded the* King *and* Queen *through much of the 1930s.*

Freight going upriver from San Francisco to Sacramento was quite different from the type coming down. Downriver, typically the steamboats carried carload lots of rice and canned goods, and the paperwork was simple. But on upriver trips, freight tended to consist of many small, individual shipments of manufactured parts and equipment, all requiring separate billing. It took the same amount of paperwork for a small package of hardware as it did for a 100-ton shipment of canned peaches. So Sacramento-bound freight clerks and their assistants had their hands full. Hundreds of bills of lading and freight bills had to be processed. On some trips, the clerks worked until 4 or 5 a.m., barely finishing before the boat docked at Sacramento.

In the small world of the steamboat, a crew member's relationship with his fellow workers took on special significance. Herb Rummel recalls that a good attitude prevailed on the *Delta King:* "We took pride in the ship we were on. And I don't think there was a man on board that, within reason, wouldn't have done nearly anything for another crew member. Before we were married, my wife-to-be would come up from San Francisco Saturday night on the *King*. She'd get off at Sacramento and go see her folks. The Filipino boys got so they knew her. I had a room reserved for her, and when they'd see her coming—two blocks away—they'd run up, get her bags, and carry 'em on board. That was nice—very nice.

"We were married on November 19, 1933, and we had a suite topside the *King* at the stern on the starboard side, a nice big room. When we came on board, Chief Steward Williams says, 'Don't come down to dinner until 8 o'clock.' I said, 'What's the matter? We'd like to come down a little earlier.' 'No,' he says, 'you come at 8 o'clock—I've got a special dinner cooked for you.' We waited. It turned out they'd cleared out the dining room. The passengers had all eaten and gone; we had the whole place to ourselves. And we had eight boys in their white jackets all waiting on us—just the two of us!"

In late 1929, Ford Motor Company came out with its 1930 version of the popular Model A (of which four million were built between 1928 and 1931). One night, Ford shipped one of these new cars to Sacramento aboard the *Delta Queen;* it was wrapped in canvas to keep the curious from seeing it before the official release date. Although that model changed little from the previous one, the company wished to create as much excitement and suspense as possible. Ina Cokeley tells a story about her father, Jack Andrews, who was chief engineer on the *Queen* that night. He knew the Model A had come aboard all wrapped up. Soon curiosity got the better of him. "What would it hurt," he asked himself, "if I went down in the middle of the night, lifted the canvas ever so carefully, and sneaked a look?"

The Swing Clerk's Long Day

In the early 1930s, the C.T. Co. employed a "swing clerk" on *King* and *Queen* upbound trips. This extra clerk handled freight paperwork starting in San Francisco and sometimes got off around midnight at Rio Vista—when the boats had a regular stop there—but usually went all the way to Sacramento.

Ray Fisher recalls: "If the upbound steamer arrived at Rio Vista first, I went ashore there and returned to San Francisco on the downbound steamer. If not, I stayed on board and continued to Sacramento. Next day, I'd return via the Sacramento Northern Railway, an electric train that crossed Suisun Bay on the Chipps Island ferry [called the *Ramon*] and delivered me to Oakland, where I took the Key Route ferry to San Francisco, arriving at 3:15 p.m."

By that time Fisher had put in a long day, having started his workday about 22 hours before and arriving just in time to report for the next upbound trip.

About midnight Chief Andrews left the engine room and headed along the freight deck to the place where the Model A sat under wraps. Only then did he realize that the people at Ford Motor Company were one step ahead of him. Along with the car, they'd sent a security guard.

In 1935 a favorite topic among crew members on the *Delta King* and *Queen* was John Ford's *Steamboat Round the Bend,* a Hollywood movie set in the deep South but filmed along the Sacramento and San Joaquin rivers. Contrary to stories often heard, neither of the *Delta* twins were in the film. But six other C.T. Co. paddle-wheel steamers were (boat names are shown on page 6). Gordon Ridley, working on the *Queen* at the time, says, "Everybody was excited about it. They all wanted to see Will Rogers and the heroine of the story, Anne Shirley; they also wanted to see how the boats had been changed to look like Mississippi riverboats. We couldn't wait to see the movie. When it came out, we all went and saw it at one of the big movie houses in San Francisco." This was Will Rogers' last film; later that year, he was killed in a plane crash in Alaska.

During the filming, *Delta Queen* purser Grandon Seal got a bit part in the movie. An accomplished cartoonist, he sketched and listened as Will Rogers exchanged tall tales with the renowned humorist and writer, Irvin S. Cobb, who was also in the movie. Seal recalled, "One session lasted eight hours and varied from personal anecdotes to the biggest whoppers I've ever heard. Both men were masters of the art and neither could be outdone by the other."

In the 1920s and '30s, the two *Delta* steamboats had their share of notable passengers. According to Arthur Snyder, *Delta Queen* purser in her early California years, President Herbert Hoover took a trip. Eldridge "Jim" Bowie, the *Queen's* last purser on the Sacramento, remembers that, after the repeal of Prohibition, Irvin S. Cobb came aboard: "He pulled out a $20 bill—big money in those days—and said, 'Drinks for everyone.'" Bowie also recalls other famous people who rode the boats, including Templeton Crocker, well-known natural history researcher, and Hollywood actor Errol Flynn.

"I always had to have my suit, coat, and tie on when the Vanderbilts were on board," says Ray Fisher. "They'd come down to Sacramento from Lake Tahoe in a couple of fancy cars—long, dark, and sleek. I was put on notice to give the Vanderbilts every possible courtesy. After all, we didn't have that many millionaires in those days."

"There were lots of celebrities," according to Gordon Ridley, "but you couldn't always tell by the way they looked. Sometimes at Sacramento they'd come on board looking like bums. At first, I thought to myself, 'If a man was a million-aire many times over, I'd think he'd look like one.' But later I realized the guy had been out hunting all week; he just wanted a bath and a good night's sleep before going to his office in the morning."

The *Delta King* and *Queen* invited passengers to take their autos with them. A few cars could be stowed forward in the bow house but most went in the regular freight area. At $3.50 one way or $5.00 round trip, the idea proved popular, particularly in the summertime and on weekends the rest of the year.

Summer vacationers who took their cars on the boat from San Francisco arrived at Sacramento in the cool of the morning. Then, if their destination was Lake Tahoe, they could continue their trip, leaving the boat early to avoid the heat of the day. Those going the other direction—to San Francisco or destinations such as Monterey and Carmel—also avoided a hot, tiresome drive by taking their car aboard. The narrow two-lane road between Sacramento and the Bay Area, zigzagging through Davis, Dixon, and other small towns, was slow and tedious. Neither highways nor cars were built for high-speed travel. And the ferries between San Francisco and the East Bay, while colorful and scenic, added extra travel time. Before the big bridges were built, an auto trip between San Francisco and Sacramento could take three to four hours.

Because the river at Sacramento usually ran well below the level of the wharf, an elevator was used to load and unload cars. To load, attendants drove the car onto the elevator at dock level, the platform then descended to freight-deck level, and the car was driven onto the boat. During loading and unloading, a few cars were lost overboard. Capt. Dewitt Hightower (interviewed by Denny S. Anspach) tells about an expensive Pierce Arrow ready to be unloaded from the *Queen* one cold morning in 1934: "The driver started to drive off the boat and didn't notice that the elevator had gone up. At the last second he slammed on the brakes, but the deck had a layer of frost—car and driver went off the edge and into about 20 feet of water. They rescued the driver and later brought the car up. We bought the car from the insurance company and made a pickup out of it, possibly the only Pierce Arrow pickup in history."

Staterooms on the *King* and *Queen* provided call buttons for room service. If you wanted an extra blanket or a late-night snack, you pressed a button that flashed a light and set off a buzzer in the purser's office. Unfortunately, the system was not child-proof. With predictable frequency, stewards answering the calls were greeted at the cabin door by children or by their embarrassed parents. History will

California riverboats (but not the Delta King *and* Queen*) star above in* Steamboat Round the Bend, *Will Rogers' last movie, filmed in 1935. At right, a cartoon by* Queen*'s purser Grandon Seal shows swing clerk Ray Fisher, one foot on each* Delta *boat. Freight clerk Gordon Ridley on fantail of the* King *displays first shad of season in '33.*

WONDER WHAT THE NEXT ABSTRACT NUMBER IS?···HOPE CAMILLI GETS A HIT TODAY··· THINK I'LL BUY SOME CINNAMON ROLLS··· HOPE WE GET MOCHA ICE CREAM TONIGHT·· WHEN'S PAYDAY? KNOCKED-DOWN GIMMACKS ARE SECOND IN THE STORE DOOR ETC - ETC.

MENU
THE RIVER LINES

STEAMER DELTA KING

W. J. ATTHOWE, *Captain*   L. FILES, *Steward*

Table D'Hote Dinner 75 Cents

SUNDAY, OCTOBER 22, 1933

SOUP

Cream of Tomato Cup Bouillon

Fruit Cocktail California Dill Pickles

SALAD

Sliced Tomatoes and Cucumbers

FISH

Baked Salmon, Brown Sauce

ENTREES

Tagliarini Mushroom Sauce

Braised Haricot of Ox Tail

French Toast, Cream Sauce

ROAST

Prime Ribs of Beef au jus

Leg of Mutton with Mint Jelly

VEGETABLES

Boiled and Mashed Potatoes

Cauliflower in Cream

Small French Carrots in Butter

DESSERT

Vanilla Ice Cream with Small Cakes

Homemade Apple Pie Lemon Cream Pie

Sacramento River Canned Peaches

ROLLS AND BUTTER

COFFEE, TEA, MILK OR ICED TEA

BEER (Eastern) 25c (Western) 20c

Additional per bottle

ARTICLES NOT ON THIS BILL A LA CARTE PRICES

Passengers are requested to report any unusual
service or attention on the part of employees. This
enables us to recognize the exceptional efficiency
which we wish to encourage in our service.

L. I. McKIM,
General Passenger Agent,
Sacramento.

Steamers also operate on Sundays
Leaving San Francisco and Sacramento at 6:30 P. M.

This 1928 photo of the King's crew was taken by crew-member Herb Rummel less than a year after the steamboat's maiden voyage. Back row (left to right): Chief Steward Williams; "Smitty" Schmidt, Second Steward; Harry Neumeyer, barber; Dan Campbell, security; Herb Rummel, freight clerk; Fred Kelly, freight clerk; B.E. "Buck" Neiger, purser. Front row: Capt. Stoffel, pilot; Paul Pohl, First Mate; Capt. William Cooley, Relief Captain; William Ely, Chief Engineer; John McGowan, Second Engineer. (Capt. George Goodell was not present.)

Look what you get for 75¢: a five-course dinner with coffee, tea, or milk.

never record the number of mothers and fathers who looked daggers at their little ones after that knock on the door.

In the late 1930s, passengers boarding at Sacramento frequently did a double take when they first saw a Russian man named Petrushka serenading the departing vessel. Standing on the wharf, dressed in colorful costume, he sang Russian songs and played his balalaika as the boat left the dock. According to Ray

They All Had Important Jobs

From the captain on down, company employees on each of the *Delta* boats had their jobs to do. The captain was responsible for the whole vessel, the crew, and the passengers. The two pilots had the responsibility of steering the boat during their respective shifts. They worked in the pilothouse, the highest and forwardmost part of the superstructure; they were assisted by the first and second mates, and sometimes by the captain.

In turn, pilots depended upon the chief engineer and his assistant in the engine room, located near the stern four decks below. The two engineers kept the steam engine operating at the speed ordered by the pilot, who used the ship's telegraph to indicate "slow," "half," or "full" speed. They, in turn, depended on the fireman to tend the boilers in the deepest part of the forward hold, directly under the stack. The fireman had to ensure that boilers held enough water and that steam pressure was maintained at 225 pounds per square inch.

Dealing closely with the passengers were the purser and his one or two assistants, who "stood the plank" collecting tickets from passengers dockside before each trip and who also served as freight clerks when aboard. If you wanted a cabin but hadn't already reserved it, you stopped by the purser's office to ask for one and pay for it. The purser kept track of all monetary transactions, including cash

received for fares, staterooms, and meals; he reported to the company auditor in San Francisco.

About eight stewards handled room service, housekeeping, and table service in the dining room. They also polished brass and woodwork. A cook, with an assistant and a helper, prepared dinners and breakfasts. Two or three deckhands, a barber, and a security officer rounded out the crew.

Officers on the *King* and *Queen* wore navy-blue double-breasted uniforms with brass buttons down the front and gold stripes on their sleeves. You could tell the levels of authority by counting the stripes—four for captain, three for pilots and chief engineer, and two for purser, first mate, chief steward, security, and second engineer. Second mates, freight clerks, and second stewards wore one stripe. All wore white navy-officer-style caps with visors, gold trim, and the C.T. Co. insignia.

Cabins for the officers occupied the far forward portion of the top deck. The captain and the chief engineer got the best accommodations. Each had a roomy cabin immediately below and just aft of the pilothouse—the captain on the starboard side, the chief engineer to port. Other officers had smaller cabins aft of these two. In contrast, stewards and deckhands were quartered below the freight deck in the hold.

Fisher, Petrushka performed there to publicize his night club across the river in Bryte, site of a sizeable Russian colony.

Capt. A. E. Anderson, president of the C. T. Co., occasionally rode his company's boats between San Francisco and Sacramento. Reportedly, he chose the *Delta King*, whenever his schedule permitted. Former passenger Frank Jaworski passes along a story about Anderson taking a trip on the *King:* "He was standing with a group of dignitaries on an outside deck, watching a steamboat that was following them. With a touch of pride, Anderson noted that the vessel behind was one of his company's boats—the *Capt. Weber*. In a few minutes, it was evident the *Weber* was traveling at a higher rate of speed. Soon it passed the *King.*" According to the story, this displeased Anderson. Within days, he issued a written order: "None of my boats shall ever pass the *King* or *Queen*."

Over the years stories tend to get bigger and better, particularly when they concern drinking, gambling, and sexual hanky-panky on river steamers. In some people's memories, incidents grow in proportion to the degree the original actions involved forbidden behavior. And, often, the more removed the teller of the tale was from the alleged occurrence, the more outrageous the story.

From time to time, one may hear references to wild parties and gambling on the *Delta King* and *Queen*. Of course, from your stateroom on summer weekends it was not unusual to hear the sounds of late-night partying—loud voices, laughter, and the banging of cabin doors. But, in most cases, the more first-hand experience the person had with the two boats, the tamer the story.

For several years in the 1930s, the two boats did have a few slot machines of the nickel, dime, and two-bit variety. The machines were locked when the boats were tied up but could be used as soon as the vessels got under way. No other company-sponsored gambling was offered, such as blackjack, poker, or roulette. Gambling on a small scale, yes—exciting riverboat gamblers with fortunes won and lost, no. During the Great Depression, revenue from the slot machines helped the C.T. Co. get through a difficult period. Rationale for their use in a state that didn't allow slot machines was that once the vessel left the dock, it was no longer under the jurisdiction of the State of California. This reasoning worked until the late 1930s, when pressure from state Attorney General Earl Warren (later to become Governor of California and then Chief Justice of the United States) closed down the machines.

A common misconception about the *King* and *Queen* is that during Prohibition liquor flowed like water—that once the boats were under way, you could order anything you wanted to drink. Not true. There were no bars on these steamers and no liquor served until after the repeal of Prohibition in 1933. Before then, people did bring alcoholic beverages with them, just as they did on trains and in many other situations. Former purser Arthur Snyder recalls a New Year's Eve in the late Twenties: "I think most everyone on board had a bottle or two in their suitcases."

Occasionally, drinking got out of hand. Former passenger Richard Audsley thinks there may still be the remains of a piano at the bottom of the Sacramento River. He recalls the incident: "In the wee hours of the morning, a group of inebriated passengers finally decided to go to bed but couldn't stop the singing and piano playing of another group. Their solution: Push the piano overboard."

But usual life on the *King* and *Queen* was far from a drunken orgy. Witness the many people who remember going with their families and still carry treasured memories of their trips. In dozens of interviews with former passengers, the subject of drinking seldom came up. And former crew members unanimously swear the company would not have jeopardized its existence by serving liquor during Prohibition. Look the other way, perhaps—serve it, never.

When the conversation turns to titillating stories of sexual happenings on the two riverboats, people often snicker and paint a risque picture. Sometimes the allegation is explicit. Other times, it's merely implied by tone of voice or arching of an eyebrow. The subject of unmarried couples taking river trips doesn't exactly lend itself to scholarly research. But we can make a reasonable assumption that the romantic environment of the boat and its overnight schedule was at least conducive to such activity. And a number of anecdotes can be found to support its existence. We just can't say how common it was.

Art Samish, a powerful lobbyist at the state capital from the 1930s almost until he was sent to prison in the 1950s, wrote a book with Bob Thomas called *The Secret Boss of California*. In it he tells about herding a bill through the two state houses. It passed the Senate and then faced the Assembly in an evening session, where the vote was expected to be close. That night, two supporters—assemblymen he referred to as Ernie and Bill—were missing. Samish describes his dismay:

"Where the hell are those bastards?" I said. "We need them." I did some sleuthing and found out where Ernie and Bill had gone. They had taken a couple of girls on a voyage of the *Delta Queen,* a steamboat that made an overnight trip between Sacramento and San Francisco.

"I'll get 'em back," I swore . . . I called my friend Bill Dwyer, who ran the *Delta Queen* and *Delta King,* and he told me the boat's schedule along the Sacramento River. Then I had the sergeant at arms call the highway patrol and tell them to dispatch a couple of officers in a car to meet the *Delta Queen* at the next drawbridge.

The highway patrolmen arrived in time to board the steamboat and haul off the two assemblymen. With sirens screaming, the patrol car hurried back to Sacramento where Ernie and Bill cast their affirmative votes for my measure.

Afterward I thanked the two men for interrupting their trysts, and I told them: "I'll have Frank Flynn drive you to San Francisco before the *Delta Queen* docks. I'd hate to have those two girls arrive with no one to greet them."

Thus ends a tale of romantic plans gone awry. But, you may wonder, what about "ladies of the evening"? Did prostitutes ride on the two vessels? I put the question to several former crew members:

Gordon Ridley, who worked close to the nerve center in the purser's office on both boats, answered, "There weren't any prostitutes doing business there, because—after all—we got to recognize who's who on the vessel. And the subject never came up."

Eldridge Bowie responded, "Wasn't a problem. We didn't worry about it, as long as there were no complaints. Capt. Cooley might ask me about a certain woman who was dressed in a certain way, and I might answer that I hadn't seen anything to make her suspect—and that she hadn't propositioned *me*."

Then we have Ray Fisher's answer: "It's conceivable that sort of thing might have happened occasionally but only if arranged before the people got on board. It would need to have been done very quietly. Capt. Anderson was a very moral person and would have fired anyone who knowingly permitted it."

To get an outside viewpoint, I asked *San Francisco Chronicle* columnist Herb Caen. He replied: "I was aboard the *Delta King* as a kid and found it very innocent. But what did I know?"

5

Beyond Comfort and Luxury

Passenger schedules and timetables for the *Delta King* and *Delta Queen* enticed travelers with a promise of "Comfort and Luxury Afloat." On their nightly trips between San Francisco and Sacramento, the two boats consistently delivered on that promise. But they offered something more.

Former passengers, while remembering the comforts, recall other things first—the excitement and romance of the overnight trip, the ambience of the riverboat, the beauty of the water scene along the way, the enjoyment of friends and family aboard—and in many cases, the small, personal happenings of the trip. Most reminiscences about the *King* and *Queen* show a warmth and fondness toward the vessels; many display a Norman Rockwell flavor.

Those who traveled on the two steamboats often hold treasured images in their minds' eyes. Brad Bowman recalls wild ducks rising out of the tules and flying across a moonlit sky. Visions of fresh flowers with fine china and silverware on white tablecloths come back to Thomas Wade. Mary Alice Carswell remembers watching fireworks as the *Delta Queen* passed the 1939 world's fair on Treasure Island and seeing the reflections shimmering on bay waters.

Christine Kirk recalls the maiden voyage of the *Delta King* in 1927. "They had a live band, and we danced most of the night." She still remembers dinner on board: "Excellent food, many courses, huge olives in garlic olive oil—and finger bowls."

Marian N.J. Cassel tells of her wedding in Sacramento to Clinton Jewett in October of 1936, and their honeymoon on the *Delta Queen* bound for San Francisco: "When we left the dock, with our friends waving, it was as if we were sailing to faraway places. As we descended the beautiful staircase into the dining room, the band struck up 'Here Comes the Bride' and bottles of champagne were brought to our table." Other passengers joined in the fun and many danced with the new bride. But when the couple decided to retire to their cabin, it just wasn't meant to be. She says, "Bells had been attached to the springs of our bed and a troop of Sea Scouts decided to spend the evening serenading us. So we gave up and went on deck to enjoy the lights of the night. We were enthralled by the Straits, the Brothers, Angel Island, and the lights of The City. In San Francisco, we rode the cable cars and ate bay shrimp out of a bag. That night, we stayed at a hotel and returned home next evening on the *Delta King*."

The year was 1927; Lindbergh had just flown across the Atlantic and the *Delta* boats had just begun their nightly cruises. Donald T. MacPherson says, "I spent two days on Pickwick Stages (predecessor of Greyhound) from Los Angeles to San Francisco where I boarded the *Delta Queen* for the overnight voyage to Sacramento. Once there, I took a taxi to the airport and boarded a 'sister ship' of Lindbergh's *Spirit of St. Louis* to fly back to San Francisco. The pilot's wife and I were the only passengers!"

Eleanor J. Melvin tells of the beautiful reflections on the water from C & H Sugar refinery at Crockett "before other bright lights stole the night." She says, "The enormous factory, at least six stories high going full blast, was something to see." She adds a word about the sounds of the trip: "I always claimed I could tell when we passed from fresh water (which rattled) to salt water (that swished)."

In 1936, Ernest Schmierer's eighth-grade class financed its own trip to San Francisco on the *Delta Queen*. He says, "I went to Houston School, south of Sacramento near Lodi, and we raised the money with a class operetta. I recall viewing a beautiful nearly-full moon from the deck of the boat and, the next day, having fun at Golden Gate Park, the zoo, and the Cliff House."

Robert L. Barber experienced the sternwheelers from two perspectives—as a teenager and as an adult. As a Boy Scout in 1934, he and his troop went to see the historic "Old Ironsides" (U.S.S. *Constitution*) on display at San Francisco. To get there, 12 Scouts and their Scoutmaster climbed aboard the *Delta King* at Rio Vista and crowded into two staterooms. On a tour of the *King's* engine room, Barber remembers being impressed by the huge pitman arms, which turned the paddle wheel. And going up to the pilothouse, he was wide-eyed at the pilot's big wheel that controlled the rudders.

Six years later, in June of 1940, Barber got married. He and his bride decid-

Soon after Delta King's *maiden voyage in 1927, Helen Fisher Perry (left) and Theresa Fisher Layton posed on the top deck. Passengers below are standing at the railing on a day cruise in 1930s.*

ed to honeymoon on the *Delta Queen* and take their 1939 Chevrolet along. But when they arrived at the Sacramento wharf with tin cans and old shoes tied to the rear bumper and "Just Married" on the car window, they attracted the attention of the "Inquiring Reporter" from radio station KFBK. Barber says, "I was only 21 at the time and a little shy. So we ended up running to the back of the boat and hiding in our cabin."

As a child, Paul E. Alexander rode the vessels to the California State Fair at Sacramento. Recalling the river scenery, he says, "It was beautiful—sometimes it seemed you could almost reach out and touch the bank. But being children, we spent a lot of time running and playing hide-and-go-seek around the boat."

Mildred Lawrence's only memory of her ride on the *Queen,* at age seven, is standing at the stern with a friend and throwing potatoes at the paddle wheel—and getting into trouble with her parents for it. Sometimes a "vegetable attack" would come from the shore. Pete Budnick says, "In the early 1930s, as young fellows we always raised a little hell. During sugar-beet season, when we heard the boat whistling for the bridge to open at Walnut Grove, we'd run out and try to throw beets down the smokestack. Never did hit the stack, but the upper deck sure took a pounding."

With a group of boys traveling to summer camp near Lake Tahoe, Bill Knorp rode the vessels from San Francisco to Sacramento on two round trips—one on the *King* in 1939 and the other on the *Queen* in 1940. He recalls the merriment when the *King* and *Queen* passed each other near the midpoint of their trips: "We sang on the outer deck, waiting for the other boat to come into view—songs such as 'The Merry-Go-Round Broke Down' and 'Smiles.' I think the predominant emotion was even more than joy—it was glee." Knorp describes another high point: "As a ferryboat fan, I was particularly thrilled to see the ferry *Cazadero* loom out of the fog one morning and run right alongside the *Queen* as we neared San Francisco. We were so close you could hear all the ferry's bells and whistles."

Claire Schluer Johnson was pre-school age, when she traveled with her family to San Francisco on the *Delta King*. She lost her prized possession—a doll—aboard the riverboat. "I responded in typical little-girl fashion, crying my eyes out until the whole ship's crew was put to work hunting for my doll. Finally, they found it, and life returned to normal."

Jack Oglesby recalls a trip in his "late pre-school years" to Sacramento. Upon arrival, he says, "It seemed sheer magic that our car appeared on the wharf, which was two stories above the deck our room was on. The river was well below the level of the levee. The magic, of course, was due to an on-shore elevator, but I didn't learn about that until years later."

Possibly the youngest passenger ever to travel on the boats was a baby born unexpectedly, November 16, 1934, on the *Delta King*. The surprised parents, Mr. and Mrs. Arthur Lancaster of Hutchison, Kansas, had expected the event to take place in December. The new addition to their family—a baby girl weighing six pounds, four ounces—was named Delta Jean.

Writing in the *Alameda Times Star* a few years ago, Alan Ward told about the special Saturday-night stops at the foot of Broadway in Oakland during baseball season in the 1930s. The paddlewheelers picked up members of the Oakland Boosters and took them to Sacramento for a Sunday doubleheader, returning from the capital city Sunday night and docking in Oakland on Monday morning. Ward says, "Most workers went directly from the dock to their jobs. We were younger then and could get along with only a small amount of slumber."

Upon occasion, the schedule of the *King* and *Queen* allowed for the needs of football fans, too. According to the Copley News Service, once a year in late November the steamers would delay their Saturday-night departures an hour or so

---

A Sight to Behold

Enjoyment of the boats wasn't confined just to their passengers. Those on shore also derived pleasure from the two stern-wheelers. George Sanchez says, "I loved to see the *Delta King* and *Queen* sail by. They could be seen at quite a distance—such a magnificent sight, all lit up like a great floating palace." At seven years of age, Betty Shannon saw the *Delta Queen* for the first time near Walnut Grove "ablaze with lights—people on deck, talking, laughing, with wonderful music in the background." She describes the sight as "the most incredible wonder of my young life."

For a special treat, Alan Henderson's father took him down to the levee below Sacramento to watch the boats go by. As he grew older, Alan went with his neighborhood friends; he says, "Riding our bikes to the river became a summer ritual."

Armando Mazzi recalls swimming under the Carquinez Bridge on summer nights and seeing the sternwheelers "with lights on and the band playing. They'd glide by like big white swans."

Although she didn't travel on the *King* and *Queen* in their California days, Betty McFerren describes them as "old friends." She says, "In the late 1930s, one or the other was always tied up at the M Street Bridge in Sacramento awaiting its nightly cruise to San Francisco. I crossed that bridge frequently when I was in school at the University of California at Davis, 14 miles west. It's funny, I recall word circulating on campus that River Lines had forbidden Davis students to ride the two boats. But I never did find out what nefarious deeds the Cal Aggies were supposed to have committed."

at San Francisco. This allowed rooters for Stanford and the University of California at Berkeley to get aboard for the return trip to Sacramento after their "Big Game" at either campus. Win or lose, they had a ride home. No mention is made of the after-game deportment of those aboard.

Because they were night boats, the *King* and *Queen* seldom offered day trips. Exceptions came at two periods. Toward the end of their commercial careers in California in the late 1930s, the boats were laid up during the winter, permitting the C.T. Co. to offer day trips at the beginning and end of the season. And in the boats' early years, before they went to a seven-day-a-week schedule, groups often chartered the vessels for Sunday outings. Organizations included the Masons, Elks, San Francisco Press Club, doctors' and dentists' groups.

Rose Callaghan tells of special Sunday cruises around the bay: "At the end of the 1920s and in the early '30s, our family enjoyed all-day affairs put on by the Ancient Order of Hibernians. The freight deck was cleared for dancing—fiddles and accordions supplied the music. It was a joyous time." She was only seven or eight at the time. But looking back now, she thinks it likely that, as the Irish celebrated their origins from such counties as Mayo, Kerry, and Cork, they conveniently overlooked the restrictions of Prohibition.

In 1939, the Deer Valley School in California's gold country housed all eight grades in a one-room schoolhouse without electricity. Miss Oates (now Dorothy

---

A Special Time on the River

While passengers were enjoying their overnight trips, the crew worked hard. But crew members also found pleasure in traveling on the river. Sometimes, it was merely a quiet moment in the darkness of the outer decks. Former freight-clerk Gordon Ridley recalls the trip upriver as especially pleasant in the early hours of the morning: "Once past the Rio Vista bridge, the river narrows . . . you can smell the fields and the blossoms along the way. On a moonlit night the scene is one of enchantment.

"On dark nights, in the small towns along the way, only an isolated light or two betrays the fact that there's another world

just before our fingertips. The pilot whistles for the next bridge—slowly and majestically it swings open. When we pass, there may be a car or two waiting on the ramp watching us and then continuing on when the span swings shut. As the sky lightens, you can see more and more, the fields, the narrow paved roads, the barns and homes—some dark and some with the activity of early-risers.

"Sometimes, as we pass, we hear birds singing in the trees—sometimes, huge flocks move from one field to the next in search of who knows what. Finally, it is light and we round the last bend."

The two boats make a rare appearance together at Sacramento in mid to late 1930s (reason for this meeting not known). Photo on right was taken during one of the infrequent day trips.

THE RIVER LINES

SAN FRANCISCO
—TO—
SACRAMENTO

Good only for one continuous passage if
used on date stamped on back hereof or on
date following.
Baggage liability limited to $100.

Form 301   *A.A. Bowman*
                        Gen. Pass. Agent

GOING   22611

THE RIVER LINES

SACRAMENTO
—TO—
SAN FRANCISCO

Good only for one passage if used within
thirty (30) days from date of sale stamped
on back hereof.
Baggage liability limited to $100.

Form 301   *A.A. Bowman*
                        Gen. Pass. Agent

RETURN   22611

Wunschel), the school's young unmarried teacher in her first year of teaching, had an idea. She would take her students by riverboat to the world's fair on Treasure Island. She says, "With the help of one mother, we loaded 12 children on the *Delta King* at Sacramento and put them in the boat's cabins, two per bunk (four per room). It was Depression time, so eating in the dining room was out—we ate sack lunches out of a suitcase. Most of the kids had never seen the ocean, the bay, a steamboat, or even the Sacramento River, and they were wide-eyed. Upon arrival in the early morning at San Francisco, I bought them doughnuts and milk at the Ferry Building. Then we had a long and exciting day at the fair." One boy, a third grader by the name of Charlie, got lost. When the boy was found, Miss Oates exclaimed, "Charlie, where have you been? I've been looking all over for you!" He paused, then answered, "I wasn't lost—I knew where I was."

As teenagers in the 1930s, Mary Botteri, Lena Myers, and Della Beltrami rode the boats, unchaperoned, to San Francisco. "We'd giggle and tell each other ghost stories all night. In the morning, we'd take off for Fisherman's Wharf. We didn't have any shipboard romances. But once someone did buy us drinks."

At grammar-school age in the late 1930s, Dorene Sewell-Johnson won a prize on a musical quiz show on the radio—a trip to San Francisco with her mother on the *Delta Queen*. "One of my most exciting memories is of the horse-racing slot machines on the boat. I remember winning time and again and people cheering me on, as though I were the jockey. We dressed up for dinner. I remember how fancy everything was. The waiters wore white jackets and dark trousers and had napkins over their arms. It all seemed like a movie to me. Upon awakening in the morning, we could hear the foghorns of San Francisco."

The *Delta King* and *Delta Queen* made good on their promise of "Comfort and Luxury Afloat." Most passengers felt they had received full measure—and more.

6

The Plot Thickens

In the late 1920s, this country still enjoyed what most people looked upon as prosperous times. But by 1929, a few observers began to notice danger signs and sounded the alarm. The building boom had ended, auto sales were off, oil production far exceeded demand, and speculation ran rampant on the stock market. Yet, up until the last days before the economy collapsed, warnings were brushed aside by optimists in high places. They assured everyone that all was well.

On October 27, 1929, Charles Mitchell, president of the National City Bank of New York proclaimed: "I know of nothing fundamentally wrong with the stock market or with the underlying business and credit structures." Two days later the market crashed, ushering in the worst depression our country had ever known.

During the two and a half years the *Delta King* and *Delta Queen* operated before the onset of the Great Depression, they produced a reasonable profit. Passenger business, in the summer at least, had flourished. And freight produced a steady revenue that substantially exceeded income from the passenger trade. But in 1930, the first full year of the Depression, the C.T. Co. lost money on its riverboats.

President Herbert Hoover's prediction in early 1931 that "prosperity is just around the corner" failed to relieve the firm's anxieties. The company had gone out on a limb to build the two steamers and now found itself vulnerable and in debt. Financing for construction of the two "million dollar boats" had created a burden, hard enough to carry in normal times. But now, a major depression was under way. Car and truck competition was beginning to take its toll—and new bridges and highways were either built or on the drawing boards. Trouble lay ahead.

The Antioch Bridge had opened in 1926 and the Carquinez Bridge in 1927 (the latter opening just days before the maiden voyages of the *Delta* boats). The Southern Pacific railroad bridge between Benicia and Martinez opened in 1930. And the two giant bridges on San Francisco Bay would open in a few short years, the Bay Bridge in 1936 and the Golden Gate in 1937.

On the plus side, competition with the *King* and *Queen* lessened somewhat when Southern Pacific, the dominant railroad company in California, went out of the riverboat business in 1930. Primarily to eliminate competition, the C.T. Co. had bought the remaining two steamboats owned by SP, the *Navajo* and the *Cherokee*. Until then, SP had competed for business on the Sacramento River. With this purchase, C.T. Co. added to its impressive fleet of vessels, already more than a dozen sternwheelers. But numbers didn't mean much. The river trade was drying up in California and elsewhere in the country. Extra vessels served no real purpose; in fact, most were already laid up at Stockton. After 1932, the *King* and *Queen* were the only boats regularly operated by the C.T. Co. A few freight boats operated by other firms remained on the river.

By 1931, the freight business had fallen off badly. To make matters worse, competition for the remaining freight was fierce; riverboat and barge operators fought for what little there was. One operator—the Fay Transportation Company, which ran diesel freight boats—was singled out by C.T. Co. and accused of unfair competition. The C.T. Co. found an ally: the Sacramento Navigation Company, a firm operating a fleet of barges and sternwheel towboats primarily on the river above Sacramento.

In late 1931, the two companies joined together and filed a formal complaint against Fay Transportation, alleging that Fay's operations were being conducted illegally, that their rates were discriminatory and unethical. The complaint, made to the state Railroad Commission (predecessor to the Public Utilities Commission), further stated that unless the situation was remedied, a disastrous rate war on the river would erupt.

At a hearing on the complaint, commissioner Fred G. Stevenot proposed that the three litigants bring their companies together under a unified operation. He said this would prevent the firms from fighting each other for existing tonnage, which was not enough to support all three under separate management anyway. The companies followed his advice.

On February 1, 1932, they set up an operating service and called it The River Lines. Their agreement did not constitute a merger. Each of the three firms—

California Transportation Company, Sacramento Navigation Company, and Fay Transportation Company—kept its own identity. But all business and equipment would be handled through one unified River Lines management. Capt. A.E. Anderson (C.T. Co. president) became chairman of the board of the new consortium. W.P. Dwyer, owner of the Sacramento Navigation Company, became its president. Norvin A. Fay (son of Nahum Fay, founder of Fay Transportation) was

A New Hope: The River Lines

THE PLAN: At first glance, it might seem that the financial arrangements of the new unified operation favored the owners of the *King* and *Queen*. Under the agreement, C.T. Co. would receive 53% of the revenue, while Sacramento Navigation would receive 27% and Fay Transportation 20%. Nothing unusual here. Because C.T. Co., with its two deluxe steamers, had more capital invested and more revenue potential, it would get the highest percentage.

But a reading of the fine print revealed a trump card in the hand of the Fays: a guarantee to their company of $50,000 per year for the first three years. If revenue during those years turned out to be extremely low, that guarantee could have been fatal to the other two companies. As it happened, however, operating efficiencies of the new River Lines paid off. In 1932, the first year of operation, all three made a modest profit.

THE PEOPLE: The heads of the three River Lines companies contrasted with one another in style and background.

Capt. A.E. Anderson of C.T. Co. had worked all his life in the steamboat business his father had founded in the last century to carry passengers and freight. Former crew member Ray Fisher describes Anderson as "a tall, very distinguished-looking man, ramrod straight—a fine old gentleman type of the old school."

W.P. Dwyer of Sacramento Navigation operated a barging business established by his father to haul firewood on the river. He had spent years on the river directing barge hands, and he displayed a rough-hewn demeanor. Fisher recalls him as "a very direct man with a businesslike manner" and then adds: "Dwyer didn't mince words. But overall he was fair and well respected."

Capt. Nahum Fay and his son, Norvin, represented the third company of the River Lines triumvirate. After steamboat beginnings, the father had pioneered the use of diesel boats to carry cargo on the Sacramento-San Joaquin River Delta. He had gained a reputation for his crusty manner but was an acknowledged expert on freight matters.

Former crew member Gordon Ridley remembers being impressed by Capt. Fay, sometimes quietly referred to as "the old fox." Ridley says, "He seemed to know all the answers." But by the time the River Lines was established in 1932, Nahum Fay was getting along in years, and his son Norvin handled most of the managerial duties. He, too, had a nickname: "Smoothie." According to Fisher, "Norvin Fay was very smooth and also very sharp. Personally, I liked him." Other former employees of River Lines were not so complimentary about the Fays. It seemed you either liked them or you didn't.

named vice-president and general manager, while his father served on the board of control.

By late summer of 1932, front-page headlines across the country dealt mostly with the harsh realities of the Great Depression and with the Democratic party's nomination of Franklin Delano Roosevelt to run against Herbert Hoover in the fall presidential election. But in Northern California, headlines also carried news of a devastating waterfront fire at Sacramento, a conflagration that destroyed almost the entire fleet of riverboats owned by one of the River Lines firms.

With the upriver trade nearly gone, Sacramento Navigation Company had laid up ten of its steamers across the river from Sacramento. Just after midnight on August 28, 1932, a houseboat resident got up to investigate a noise. He was shocked at what he saw—flames pouring from the windows of one of the riverboats. Soon sparks and glowing embers ignited other vessels; smoke and cinders engulfed both sides of the river. In one of the most spectacular fires in anyone's memory, crowds watched as tall smokestacks tumbled, pilothouses crumbled, and oil tanks exploded. Of the ten boats, only the *Dover* and *Red Bluff* could be towed to safety. The rest burned to the waterline. Since the steamboats were already out of service, the fire had no immediate effect on River Lines operations. Rumors circulated that the fire was planned in order to collect insurance. But, as far as is

known, no charges were filed.

As if the C.T. Co. and River Lines didn't have enough trouble already with the depressed economy and increased car and truck competition, labor unrest in the Bay Area added new woes in 1934. On May 9, the first great maritime strike of the 1930s began. The strike wasn't aimed at the *Delta King* and *Queen* and did not shut them down at first. But, according to C.T. Co. historian Bill Stritzel, this dispute cost the company dearly, coming as it did at the busiest time of the year when the boats were working to capacity. The *King* and *Queen* soon had to cancel their runs—they had no freight to pick up or deliver.

Former freight-clerk Ray Fisher got curious one day during the early part of the strike and stepped outside the River Lines office in San Francisco. "I decided to go down a couple of blocks from Pier 3 to buy a candy bar at one of the other piers. Just as I was about to go back into the office, a big touring car with four or five big, burly guys pulled over. They looked like Al Capone goons; they asked me what I was doing there. Not wanting to let them know I had any connection with the maritime scene, I meekly replied that I had come down from Sacramento and thought I'd have a look at the waterfront. They told me, 'This is no place to be—there's a big strike on.' 'Oh, gee—thank you, thank you!' I said. They drove off, and I scuttled back into the River Lines office, a little wiser for the experience."

In August 1932, fire (opposite page) destroys eight River Lines all-wooden steamers; the King *and* Queen *were not directly involved. In July 1934, San Francisco's water-front is rocked by violence, as police and strikers battle; governor calls out National Guard. Though strike is not aimed at* Delta *boats, it costs them dearly, coming at their busiest season.*

Harry Bridges, founder of the International Longshoremen's and Warehousemen's Union, led the 1934 strike that began in San Francisco as a dispute between steamship lines and the men working the docks. Soon the longshoremen were joined by other waterfront unions, including the Teamsters, Sailors Union of the Pacific, Marine Cooks and Stewards, Marine Firemen, and Marine Workers' Industrial Union.

The employers announced they would reopen the San Francisco waterfront by force. In early July, the dispute grew ugly. Policemen tried to open the waterfront, firing guns and tear gas at strikers, who were armed with bricks, clubs, and railroad spikes. Four days of riots followed. On July 5—later termed "Bloody Thursday" by the union—the police killed two men and injured dozens. "Blood ran red in the streets of San Francisco," the *Chronicle* reported the next day, calling it "the darkest day this city has known since April 18, 1906 [the big earthquake and fire] as 1,000 police battled 5,000 longshoremen."

Governor Frank Merriam called out the National Guard to patrol the Embarcadero. Later, thousands of men and women marched up Market Street with the coffins of the two slain union men. On July 17, an estimated 125,000 people walked off their jobs in a general strike that stopped the city dead in its tracks for three days. Finally, on July 31, 1934, San Franciscans gave a collective sigh of relief as the waterfront strike ended—83 days after it began in early May.

Now the *Delta King* and *Queen* could operate again. But only for a year. In July of 1935, a bargemen's strike shut down river operations for three months. Because River Lines cargo was trucked between Sacramento, Stockton, and San Francisco by the Teamsters Union, which was not on strike, the freight went through. But the strike proved to be another big blow to C.T. Co., both in terms of lost revenue that could never be recovered and in the way it reinforced the growing image of trucks as a superior method of transport.

The bargemen's strike turned out to be "blow one of a one-two punch." An event the year before, though it took place on the East Coast, affected the two *Delta* boats now in 1935. When the steamship *Morro Castle* burned and went aground near Asbury Park, New Jersey, 125 people lost their lives. This disaster prompted a safety program by the Coast Guard. New regulations caught up with the *King* and *Queen* right after the bargemen's strike.

The Coast Guard ordered the drydocking of both vessels for thorough inspection of hulls, and it mandated the installation of fire sprinklers. When this work dragged on into the fall, River Lines decided to lay up the two boats for the

In these pictures, boats are "peddling"—the daily pick-up and delivery of large shipments on San Francisco waterfront after passengers disembarked in morning. Above photo shows Coit Tower and Telegraph Hill in mid to late 1930s. Below, that lonely pier will soon become an integral part of the San Francisco-Oakland Bay Bridge, which opened in November 1936.

1934 advertisement above promotes travel by Bay Area passengers to Sacramento; fares reduced for Depression (compare to prices in early ad, page 40). In late 1930s, boats begin winter layovers; thus the 1938 ad at right, which announces resumption of service; fare is still $1.95 round trip.

Sail 6:00 p. m. Enjoy delicious, well-served dinner. Relax a few hours on deck. Listen or dance to good dance music. Play cards in richly furnished lounge or smoking room. Then deep refreshing sleep "a million miles" from traffic odors, noise, dirt—in your "ocean liner" stateroom. Arrive 5:30 a.m.... sleep as late as you like (breakfast 'til 8:30). Arise rested, refreshed ... ready for a full day of business or pleasure.

California's only over-night water trip.

ROUND TRIP $1.95 • STATEROOMS $1 to $5
Take your car for less than it costs to drive

The **RIVER LINES**
Pier 3   SUtter 3880

At Sacramento cars were loaded and unloaded by elevator on dock.

winter. Service didn't resume until spring. Consequently, the vessels stayed out of service for a total of nine months in the 1935-36 period. This meant another serious loss in revenue and another nail in the coffin of the last two riverboats carrying passengers and freight on California waters.

The outlook for C.T. Co. was grim. Not only had the two strikes and dry-docking cost the company money it could never get back, but there seemed little hope for a better future. Roads were getting wider, straighter, faster. New bridges had been built, and more were coming. Trucks competed for freight; more people owned cars. The Great Depression had substantially reduced passenger and cargo business. And, according to Bill Stritzel, strikes in the 1930s not only lost revenue for the company, but they also destroyed a critical lifeline. The strikes ended the important long-time passenger and freight connection between river steamers and coastal vessels.

In the fall of 1935, the C.T. Co. declared bankruptcy. The company filed for reorganization under the federal bankruptcy law, which permitted it to hold off its creditors for a period while reorganizing its affairs under supervision of the court. Almost two years would pass before the state Railroad Commission would approve a reorganization plan. In the meantime, the two sternwheelers continued as best they could.

On April 1, 1936, when the *Delta King* and *Queen* resumed service after their nine-month layover, the initial trips seemed almost like maiden voyages again. The *Queen* steamed out of Sacramento with a party of a hundred business-men and their wives on a cruise sponsored by the Sacramento Chamber of Commerce. Upon arrival the next day in San Francisco, Mayor Angelo Rossi and a delegation of city officials met the boat and greeted the Sacramentans with cheer-ful words and firm handshakes.

The elation didn't last long. Labor strife returned to plague the River Lines and C.T. Co. In October, just six months after the *Delta* boats had resumed ser-vice, another major strike hit the San Francisco waterfront. The two steamers were forced to shut down for about three months.

The 1936 strike produced one episode long remembered by the C.T. Co. employees involved. When the labor dispute began, the *Delta Queen* was docked at Sacramento and the *Delta King* at Pier 3 in San Francisco. The owners worried that if the *King* sat in salt water too long, barnacles would grow on the hull. Because this would put a drag on the boat and waste fuel, they decided to take the vessel to Stockton and dock it in fresh water for the duration of the strike.

With no passengers or freight to carry, the *King* needed only a skeleton crew. On November 1, a small, select group assembled: Capt. Howard King as pilot, a first mate and his deckhands, and Jim Burns as engineer. Burns had many years of experience and, as Port Engineer for C.T. Co., had supervised the building of the *King* and *Queen* a decade before. While the engine room was in good hands, a fireman was needed to tend the boilers. Jim Burns telephoned his son, John, who had worked full time as fireman on company boats from 1930 to 1933 and as relief fireman in later years. "Can you help us out, John? We want to take the *King* up to Stockton tomorrow, and we need your help." John paused a moment, then replied that he would take a day off from his job and join the crew.

John recalls the strikebound waterfront at Pier 3 as "a tough place—nothing but a bunch of clubs, guns, and knuckles." At the end of their phone conversation, his father told him how to avoid the strike lines. "Go up to Pier 27, and I'll have someone meet you with a rowboat. I'll have it there by 10 tonight." Because Pier 27, known as the "potato boat dock," wasn't an active pier at that time, it wasn't being picketed. It made a safe place to meet.

At the appointed hour, John Burns was rowed in darkness a half mile to where the *Delta King* was docked. John, an agile young man, climbed up the paddle wheel, slipped into the engine room, and met with his father and Capt. King to discuss plans. They decided to get some sleep and leave for Stockton early in the morning.

Since it would take four hours to get steam up for departure, John started his job soon after midnight. By daybreak on November 2, everything was ready. The captain telegraphed the engine room, "Slow speed astern." With a churning of the paddle wheel, the *King* backed into the bay.

All seemed to be going well as the bow came around and pointed north toward the intended route. John went aft for a minute to inspect the machinery section. On returning to the boiler room, he routinely scanned the sight glass on the boiler. He expected it to show a sufficient level of water, just as it had moments before. Instead, the glass was completely empty! He recalls, "I knew I had to act quickly to avoid a disaster. So I shut down the fire and ran back to the engine room and shouted to my dad, 'I shut 'er down! There's no water in the sight glass!' My father quickly called up to Capt. King, who immediately set the telegraph to the 'Stop' position."

With quick hands, Jim Burns closed the throttle, cutting off steam to the engines. Without power, the boat drifted. While the vessel was adrift, father and son tried to go below to find the cause of the problem. This proved impossible, since the cavernous machinery section was now cloaked in total darkness and filled with steam.

Within minutes, those aboard the drifting steamer would experience a strange adventure, the kind that had only a one-in-a-million chance of happening in the first place. Like the *Titanic* and the iceberg, it seemed the *Delta King* was destined to cross paths with a unique landmark in the bay.

Wind and tide had taken charge. It so happened that those two forces joined together in just the right combination to run the helpless sternwheeler aground on Alcatraz Island, otherwise known as "The Rock." Here the venerable riverboat sat stranded under a rocky cliff that rose up to the "escape-proof" federal prison, where Al Capone and other notorious convicts were serving their time.

The paddle wheel and part of the stern had caught on a gravelly beach. Fearing serious damage, the captain asked John to go over the side and inspect the hull and the wheel. John recalls, "I dived down several times on both sides—went down about five feet and couldn't see any obvious damage. After the last dive, I was standing on the beach when suddenly I hear this loud bull horn above me, 'Get back on the ship—get back on the ship.' I looked up and saw a dozen prison guards with Thompson submachine guns pointing at me. I climbed the wheel and got back on the *King*—pronto!"

While this drama was unfolding, word of the mishap reached the Coast Guard, which sent for a Crowley Red Stack tug. Meanwhile, the father-and-son team inspected the machinery and found the cause of the problem. Debris had caught in the sea well, where water was supposed to flow in and go to the condenser, thus robbing the boilers of water.

Within an hour help arrived. The steam tug *Sea Lion* secured a tow line to the steamer, pulled it free, and towed it back to Pier 3. Later that day, Jim Burns and Capt. King decided the vessel could cruise again. Just after dark, the *Delta King* left San Francisco for an uneventful trip to Stockton. No side trips this time.

As a backdrop to that day's events, two engineering marvels on the bay loomed high, a reminder the world was changing. The San Francisco-Oakland Bay Bridge had just been completed and would open in ten days. The Golden Gate Bridge was nearly complete and would open the following spring. Soon cars and trucks by the thousands would pour over these spans. Beautiful and majestic as they must have seemed, these structures represented two more coffin nails for the *King* and *Queen*.

1938 steamboat race between **Delta Queen** *and* **Port of Stockton:** *That's Myrtle Loheit Duensing, "Miss Sacramento," atop the* **Queen;** *historian Julian Dana stands behind her. Below, at Freeport Bridge,* **Queen** *holds slight lead.*

End of an Era

By the late 1930s, the *Delta King* and *Delta Queen* were living on borrowed time. And, in a sense, the whole country was, too. Still reeling from the effects of the Great Depression, Americans were becoming increasingly aware of threats from outside their borders. Many felt the nation was headed toward a worldwide conflagration.

Yet an air of innocence remained. Certainly, for many people, there was a degree of denial as they tried to forget their troubles and the stark realities of the world. They went about their daily lives as best they could. Now and then, when they could afford to, they tried to escape for a day or two of diversion and relaxation. For Northern Californians, that sometimes meant a trip on the *Delta King* or *Delta Queen*.

On weekends in the good-weather months, a fair number of passengers continued to ride the two sternwheelers. They still enjoyed the romance, the ambience, the get-away-from-it-all feeling of the overnight voyage. Passenger traffic was brisk each year during the State Fair at Sacramento. Occasionally, too, Sacramentans took weekday trips for shopping or a show in "the city." Also a few businessmen, legislators, and lobbyists stuck with their habit of using the boats to arrive fresh and rested for a full day's work at their destination city.

While passengers were aware of their own economic problems and the worries of those around them, most were unaware of the riverboats' fragile hold on life. To many, it seemed these inland steamers had become an institution that would go on forever. But evidence to the contrary appeared all around, as more people owned cars, freight-laden trucks could be seen everywhere, and the two big

bridges on San Francisco Bay neared completion.

From the mid-1930s on, as the *King* and *Queen* steamed on the bay, passengers and crew witnessed an amazing trio of projects under way—true engineering marvels, the likes of which hadn't been seen before and haven't been seen since. First, they saw construction of two of the largest bridges in the world, the San Francisco-Oakland Bay Bridge and the Golden Gate Bridge (the latter linking San Francisco with Marin County). Then, they observed the creation of what was billed as the biggest man-made island on earth: Treasure Island. The future for the two boats was to become irrevocably tied to these projects.

When finished, these immense undertakings would have their individual effects on the *Delta* boats. The bridges' effect would be negative; eventually, the steamboats would lose passengers and freight. Treasure Island's effect, on the other hand, would be positive; it would help to keep the vessels operating.

This new 403-acre island in the bay was to be the site of a world's fair: the Golden Gate International Exposition. At a time when the C.T. Co. was barely able to hang on financially, the coming fair became a rationale for keeping the boats in service. The company hoped that patronage by fair-bound passengers would make its riverboats profitable again.

Construction on the Golden Gate Bridge began in early 1933, and work to span the bay between San Francisco and Oakland began six months later. The Golden Gate structure, the longest suspension bridge in the world at that time, cost $35 million. The eight-mile-long Bay Bridge, though started later, opened first. It cost $77 million.

The **King** *and* **Queen** *offered only a few day trips: Sunday charters in their early years; then in late 1930s, day trips at start and end of seasons.*

The possibility of crossing the bay to link San Francisco and Oakland had been discussed for half a century. Finally, that long-awaited bridge was built, and it opened on November 12, 1936. In *Treasure Island,* a book about the fair and the bridges, Richard Reinhardt writes: "According to the [Oakland] *Tribune,* the opening of the Bay Bridge was the greatest civic event in the Bay Area since the end of the World War. There were fireworks and school holidays, radio broadcasts, football games, chain-cuttings, ribbon snippings and day-and-night parades. The newspaper coverage was prodigious."

As for early thinking on the other bridge, Reinhardt says:

Since the end of the Great War, people in Northern California had been talking more or less seriously about building a suspension bridge across the Golden Gate. Hundreds of professed experts said it could not be built (on engineering grounds), should not be built (on aesthetic grounds), and probably would not be built (on financial grounds). But the counties to the north of the straits joined the city in forming a bridge district, and the voters approved a bond issue . . .

After four years of construction, the Golden Gate Bridge was completed, and the public was invited to inspect it on May 28, 1937. Reinhardt describes the throngs that descended, beginning early in the morning:

A few had come on horseback, roller skates or bicycles . . . one man was strutting back and forth on stilts. Many had come directly from an all-night ball at the Civic Auditorium, where George Jessel told jokes and Al Jolson sang. When the toll gates opened at 6:00, the crowd rushed forward with a shout of joy . . . By nightfall, 200,000 votaries had trod the span of gold.

Ferryboats that plied the bay alongside the new spans were soon taken out of service. But the bridges' effect on the *King* and *Queen* was more gradual. The *Delta* boats held on bravely in a world quite different from the one in which they were born. They even managed to add new excitement to the bay and river scene.

On June 26, 1938, the *Delta Queen* thrilled passengers and spectators alike—and received good press in the bargain—when she got into a good old-fashioned steamboat race. It was California's first in half a century. Representing Sacramento, she raced 17 miles downriver from that city to the town of Clarksburg, competing against *Port of Stockton* (formerly *Capital City*) which represented Stockton.

Robert W. Parkinson, who rode on the *Queen* that day, recalls that the boat left Sacramento with 900 passengers, who paid 50 cents each. The finish was extremely close. At first, officials declared the race a dead heat. Then they ruled in favor of the *Port of Stockton,* saying she had won by a whisker. *Delta Queen* fans protested. They claimed the large number of passengers on their boat had created a handicap in competing against a vessel without passengers. Parkinson says, "The *Port of Stockton* had no passenger license, but some people were aboard, apparently company employees and families." In any case, Sacramento mayor Tom Monk immediately challenged Stockton to a rematch, setting the stage for another race the following year. The next contest would prove to be a more lengthy and better-publicized event between the royalty of the river, the *Delta King* and *Delta Queen*.

ALL ABOARD FOR ADVENTURE!

Delta Queen, sponsored by Sacramento, vs. Delta King, sponsored by Stockton —racing to Treasure Island.
Golden Eagle vs. City of St. Louis racing on the Mississippi.
All four boats racing against time for the CHAMPIONSHIP OF AMERICA

NATIONAL
STEAMBOAT RACE
Saturday, April 22nd.

Here's your 20th Century adventure with Old Man River! Paddle-wheels slapping— smokestacks pouring—gaiety at the helm and excitement dead ahead!

Plan to be "on deck" when your favorite swings into the stream. National and international newsreel cameramen will be on hand to "shoot" you. Costume parties will be aboard—dancing—entertainment—re- freshments—will key you for the grand fi- nale at the Fair.

Boats dock right at Treasure Island. Special "doin's" there will help you celebrate the race. From start to finish, it's going to be FUN, spelled in capitals, and underlined with thrills!

ROUND TRIP FARE ... $3.50
ONE WAY   ... 2.50

Delta Queen leaves Sacramento at 8:00 a.m. Delta King leaves Stock- ton at 9:00 a.m.—race to the Fair arriving around 6:00 p.m.

Both boats leave Treasure Island at 11:00 p.m. that night. Round trip tickets also good on Southern Pa- cific trains (special late train to Stockton). If you wish, you may spend the week-end at the Fair, re- turning Sunday night by boat (Sac- ramento only) or train.

$50 CASH PRIZES
for the best old time costumes on each boat
Be sure to get "rigged out"—you may win

BUY YOUR TICKETS at any River Lines office. Pier M, Sacramento • El Dorado & Channel Sts., Stockton • Pier 3, San Francisco. Reservations going fast. Don't wait until the last minute to get your tickets ... you may miss the fun.

1939: First and only race between Delta King *and* Delta Queen.

Boat race receives nationwide public- ity: newspapers, radio, newsreels. It all helps promote the Golden Empire Centennial, cities of Sacramento and Stockton, River Lines, and world's fair on Treasure Island.

Souvenir Ticket
River Boat Race
S. S. DELTA KING
vs.
S. S. DELTA QUEEN

April 22, 1939

STOCKTON
TO
TREASURE ISLAND
The Historic River Route of the 49'er

This is to Certify that

was aboard the million dollar de lux
S. S. Delta King

The 1939 steamboat race grew into a major undertaking sponsored by the California State Chamber of Commerce, the Sacramento Golden Empire Centennial, and the Golden Gate International Exposition. The two boats started from different cities and came down separate rivers until they met for a race to the finish line. The *King* steamed down the San Joaquin from Stockton, while the *Queen* cruised down the Sacramento from the city of Sacramento. Meeting near Pittsburg, the paddlewheelers then raced to Treasure Island, where the fair had opened just two months before.

Had plans worked out as originally conceived, the big steamboat race would have been even more of an event, involving at least five vessels. At a meeting in February 1939, California's Governor Culbert L. Olson issued a challenge to the governors of New York, Ohio, and Missouri—states with cities on the Hudson, Ohio, and Mississippi rivers. He invited them to pit their best craft on a time-elapsed basis (meaning a miles-per-hour comparison) against the two California boats.

As it turned out, just three boats participated. One boat east of the Rockies raced with the *King* and *Queen* to determine, as the *Sacramento Bee* put it, "the supremacy of river steamers on major streams of the United States." The *Golden Eagle,* a Mississippi River packet, traveled from St. Louis downriver about 130 miles to Cape Girardeau, Missouri. The *Delta* twins represented the main naviga-ble rivers of the Golden State.

On race day, April 22, 1939—proclaimed Inland Steamboat Day in California by Governor Olson—the *Delta Queen* left the M Street wharf in Sacramento at 8:25 a.m. with Capt. William Cooley in command. Capt. Cooley expressed confidence in the *Queen* but spared her whistle to conserve steam. The *Delta King,* with Capt. William J. Atthowe commanding, left the dock on the Stockton Channel at 9:32. Capt. Atthowe sounded the *King*'s whistle in one long blast and predicted, "It's in the bag!" The *Queen*'s earlier departure time came because of her longer course to the rendezvous point (according to the *Sacramento Bee,* the *Queen* covered 105 total miles, the *King* 90).

On board the *Queen* rode 500 to 600 jubilant passengers, including mayors, councilmen, city managers, newspaper reporters and photographers. The *King* car-ried a capacity crowd of 800 to 900 similarly excited people. Adding a festive touch to the occasion, many of the passengers on both vessels dressed in western pioneer costumes.

Dewitt Hightower, who stood at the *Delta King*'s wheel as relief pilot with

MENU

GOLDEN GATE INTERNATIONAL EXPOSITION
SAN FRANCISCO · 1940

★ THE DELTA ROUTE ★
COMFORT AND LUXURY AFLOAT

Sail the romance-lanes of '49
...the great Sacramento River...
in modern luxury!

Our steamers dock at Pier 3, only
one block north from the ferry boats
which take you to the Golden Gate
International Exposition on Treasure Island, in San Francisco Bay.

1939 World's Fair

OVERNIGHT SERVICE BETWEEN
SAN FRANCISCO
SACRAMENTO
RESTFUL
LUXURIOUS
ECONOMICAL

The RIVER LINES
San Francisco · Sacramento

The RIVER LINES
San Francisco · Sacramento

SUtter 3880   CApitol 7600
RESERVATIONS AT ANY TRAVEL AGENCY

SUtter 3880   CApitol 7600

*Menu and flyer promote trips to world's
fair on Treasure Island. History of the
King and Queen is intertwined with fair:
Passengers and crew witness the island
under construction; promise of extra business keeps the boats running during fair;
the 1939 race ends there.*

*Below, King slightly ahead of Queen at
Carquinez Strait, passing Crockett, and
winning race at Treasure Island (bottom).*

Capt. Atthowe on race day, gives this firsthand account of the early part of the race (in an interview by Denny S. Anspach):

> We met the *Queen* around noon at the head of Suisun Bay. The race officially started between Pittsburg and Van Sickle Island. For a while, the *Queen* was ahead of us—then we'd edge up and stay maybe 100 yards apart. After we got down into the Carquinez Strait, we got ahead of the *Queen*. Then the *King* stayed ahead of her most of the way, although she'd creep up and drop back. We were turning about 17 "revs" on the wheel. [He refers to the *King*'s paddle wheel turning 17 times a minute.]

As reported the next day in the paper, the first-and-only race between the *Delta King* and the *Delta Queen* went like this:

> The Queen spurted into an early lead and held it as far as Port Costa, where the King overtook and passed her. The Queen caught up again at Rodeo, and from there to Richmond the rivals churned furiously, white water trailing their sternwheels, with not a boat length between them at any moment. A final burst of speed in the bay stretch brought the King in the winner.

The *Delta King* crossed the finish line, an imaginary line between Treasure Island's Tower of the Sun and Coit Tower on San Francisco's Telegraph Hill, at 6:04 p.m. The *Queen* came right behind. Both docked at Treasure Island's west ferry terminal, and their passengers streamed ashore to enjoy the fair. For those unable to ride the boats or watch from shore, the race was broadcast on radio (by 1939 almost everyone had a radio). The *Sacramento Bee* station, KFBK, covered the beginning with announcers aboard each boat and then broadcast the finish from the deck of the *Delta Queen*. Radio coverage even went out to the rest of the nation over the NBC's Red Network. Later, movie audiences across the country saw the race in newsreels.

What about the *Golden Eagle?* In the excitement of the finish at Treasure Island, nearly everyone had forgotten about the third boat. Later it was announced that the winner, on a time-elapsed basis, was the Mississippi River entry, which maintained an average speed of 13.8 miles an hour. The *King* averaged 11.54, the *Queen* 11.4. Apologists for the comparatively slow time of the California entrants said the two boats had to buck an incoming tide for the last 55 miles. Their competition on the Mississippi had traveled with the current.

Regardless of the circumstances, the *Golden Eagle* had won the unofficial steamboat racing championship of the United States. The *Delta King* had to settle for being best in the West. Yet everyone seemed happy. The River Lines had called attention to their boats, the fair and sponsoring cities had received publicity, and the participants appeared to have enjoyed themselves immensely.

Such light diversions seemed particularly welcome in the 1930s, a decade that had opened with the reverberations of a financial crash and that would close with the rumble of distant gunfire. It was a time of simple pleasures—listening to favorite radio programs, *Amos 'n' Andy* and *One Man's Family;* going to your neighborhood movie house to see the Marx Brothers, Janet Gaynor, Clark Gable, Shirley Temple; dancing to the recorded music of Glenn Miller, the Dorsey Brothers, Benny Goodman, Count Basie; hearing the latest hits on your radio, Ella Fitzgerald singing "A-Tisket A-Tasket," Martha Tilton's "And the Angels Sing." It was an era that, in hindsight, often seems simple and unsophisticated. Yet, near the end of the decade, it produced two timeless motion pictures: *Gone with the Wind* and *The Wizard of Oz.*

By the time of the 1939 steamboat race, the Treasure Island fair had been open for two months. But the initial construction work on the man-made island had begun in 1936 with funding by the WPA and PWA (agencies of Roosevelt's New Deal). The original idea for the fair had been conceived three years before that. So, for better or for worse, the island and the fair were phenomena born in the Thirties that came of age in the Thirties. War had begun in Europe before the fair's first season ended in 1939, putting a damper on festivities. And both that year and the next, the New York World's Fair competed for visitors. San Francisco's fair had its problems and its share of detractors. But a lot of people had a lot of fun the two years it was open. And the fair did help the two riverboats stay in business.

In 1939 and 1940 the River Lines promoted the *King* and *Queen* as a convenient way for Sacramentans and other valley folk to get to the fair. The company used artwork depicting the Tower of the Sun on the cover of its menus. And an advertising flyer announced, "Overnight service between San Francisco and Sacramento—restful, luxurious, economical—our steamers dock at Pier 3, only one block north from the ferry boats which take you to the Golden Gate International Exposition on Treasure Island." During the months of the fair, passenger business on the *Deltas* improved considerably.

Half a century later, the *San Francisco Chronicle* ran an article headlined: "Remembering the 'Magic City.'" Reporters Harre W. Demoro and Carl Nolte summed up the fair this way:

> On a chilly morning 50 years ago, a fairyland world's fair opened on
> Treasure Island, its visitors gazing optimistically toward a future that
> would never arrive. The Golden Gate International Exposition was a
> beauty, a shimmering magic city on a 400-acre man-made island in the
> middle of San Francisco Bay.
>
> However, there was no fairytale ending to the Pageant of the Pacific,
> as the exposition was called. The fair lost millions of dollars and was
> overshadowed by the approach of World War II. Its mid-bay site became
> a Navy base rather than, as intended, San Francisco's airport. . . .
>
> The idea was to tell the world that the great bridges were finished, that
> the economic depression was over in San Francisco. When the gates were
> unlocked with a jeweled key on February 18, 1939, people who had seen
> bread lines and soup kitchens gawked . . . Even when the wind was blow-
> ing, and it almost always was, most visitors thought the fair was swell.

Although the *Delta King* and *Queen* did a brisk business carrying fair-bound
passengers, attendance in 1939 turned out below expectations. Toward the end of
the fair's first season, Benny Goodman and his band arrived, adding new excitement. Some people thought the "King of Swing" saved the '39 fair.

Writing about the following year, *San Francisco Chronicle* columnist Herb
Caen said:

> By 1940 . . . the professionals were in charge. Billy Rose's Aquacade, with
> Esther Williams and Johnny Weissmuller, was a sensation. So was the
> Folies Bergere . . . but the fall of Paris seemed slightly more important.
> The war was heating up, and one after another, invaded countries closed
> their exhibits. On closing night, as we drove onto the bridge, we looked
> back at the glorious lights as they slowly faded into blackness and real-
> ized that the time of innocence was over . . .

Caen recalled the desolation he felt at the moment the island flickered into
darkness: ". . . and you knew, suddenly, that an era had ended for a generation
that would never be young again."

On the same day the fair closed—Sunday, September 29, 1940—the *King*
and *Queen* made their last trips of the season. Although no one knew it at the
time, as fate would have it, these were to be the final voyages the legendary pair
would ever make between San Francisco and Sacramento.

That Sunday, contrary to their normal schedules, *both* steamboats started from San Francisco. The *Delta Queen* left Pier 3 at 9 a.m. on a special daylight cruise to Sacramento, while the *Delta King* left at the regular evening departure time.

Then, with a blast of their whistles, an institution came to an end. The last of California's beloved night boats had made their final runs.

Last day of 1940 fair is also last day for the King and Queen. Words "until next Spring" imply boats' return in 1941. But fate decides otherwise.

Special

DAYLIGHT CRUISE

to Sacramento
SUNDAY, SEPTEMBER 29
marking
Suspension of Passenger Service
until next Spring

Come one . . . come all . . . for a grand day of fun and festivity as you cruise up the placid Sacramento to the historic State Capitol. Be sure you're on board when the Delta Queen leaves San Francisco Sunday morning, September 29, on her last passenger sailing of the year. It's a golden opportunity to see California's own "Ol' Man River" as only a daylight cruise can reveal it. Music — dancing — entertainment — good food — refreshments. *Buy your tickets now — we had to turn down hundreds on our last Daylight Cruise.*

HERE'S THE DAYLIGHT CRUISE SCHEDULE
Leave San Francisco 9 a.m. Sunday, September 29, from Pier 3. **Arrive Sacramento** 8 p.m. **Leave Sacramento** by special Southern Pacific train 9 p.m. (there'll be a dance car, club car and diner attached so the fun still goes on). **Arrive Oakland** 11:20 p.m.
Or you can buy a boat ticket only, take your car on board at special low rates, and drive back to Oakland.
Staterooms for day use at moderate prices.

SPECIAL DAYLIGHT CRUISE
$2.50 ROUND TRIP
GO BY BOAT RETURN BY TRAIN
$1.50 ONE WAY
(Meals, staterooms, additional)
Special auto rate $2.50 plus fare. Take your car on the boat and drive back.

For Information or Reservations, See Your Travel Agent, or
PIER 3, S.F. THE RIVER LINES SUtter 3880
Uptown Ticket Office: American Express, 253 Post St., Phone EXbrook 1083

Naval reservists, called to active duty, report aboard **Delta Queen** *(above) at Yerba Buena Island and on* **Delta King** *(right) at Naval Net Depot, Tiburon, both on San Francisco Bay. Joe Cornyn is shown holding a life preserver.*

8

The Royal Pair Joins the Navy

By the time the *Delta Queen* completed her special daylight cruise from San Francisco on Sunday, September 29, 1940, it was evening and already dark in Sacramento. The captain and his crew landed her with the aid of wharf lights and the searchlight atop the pilothouse, just as they did for their early-morning dockings at the darker times of the year. The *Queen* tied up in the usual spot at the River Lines dock, downstream from the Tower bridge, and discharged her passengers and freight.

Early Monday morning the *Delta King* arrived at Sacramento, finishing a regular overnight schedule and ending the two boats' more-than-13-year reign on the river. The *King's* arrival also marked the end of more than 90 continuous years of steamboating on the Sacramento River, dating back to the Gold Rush.

Dewitt Hightower, pilot on the *King's* final trip, moored the vessel at the old Southern Pacific dock just upriver from the bridge (the *Queen* occupied the usual spot). The *King* and *Queen* together at Sacramento was a rare sight. But it didn't last long. On Monday night, the *Queen* steamed down to Pier 3 in San Francisco. Shortly, she would begin a dramatic new episode in the lives of the two sternwheelers—the Navy years.

The war in Europe had been under way for a year when the boats made their final trips in September of 1940. By that time, France, Belgium, Denmark, Norway, Luxembourg, and The Netherlands had surrendered to Germany (Poland had been overrun the year before). The Nazi war machine seemed unbeatable. Although the United States wasn't yet officially involved in the war, it had shifted its focus from neutrality to preparedness. Following President Roosevelt's lead, the country had begun to expand its armed forces, build defense plants, and give the Allies much-needed military aid.

In the months before the last trips of the *King* and *Queen,* the Navy had negotiated a short-term charter with River Lines to use the two boats over the winter (for the preceding several winters they had been laid up anyway). Barracks space being in short supply, the vessels offered an instant solution. Under this arrangement, River Lines received a temporary permit from the state Railroad Commission to discontinue commercial service, and the Navy obtained a six-month lease on the boats for use on San Francisco Bay. After that, the Navy was to return the *King* and *Queen* in time for regular passenger and freight service in the spring and summer of 1941.

At least, that was the plan. Newspaper ads in September 1940 promoted the daylight trip of the *Queen* as "her last passenger sailing of the year" and referred to "suspension of passenger service until next spring."

Long before the Treasure Island fair closed, the Navy realized what a highly desirable site the island would be for a naval base. Accessible and close to other naval operations around the bay, it could function as a combined receiving station and distribution and training center. But the island belonged to San Francisco. After long negotiations, the city agreed to let the Navy use the land for the duration of the emergency. Treasure Island could now be converted into a major base. And the *Delta Queen,* first of the two boats to go into active service, would play an important role.

A few days after arriving at Pier 3 in San Francisco, the *Queen* steamed over and tied up at Yerba Buena Island—in earlier times known as Goat Island—where she sat in a lagoon called Port of the Trade Winds. There, Navy recruits would have a view of the famous *China Clipper* and other flying boats taking off from the Pan American World Airways base, just across the lagoon at Treasure Island. Five years before, the *China Clipper* had made its first flight to the Philippines. And just the past year, the giant flying boat had flown orchids from Hawaii to the world's fair on Treasure Island. Historical footnote: Pan Am was founded in 1927, the same year the C.T. Co. put the *King* and *Queen* into commercial service—one company at the beginning of a new transportation era and the other company near the end of an old one.

Under the command of Lt. Commander John H. Heinz, the Navy established the *Queen* as a receiving ship for naval reservists activated by President Roosevelt's order declaring a limited national emergency. The first group—First,

Second, and Third Divisions from San Francisco—came aboard on October 16, 1940. That date also had national significance: It marked the first day of Selective Service, the beginning of registration for the draft.

At 8:30 on Monday evening, October 14, a telephone rang in Sausalito; it belonged to Navy reservist Carl Heynen. Picking up the receiver, he heard the no-nonsense voice of reserve Ensign John Hoefer: "Heynen, you are to report for active duty on Wednesday morning at 0800." Calls like this were being made all over the Bay Area. Within a few days, almost 300 men from the San Francisco, Oakland, San Jose, and Santa Cruz areas received orders to report for active duty—some to report immediately, others days or weeks later.

On October 16, 1940, the Queen, *tied at Yerba Buena Island, became home to scores of new recruits. A month later, the* King *took aboard its first Navy crew at the Naval Net Depot, Tiburon. In mid-1941, the* Queen *moved to a new dock on Treasure Island.*

Some young men got their orders at the regular weekly meeting of their reserve units. Bob Neilan tells of being activated at his meeting of the Third Division on October 15. He says, "We reported the next morning at 0800 to the Lincoln Building at Market and New Montgomery [San Francisco]. We carried our sea bags and bedding down to the Embarcadero, where they put us on a Navy tug and took us to Yerba Buena Island and installed us on the *Delta Queen*."

Lee Mineau, another reservist, speaks of the luxuries enjoyed by the men when they first went aboard the *Queen*. "The civilian galley crew and stewards from the River Lines still worked on the boat. We had white tablecloths on the dining tables and the ship's best china and silverware—and Filipino stewards in white jackets waited on us. But that lasted only a few days. Then reality set in— we got regular Navy chow and did mess duty." The *San Francisco Chronicle* said sleeping arrangements on the *Queen* also had pampered the new recruits:

Each of the officers found himself with a separate cabin, complete with shower—and as for the ranks, some of them got showers, too. It is not

Proclamation

WHEREAS,   On October 16, 1940, the 1st, 2nd and 3rd Divisions of the San Francisco Naval Reserve were activated by President Roosevelt's order declaring a limited emergency. These patriotic San Franciscans reported (to a man) within twelve hours aboard the Sacramento River boat, Delta Queen, which was made fast to the east side pier of the Yerba Buena Island Naval Station; and

WHEREAS,   After a few weeks additional training the San Francisco Naval Reservists were ready for sea, many serving on four stack destroyers, minesweepers, and patrol craft and at the declaration of World War II were augmented into the fleet that blasted its way into Guadalcanal, New Guinea, and the Philippine Island liberation; and

WHEREAS,   After the war these San Francisco Naval Reservists returned to San Francisco and their civilian pursuits, many becoming leading figures in our community in sports, government services and business; and

WHEREAS,   On October 18, 1980, these patriotic San Franciscans will gather for their fortieth reunion at the Officers' Club at Treasure Island;

NOW, THEREFORE, I, Dianne Feinstein, Mayor of the City and County of San Francisco, do hereby proclaim October 16, 1980, as DELTA QUEEN/NAVAL RESERVE DAY in recognition of the valiant deeds of these men and the many young San Francisco Naval Reservists who follow in their footsteps.

IN WITNESS WHEREOF, I have hereunto set my hand and caused the Seal of the City and County of San Francisco to be affixed this fifteenth day of September, nineteen hundred and eighty.

Dianne Feinstein
Mayor

Cartoon in February 1941 San Francisco Call-Bulletin ribs the reservists. At left, proclamation in 1980 by then-Mayor of San Francisco Dianne Feinstein marks the 40th reunion of Navy men who served on the Delta boats (group's insignia is shown above).

exactly Navy tradition for sailors to have twin beds, or beds of any kind for that matter, but the citizens-turned-sailors have them, anyway.

The first wave of 230 reservists who came aboard the *Delta Queen* received various assignments. Some used the boat as their barracks while building the Navy's big new base on Treasure Island. Many stood fire-and-security watches in the now-rat-infested former fair buildings. Some took training classes aboard the *Queen,* learning to be signalmen and quartermasters, while others were sent to training duty on Eagle boats and former purse-seiners now converted to minesweepers. Still others became crew on the patrol craft *Argus* that used the *Queen* as its operating base. As space for personnel opened up on the sternwheeler, new reservists reported aboard. It was a busy place. In December 1940, the *Delta Queen's* own Navy newspaper *Weekly Sweeps* suggested a new name for the boat: "Grand Central Station."

In his diary, reservist Edwin Morgan described the cacophony of noises, including foghorns, that kept him awake one night when the fog blew in from the Golden Gate: "Bossie (sounds like a sick cow) and Big Bertha blared in chorus with the bell buoys and whistles." Later came a steady roar from the *China Clipper* warming up nearby. His entry concludes, "Very little sleep."

Elsewhere on San Francisco Bay, near the town of Tiburon in Marin County, workmen were preparing an old Navy coaling station to serve in a revised capacity; it would be the new Naval Net Depot. There, in a program of national preparedness, an antisubmarine net would be constructed and placed across the Golden Gate. Similar nets for other West Coast ports and U.S. bases in the Pacific, along with anti-torpedo nets, would also be produced.

A short time after the October call-up of reserves, the *Delta King* steamed to the Tiburon base and docked there as a floating barracks for sailors who would be building the nets. On November 11, about two dozen reservists from the *Queen* transferred to the Net Depot on a minesweeper and went aboard the *King*. Those recruits became the riverboat's first Navy crew.

Ed O'Brien, who was Bosun's Mate First Class, tells a story of the reservists' first days on the *Delta King* that even surpasses the tale of the first, easy living, white-tablecloth-days on board the *Queen*. During an off-duty hour, he and a shipmate, George, noticed a small button in their cabin and wondered what it was for. Out of curiosity, George pressed it. Within minutes, a Filipino steward knocked on the door: "You want something?" Assuming this was someone's idea of a joke, George played along. He said, "Sure, how about a ham sandwich for O'B and me—a piece of pie and some coffee." They were wide-eyed a few minutes later when the steward arrived with their order. When asked to sign for room service, George hesitated a second. Then, thinking quickly, he signed "W.T. Hatch" (in Navy lingo, that's short for watertight hatch).

As it turned out, over the next few weeks many other crew members, officers and enlisted men alike, enjoyed similar luxuries. Room service on the *King* worked quite well. That is, until River Lines sent the first monthly bill to Navy headquarters. Then the proverbial something "hit the fan." When it became evident that Navy brass had absolutely no sense of humor about this affair, the men quickly emptied their pockets and paid the bill. From then on, the sailors ate regular Navy chow—without room service.

Reservist Bob Cunningham tells about "the case of the purloined pies." He had made his daily run with the Navy truck to Yerba Buena Island to pick up food from the *Delta Queen* commissary and had just come back to Tiburon with a load of pies for the *King's* galley. He parked on the dock and left the truck for a minute. When he returned, the pies were gone. Cunningham had great difficulty convincing his superiors that he wasn't somehow responsible. Many years later at a Navy reunion, the truth came out: the "black gang" (engineers, firemen, and water tenders) had committed the perfect crime, taking the pies for their secret and personal use.

The *King's* former Navy crew often tell of an overabundance of carrots on their menu day after day: carrots for lunch and carrots for dinner, in every imaginable combination. Vic Chernoff, chief commissary steward, became the scapegoat. The sailors named him "Creamed Carrots Chernoff," after the way he most often served the vegetables. He, in turn, blamed commissary headquarters for the problem.

All the gripes about life on the *Delta King* didn't pertain to culinary annoyances. Crew quarters in the boat's hold presented problems, too. Reservist Frank Cummings reports, "My most enduring memory was the bedbugs. Man, they almost ate us alive. Our bodies were so covered with welts that we at first thought we were in the middle of a measles epidemic." According to Stan Haynes, "We tried wiping down the coil springs with gasoline. We even used blowtorches." Eventually, fumigation took care of the problem.

All distractions aside, much work had to be accomplished at the Tiburon Naval Net Depot. Under the iron-fisted guidance of Commander Stanley M.

Haight and the tough-but-respected direction of his executive officer William DeFries, crews began the monumental task of building and placing an antisubmarine net across the Golden Gate. When completed, the net—seven miles of steel netting that would stretch from the San Francisco Marina to Sausalito and would weigh 6,000 tons—had to be strong enough to stop an enemy sub. It also had to withstand the awesome power of the tides when tons of sea water, up to a hundred feet deep, pushed through the Gate at more than six miles an hour. A series of concrete "clumps," weighing 15 tons each, would anchor it.

A group of regular Navy men began building the nets. Soon reservists toiled alongside them on "the slab," the big concrete work area at Tiburon. By all standards, the work was grueling and unglamorous, even though the workers lived on a once-glamorous riverboat. At times, inmates from nearby San Quentin provided help from inside their prison walls.

The Net Depot had been commissioned in August of 1940. In July almost a year later, the Navy laid down the first mooring buoy for the Golden Gate net. But formal authorization from President Roosevelt didn't come until mid-September 1941, when the net was already well along in construction.

In June of that year, the first two net-tender vessels, the newly-built *Catalpa* and *Aloe,* had sailed down from the Northwest to Tiburon. These craft and their crews began to install the net and later handled its maintenance. Shortly, a third tender, the *Chinquapin,* arrived—and a bit later, the *Ebony.* A number of reservists from the *King* were assigned duty on these four vessels.

By the time the Japanese attacked Pearl Harbor on December 7, the net at the Golden Gate was virtually complete. During the following three days, crews worked around the clock to finish it. Carl Heynen recalls seeing men "falling asleep at the winches" during those 72 hours. Later, the Navy reduced the size of the openings in the nets to prevent Japanese mini-subs from slipping through.

Two "gate ships," the *Eider* and the *Dreadnought*—hulks without engines as they didn't need to move—guarded the entrance to San Francisco Bay. They opened the net at a designated spot, close to the city shore, to let friendly craft pass in and out of the harbor.

During the early months at Tiburon (in the waning days of 1940), the reservists had come to a realization. Though they were still in the Bay Area, life at the Net Depot was vastly different. Most of them had lived close to the action in cities and suburbs. Now, not only were they isolated from city life, but even the small town of Tiburon lay several miles away. Small wonder that the new sailors called the base "Little Siberia."

What's more, with the strictest of Navy discipline at the base, the Net Depot soon developed another name: "Haight's Concentration Camp." It seemed Commander Stanley Haight was the kind of military officer that servicemen love to hate (no pun intended). He was known for his brusque and tactless manner. For example, the day Ensign John Hoefer reported for duty at Tiburon, Commander Haight told him, "If I don't like you, I'll send you to China." Though miffed at the time, Hoefer came to respect Haight for what was accomplished at the base.

Reservist Joe Copeland remembers that one weekend some creative-but-foolhardy sailors posted signs along the winding country road to the base: "3 miles to Haight's Concentration Camp"; "2 miles to . . ."; "1 mile to . . ."; etc. When Commander Haight discovered the signs, he was furious. Unable to single out the culprits, he restricted every last man on the base for a week (no liberties). In discussing their former commander, men who served at the Net Depot often describe him in terms that make him seem arbitrary, harsh, even tyrannical. In any case, the task assigned to the commander was performed—nets were constructed for the bay and many other ports, and the difficult installation across across the Golden Gate was completed.

The reservists complained about many things, but they were unanimous in praising one particular reserve officer, Lt. (jg.) Charles J. McWhinnie. As the commanding officer of Naval Reserves, Second Division, in San Francisco, McWhinnie went aboard the *Queen* with his men on October 16. Joe Cornyn recalls, "Late that first night he came around to see that all the men had a spot for the night in the cramped quarters. He was always concerned about his men, thinking of their welfare—always calm, never got excited." Bob Neilan says, "Lt. McWhinnie was one of the reasons I volunteered to go to the *King* at Tiburon. He was the finest officer I ever served under." Frank Cummings calls him "the epitome of what a naval officer should be." McWhinnie became the first commander of the net tender *Catalpa,* then went to a destroyer, and retired many years later as Rear Admiral.

In April of 1941 a little-noticed action took place: The Navy renewed the leases on the *Delta King* and *Queen* for another six months. Thus ended any chance the two boats would return to commercial service for the coming season, as advertisements had promised the previous September. For the first time since Gold Rush days, a year would pass without steamboat passenger service on the inland waters of California.

Soon after the leases were extended, the Navy built a special dock for the *Delta Queen* on the east side of Treasure Island and moved her there, less than a mile from her old moorings at Yerba Buena Island. At the new dock she would perform much the same duties as before but in a more convenient place. An improvised Navy band, composed of one sailor strumming a banjo and another pumping an accordion, celebrated the *Queen*'s move.

By the summer of 1941, the civilian world began to miss the *King* and *Queen*. In an Independence Day report, the *San Francisco Chronicle* said, "It was the Fourth of July and for the first time in the history of Western steamboating, no holiday excursion disturbed the broad Sacramento as it flowed gently to the sea. National defense had taken the River Lines' spacious *Delta King* and *Delta Queen* off the river, ending—perhaps forever—those Independence Day cruises between San Francisco and Sacramento."

The two sternwheelers remained at their docks, the *Queen* at Treasure Island and the *King* at Tiburon, until the fall of 1941. Then, as their second lease had expired and since the Navy had built enough barracks space, they were given "honorable discharges" and returned to River Lines. The first week in November, just a month before Pearl Harbor, the *King* and *Queen* steamed away from their respective Navy docks. They headed for Stockton and the hope of a promising new civilian life that—due to Japanese plans in the Pacific—would never come.

Upon arrival at Stockton, the boats tied up at the C.T. Co. maintenance yard, but only temporarily. Before the vessels' return, the company had made a major decision: instead of putting the *King* and *Queen* back into service, it would sell them. River Lines had already applied to the state Railroad Commission for permission to permanently discontinue passenger service. Now it announced that the two sternwheelers had been sold to the Isbrandsten Steamship Co. of New York. Reportedly, the price was $250,000 for both.

According to the *Sacramento Bee* of October 15, 1941, and the *Stockton Record* of November 22, the new owner planned to tow the vessels to the East Coast via the Panama Canal for use as excursion boats on the Hudson River. But on December 6, the *Waterways Journal* of St. Louis quoted an Isbrandsten freight agent who said the boats probably would go into packet service on the Mississippi and Ohio rivers between Cincinnati and New Orleans. Shortly, however, any questions about their intended destination would prove academic.

Workmen at Stockton began boarding up the boats for towing on the open sea. Starting first with the *King*, they installed wood sheathing on the foredecks

In November 1941, the Navy, which had leased the King and Queen, returned them to River Lines. Both boats were sold to Isbrandsten Steamship Co. and prepared at Stockton for towing on the open sea. In these photos, the Queen has freight-deck windows covered, while the King appears fully boarded up. Pearl Harbor attack ends all plans.

and along the sides to prevent ocean waves from swamping the vessels. The *Delta King* and *Delta Queen* were moved to the south side of the channel and docked stern-to-stern. There, awaiting departure, the legendary sternwheelers sat across from the shipyard where their lives had begun not so many years before.

Then on December 7 came the grim news that no one expected to hear but that no adult alive at the time would ever forget: Japanese planes had attacked Pearl Harbor.

The King *and* Queen *begin wartime duty in San Francisco Bay Area carrying wounded from ships to Navy hospitals. Early designation is Yard House Boat. As troop shuttles, the boats later become Yard Ferry Boats: the* King *was YFB-55, the* Queen *YFB-56.*

9

Paddle Wheels in Wartime

During the year before the Japanese attacked Pearl Harbor in 1941, Lt. William DeFries made his presence felt as executive officer at the Naval Net Depot. Big, bluff, and noisy—but respected by his men—he got into every aspect of base operations at Tiburon. Known as "Kinky" DeFries because of his curly red hair, he had retired earlier after 30 years of Navy service and then had been called back for the national emergency.

Reservist Frank Cummings describes DeFries as "the driving and guiding force behind the entire base . . . not above getting his hands dirty if help was needed . . . a tough old guy, a hell of a sailor. He just looked like United States Navy. In fact, just to look as him, you knew he had a girl friend named 'Olive Oyl.'" Cummings remembers DeFries on the morning of December 7, 1941: "I can still picture this giant of a man broken-voicedly breaking the news to us about Pearl Harbor with tears streaming down his face."

The first bombs fell Sunday morning at 7:55, Hawaii time. It was late morning when the news reached the West Coast. Reservist Dan "Dusty" Rhodes says that, by evening, his vessel—the net-tender *Aloe* armed with a 3-inch deck gun and two 30-caliber machine guns—was assigned to patrol the San Francisco-Oakland Bay Bridge as an emergency air-defense measure.

In a speech to Congress the next day, President Franklin D. Roosevelt called December 7 "a date which will live in infamy," and the United States declared war on Japan. At 6:15 Monday evening, San Francisco experienced its first blackout when false reports came that enemy aircraft had been detected coming in over the Farallon Islands. Within 24 hours, news arrived that the Japanese had attacked the

Philippines, Thailand, Malaya, Hong Kong, Singapore, Guam, Midway, and Wake Island. The *Delta King* and *Queen,* poised at Stockton for departure from California, would soon find these plans canceled and a return to Navy duty.

The 360 carrier-based planes that hit Pearl Harbor dealt the U.S. Pacific fleet and Hawaii's air defense a crippling blow. The attack sank 18 ships and destroyed 174 planes on the ground. The fleet lost battleships *Oklahoma, Utah,* and *Arizona* (the latter now a memorial). Heavy damage was inflicted on other ships including battleships *California, West Virginia, Nevada, Tennessee, Maryland,* and *Pennsylvania*—plus three cruisers and three destroyers. The human toll was staggering: In those two tragic hours on December 7, the United States suffered 2,403 dead and 1,178 wounded, a total of more than 3,500 casualties.

With a large number of wounded, many bearing extensive burns, military and civilian hospitals on the Islands were overtaxed. As soon as ships became available, the Navy decided to send a number of injured to the mainland. It was then, in the dark days of our early involvement in the war, that the *King* and *Queen* were rushed back into Navy service as emergency hospital transports on the bay.

As the first vessel from Hawaii with several hundred injured men steamed toward San Francisco in mid-December, the Navy worked quickly to get the *Delta King* ready to meet it. Reservist Frank Larson, a Lt. (jg.) at the time, recalls:

> At the last minute, I was chosen as the officer in charge to take the *King* to meet the ship. We met the transport at a San Francisco pier, pulled alongside, and took the injured directly onto the *King*. A hatch on the ship opened up at the level of our cargo deck to let them come aboard. Some were ambulatory, some came on stretchers. Many were in bad shape—burn victims, injured, and some psychiatric cases.
>
> With the help of a lot of Red Cross ladies, we put the men in folding beds on our cargo deck and in the various cabins. Then we headed for the naval hospital at Mare Island [on the bay at Vallejo, about twenty miles north of San Francisco]. In a couple of hours we arrived at the dock where ambulances were waiting to receive our load of wounded.

Unfortunately, more casualties existed than could be brought to the mainland on one trip, and the military found itself short on vessels. About ten days later, the *King* was called on again to meet the same ship which, by then, had made a round trip out to Hawaii and back with another load. After that, Larson says the *King* met the transport one more time, making a total of three times the sternwheeler served as temporary hospital craft. Though he doesn't recall the ship's name, most likely it was the ocean liner S.S. *President Coolidge,* pressed into military service after Pearl Harbor. The *Coolidge* had begun a trip from China with a load of civilian passengers before the Japanese attack and had stopped by Honolulu on her way to the states.

Carl Slattengren, a Fireman Second Class injured when the destroyer U.S.S. *Shaw* was bombed, describes his arrival at San Francisco aboard the *President Coolidge* on Christmas day 1941:

> "I was suffering from a shrapnel wound plus first, second, and third degree burns. But when we docked, I managed to walk off the ship by myself. No one noticed me. I got onto the *Delta King,* which was standing by, and I crawled into a bunk. Sometime later a nurse found me and scolded, 'We've been looking all over for you—you're supposed to be a stretcher case!'"

The *Delta Queen* also carried Pearl Harbor wounded. Capt. Dewitt Hightower, River Lines pilot before the war, remembers taking the *Queen* to meet the S.S. *Mariposa* at Pier 32 in San Francisco in circumstances like those of the *King.* The Matson liner had just been taken over for use as a military transport. Hightower said that four or five hundred beds for the injured had been set up on the *Queen's* freight deck. After loading, the boat steamed to Mare Island, delivering the patients to the naval hospital there. A similar account is given by W.B. "Bud" Atthowe, who had been captain of the *Pride of the River* for the C.T. Co. (his father, W.J. Atthowe, was captain of the *King* in the 1930s). Capt. Atthowe recalls a somber scene when he piloted the *Delta Queen* to Mare Island with a load of wounded in the early days of the war.

One week after Pearl Harbor, the Navy had formally acquired the *Delta King* and *Queen* for the duration of the the national emergency and had compensated the Isbrandsten Steamship Co. accordingly. The boats were placed "in service" as district craft but not "in commission," and Navy crews were assigned to man the craft. They were classified as Yard House Boats (which meant for barracks use). The *King* was listed as YHB-6, the *Queen* as YHB-7, although both also retained their names while in Navy service.

In early 1942, after finishing emergency hospital duties, the *King* reportedly spent a short time at the Mare Island Naval Ammunition Depot as barracks for ammunition-handling crews. Then the vessel, returning to familiar territory on the Tiburon peninsula, docked at the Naval Net Depot, where it served as barracks ship until late fall. The *King* then went to Bethlehem Steel in San Francisco and tied up alongside the U.S.S. *Pennsylvania* for about three months, where the sternwheeler housed that battleship's crew while shipyard workers overhauled the ship.

Navy quartermasters learn to operate the venerable steamboats; that's Gene Johnson at the wheel of the Queen.

The *Queen* also found a new home in 1942. She spent the year at Government Island on the Oakland Estuary, ending with a brief stay at the site of the old Neptune Beach amusement park on the west end of Alameda. The Navy had loaned the boat to the U.S. Maritime Service for its officers' training school conducted by the Coast Guard. Of the school's enrollment of 400, about half slept on the *Queen*. But all went aboard at mealtime and for recreation.

1942 proved to be a tough year for America and the Allies. The Japanese over-ran Burma, Malaya, the Netherlands East Indies, the Philippines, Singapore, and Thailand. By mid-year the Japanese empire reached its peak, spreading itself from the East Indies in the South Pacific to parts of the Aleutian Islands in Alaska. And, in the European theater of war, the Axis forces extended their control from Norway to North Africa and from France to western Russia. The outlook was bleak.

Yet on April 18, 1942, a fleet of 16 Army B-25 bombers, led by Lt. Colonel Jimmy Doolittle, gave America's morale a boost. The planes took off from the carrier *Hornet,* flew 650 miles over water, and jolted the Japanese by bombing Tokyo, an "impossible feat." Then in June, the Battle of Midway provided a needed victory for the United States in the Pacific. And in August our marines landed on Guadalcanal. The tide was slowly turning. Early in 1943 President Roosevelt and British Prime Minister Winston Churchill conferred at Casablanca, Morocco, and announced that the Allies would accept nothing short of unconditional surrender

The King *in 1944 docks at Stockton to
pick up Sea Scouts for trip to San Francisco.*

from the Axis nations.

In 1943, the *Delta King* and *Queen* again played new roles. Early in the year, the *King* (temporarily inoperative) was towed to Redwood City, there serving as barracks for PT boat-crew training. The stay was brief. By mid-spring the *King*—destined to become a bay transport along with the *Queen*—was towed to Moore Drydock in Oakland for overhaul. After a month of work, the *Delta King* emerged fully operational.

The *Queen,* back from the Maritime Service and in Navy hands again, received her own overhaul of machinery and electrical components. Now, both sternwheelers were in top-notch condition and ready for their new life as military people movers. With their renovation, they had received new coats of paint—naturally in Navy gray. No longer were they the gleaming white steamers of their Sacramento River days.

By the summer and fall of 1943, the *King* and *Queen* were proving their worth by shuttling sailors and soldiers between piers around the Bay: Treasure Island, Alameda Naval Air Station, Fort Mason, and San Francisco. Most frequently, they ended these trips at San Francisco piers, where the men were loaded onto transports bound for the Pacific. Occasionally, the two boats made longer trips to pick up Army troops from Camp Stoneman at Pittsburg, where the bay meets the river 40 water miles northeast of San Francisco.

On D-Day—June 6, 1944—the Allied forces, with the greatest invasion force in history, hit the beaches at Normandy, France. Although the war didn't end until 1945, the "longest day" was the beginning of the end for the war in Europe. In this country, troops continued to be sent overseas—and on the West Coast that meant destinations in the Pacific. Jack Oglesby recalls riding as a soldier on the *King* or *Queen* from Camp Stoneman to San Francisco in July 1944. He offers this description from his 96th Division history book of troops leaving aboard "two old river steamers":

> Had the departing passengers not all been dressed in the regalia of their deadly trade, it might have been the sailing of a Caribbean cruise ship, for the band was at the dock and the whole thing had the air of slightly hollow festivity. The residents of the towns that lined the Sacramento River [Suisun Bay and the Carquinez Strait] well knew the mission of those boats, and hundreds of them waved a friendly "God bless you.". . . All along the route, river tugs barked sharp salutes.

On July 5, 1944, the Navy belatedly recognized the transport duties of the two vessels by reclassifying them as Yard Ferry Boats (they had been Yard House Boats). The *King* became YFB-55, the *Queen,* YFB-56.

Just twelve days after that reclassification, Lady Luck smiled on the two boats. Although their route to Camp Stoneman passed right by Port Chicago and they had even been known to stop there, both vessels were elsewhere when the ammunition depot blew up on July 17 in the worst home-front disaster of the war.

The Port Chicago blast killed 320 men and wounded almost 400, destroyed two ships, and leveled the nearby town. The explosion set off a 30-foot tidal wave across Suisun Bay. Windows were shattered in the St. Francis Hotel in San Francisco; buildings shook in Petaluma. The blast, which registered on seismographs in Nevada, may have been the largest man-made explosion in the world to that date. According to the *San Francisco Chronicle,* only the atomic bomb set off a year later was bigger. You can imagine what the blast would have done to a paddle-wheel steamer, with wooden superstructure and flat bottom, passing by a quarter mile away.

On September 5, 1944, less than two months after the blast, the *Oakland Tribune* reported that 300 Sea Scouts took a weekend trip from San Francisco to

Stockton on the *King:* "Off Port Chicago, scene of the recent Navy ammunition ship explosion, the *Delta King*'s engines were stopped for a solemn ceremony in tribute to the the men who lost their lives in the blast. The boat's flag was lowered to half staff and a wreath was tossed on the water while the bugler sounded taps."

The *King* and *Queen* weren't the only California paddle-wheel steamboats used by the military. The *Fort Sutter* and *Port of Stockton* (formerly *Capital City*)—predecessors to the *King* and *Queen*—also served on the bay, as did the *Crockett* (formerly *H.J. Corcoran*). And the former sternwheel steamer *Isleton,* with her diesel engines and twin screws, joined the Army as the *Army Queen*. Several bay ferries, former Southern Pacific and Key System double-enders, also saw service with the Army, Navy, and Maritime Commission. In addition, the Catalina Island steamers *Catalina* and *Cabrillo* came up from Southern California to serve the Army on the bay. All of these vessels crossed paths with the *King* and *Queen* at one time or another during the war.

Jukeboxes played "Begin the Beguine," "Moonlight Cocktail," and songs spawned by the war—"White Cliffs of Dover," "Don't Sit Under the Apple Tree," "I'll Walk Alone." Moviegoers went to see *Casablanca,* the film few expected to be a hit but that turned out a classic. It was a time of great courage, determination, and sadness—a time of new experiences on the home front, including blackouts and air raid drills, food and gas rationing, victory gardens, women in war plants, and gold stars in windows for sons lost in combat. And a time of internment camps for American citizens of Japanese ancestry. It was a time that seemed to bring out the best and worst in human behavior.

In the final years of the *Delta King*'s Navy service, Lt. Charles Fleming commanded the vessel. The officer in charge of the *Delta Queen* was Chief Warrant Officer Mullen, later succeeded by Lt. (jg.) Webb. But worthy of special note was the service of a certain Seaman First Class Branwell Fanning, who went aboard the *Queen* in the spring of 1945. His tour of duty turned out to be more significant for what he wrote about it later than for what he did while on the boat. Fanning's book *The Wartime Adventures of the Delta Queen* describes, with a light touch, some of the happenings near the end of the war. In the book, a "letter to his parents" begins:

Dear Mom and Dad,
　　After 1½ years in the Navy, I'm finally going aboard ship. At least I think that's what it is. The Navy has spent a lot of hours teaching me that

it is not a boat unless it can be hauled aboard a ship. But my new assignment is officially called a Yard Ferry Boat, the YFB-56. . . . Well, the Navy doesn't own a ship that could haul this boat aboard.

You know how I've always dreamed of serving aboard a destroyer or an aircraft carrier? Well, the YFB-56 is as long as a destroyer and has a flat top like a carrier, but it also has a flat bottom, so we can't even go near the Golden Gate for fear it will turn turtle. The flat top isn't big enough for airplanes, and it's not fast like a destroyer, either. In fact, its speed depends more on the wind and tide than on its own machinery.

Fanning tells of the Delta Queen being loaded with more than 3,000 men—many times the normal passenger load and probably exceeding safe limits. Almost 2,000 were crowded, shoulder to shoulder, on the freight deck. The rest rode on decks above. He describes the excitement after the regular skipper was assigned to another ship:

> After he left, we knocked down some of the best piers ever built in San Francisco Bay! Handling a "box kite" like the *Queen,* with 30-knot winds and 7-knot tides working against it, and trying to dock, loaded down with 3,200 passengers, required skill and experienced handling technique. More than one of our passengers, returning from four years in the Pacific, commented that the final trip across San Francisco Bay was the most hair-raising part of the war.

We can surmise reasons for the Navy's navigational problems. It could be partly that their quartermasters just weren't used to handling paddle-wheel riverboats. Granted, with her flat bottom, shallow draft, and high wooden superstructure, the *Queen* was tricky to handle. But, probably also important, the Navy was not carrying freight on the boat as in her commercial days. Back then, the weight was distributed evenly and kept low, so the freight acted as ballast. Instead, the Navy was carrying an undependable and unpredictable commodity—human beings in large numbers, many of whom rode above the freight deck.

One of the *Queen*'s duties was serving as liberty boat for sailors who had just returned from overseas to the submarine base on the Tiburon Peninsula (near the Naval Net Depot). After long months at sea in a submarine, these men were ready for San Francisco even if San Francisco wasn't ready for them. Fanning tells us: "Although the sub crews were in good shape when we picked them up in Tiburon, when they returned on board in San Francisco about midnight, it was a different story. From about 11:30 on, there was a steady stream of shore patrol paddy wagons pulling up on our dock. Limp bodies would be carried aboard and lined up on the cargo deck . . . uniforms were invariably torn, tattered, and messed. . . ."

Fanning describes the difficulty of painting the paddle wheel on the *Queen* when she was in drydock:

Climbing around inside that thing was an experience! Painting it was nearly suicidal . . . The 26-foot wheel was about 10 feet off the bottom of the dry dock, so that when sitting astride the top blade, painters were about 3½ stories above the dock floor. No nets or safety lines . . . The real problem was that we were not born with enough hands. If you had the paint bucket in one hand, and the brush in the other, you couldn't hang on. Hanging by one hand and painting with the other left you without paint. . . . once you were launched out onto one of the upper blades, there was no turning back. You moved backwards, and facing you was the blade you painted. With wet paint in front of you, the only course was to keep painting. . . .

During the historic weeks from April 25 to June 26, 1945, when the United Nations founding conference met in San Francisco, the *Delta Queen* played the role of international hostess. She took delegates on frequent sightseeing trips around the bay. Fanning says: "Delegates from the 51 nations, often resplendent in exotic apparel typical of their countries, were the honored passengers. A heady experience for a simple riverboat to be suddenly in the international limelight."

Since President Roosevelt died on April 12, 1945, he did not live to see the end of the war in Europe. V-E Day (Victory in Europe) was officially proclaimed by President Harry S. Truman on May 8, 1945. On August 6 the United States dropped an atomic bomb on Hiroshima and, three days later, another on Nagasaki. The Japanese accepted Allied terms on August 14 and signed the surrender on September 2, since then declared official V-J Day.

With the war over, the *King* and *Queen* took part in Operation Magic Carpet, which returned servicemen to the United States. Now, instead of ferrying sailors and soldiers to San Francisco for embarkation on transports headed to the Pacific, the *King* and *Queen* moved men from the ships back to various shore installations around the bay. In less than a year, the big crush of returning servicemen ended.

One of Bran Fanning's last experiences on the *Queen* involved Alcatraz, the infamous island on the bay where the *King* had run aground ten years before. Early in 1946, several of the toughest prisoners at the penitentiary tried to escape. They had guns and were holed up in a cell block. In another of Fanning's "letters to his parents," he wrote: "The escape was so meticulously planned that it was assumed the prisoners had lined up a get-a-way from the island by boat. They had to be stopped, and guess who got the patrol duty? That's right, the *Delta Queen* became a large and very stable gun platform for sharpshooters. So we circled the island all one day. . . . [though no shots were fired from the boat] the *Delta Queen* finally got into combat, even if it was a little late, *and* the wrong war."

As a footnote to the wartime use of the *Queen,* Fanning comments that, in spite of some damage inflicted on the boat, the Navy probably did more to save her than to harm her. Not only did the Navy replace hull plates on the entire bow, but it also installed a new piston in the high-pressure cylinder of the steam engine. It's unlikely a private owner could have afforded such repairs.

By the time of the Alcatraz escape attempt, the usefulness of the *King* and *Queen* to the Navy had nearly come to an end. According to former Navy crew member Bob Guest, early in 1946 the *King* was stripped of all Navy furnishings at a San Francisco dock. A bit later, the Navy delivered the vessel to the War Shipping Administration for lay-up at the Reserve Fleet on Suisun Bay, usually called the "mothball fleet." Here, about 30 miles northeast of San Francisco, the Maritime Commission was storing surplus ships as they came out of service. Navy records show the *Delta King* officially out of service on April 4 and stricken from the Naval Vessel Register on April 17.

The *Queen* was still operating, but by now her crew had dwindled to 35 men, about half the number at the peak of her duties. The men had less and less to do. Soon the Navy discharged the cooks and closed the galley. The *Queen* was down to her last officer, Chief Warrant Officer Natalino A. Carilli, formerly third in command. On August 20, 1946, as the last skipper, he had the solemn duty of delivering the vessel to the mothball fleet. The craft was stricken from the register on August 28.

Officers of the Reserve Fleet headquarters at Suisun Bay reported that the *Delta Queen* was the only one of the huge fleet of mothballed ships that had arrived under its own power. They said she was unique—she had come and "laid herself up."

10

The Departure of a Queen

The mothball fleet—Suisun Bay, Benicia, California—late summer 1946. A vast sea of more than 500 phantom-like gray ships, no longer needed by the Maritime Service and the Navy, stretches out across the water as far as the eye can see. It's a somber collection of craft, sometimes called the "ghost fleet." Sitting among these cast-off vessels, the unmanned and lifeless *Delta King* and *Delta Queen* rock in the afternoon westerlies and tug gently at the anchors that hold them, bow and stern.

Dwarfed by the ships around them, the two river steamers await an unknown fate. Six months before, Norvin Fay, general manager of River Lines, said he was doubtful the *King* and *Queen* would ever again operate on regular schedules between San Francisco and Sacramento. "The high cost of labor and greatly increased operating expense," he explained, "would prohibit their operation on a year-round basis." And he held out only a slim hope that the company might buy back one of them from the Maritime Commission for use as a summer excursion craft. After only 19 years of service, would the two finest riverboats ever built remain idle? Or worse yet—would they end up on the scrap heap?

The week before Labor Day, a scenario was unfolding over two thousand miles away that would have a profound effect on the future of one of these steamboats. In Cincinnati, Capt. Tom Greene and his wife, Letha, boarded a train bound for California to look at the vessels, with the intent of possibly buying one. The Greenes represented a steamboat dynasty on the Mississippi and Ohio rivers: Greene Line Steamers, founded by Tom's father in 1890. Over the years, the company had owned and operated 26 river steamers, including the *Chris Greene, Tom Greene,* and *Gordon C. Greene.*

Capt. Greene spent five days at the mothball fleet inspecting the *King* and *Queen*. He liked what he saw and wrote a letter to his good friend, Capt. Frederick Way, Jr. Way later authored a book, *Saga of the Delta Queen,* which quotes Greene's letter: "First, we boarded the Delta Queen. Both boats are dressed up in their war paint (Navy gray) but still you couldn't fool an old Mississippi River packet man, for it was easy to see she (the Queen) was a winner." He went on to tell about the boilers and decks, the beautiful stained glass, the grand staircase and fine woods. Clearly, Greene wanted to buy one of these steamboats as soon as the Maritime Commission put them on sale. Returning to Cincinnati, he held a number of meetings to discuss and confirm his already-made decision.

The *Delta King* went on the auction block first, with bids to be opened on October 18. The vessel would go to the highest bidder, unless that bid was deemed too low by the Maritime Commission. Just two bids were received: a bid of $26,350 by Greene Line and the high bid of $60,168 by the Southeast Asia Importing & Exporting Co. of Siam. Capt. Greene had lost that round. One down, one to go.

When the *Delta Queen's* turn came on November 20, Greene added about $20,000 to his previous offer. He bid $46,250, which turned out to be plenty—his was the only bid. The Commission confirmed the sale on December 17, 1946, and gave him 30 days to accept delivery. This wasn't much time. Up to that point, Greene had given little thought to the herculean task of getting the *Queen* to New Orleans. He had a vague notion that the vessel would go out the Golden Gate, down the coast and through the Panama Canal, to New Orleans, then up the Mississippi and Ohio rivers. But *how* this would be accomplished was one huge question mark.

In his book, Capt. Way offers a sobering thought about the hazards of taking such a large boat to sea:

> A small steamboat has one pat advantage at sea, for even though she may toss like a cork she has water under her hull at all times. The Delta boats, although built of steel, introduced a new risk. Two waves might get under a hull 250 feet long, one wave holding up the bow and the other holding up the stern, thus removing all support under the middle and presenting a situation the original builder gave no heed to.

In other words, the trip could end in disaster as the boat suddenly breaks in half. At this critical point, Tom Greene called on Fred Way for help. The two men had gone through various river experiences together, including steamboat racing back in the late 1920s with Capt. Way's river packet *Betsy Ann* pitted against Greene Line steamers. Both had ridden with Tom's father, Gordon C. Greene, in the pilothouse of the *Greenwood*—they had almost been raised side by side on the river. It was natural that they face the coming challenge together.

Seeing the *Queen* for the first time, Way remarked, "She's going to be some pumpkin in Cincinnati, Tom." Yet he had misgivings. Neither he nor Greene had experience in taking a flat-bottomed steamboat, built for river travel, on the open seas. At first, they toyed with the idea of taking the *Queen* to sea under her own power, using steam and paddle wheel all the way to New Orleans. The U.S. Coast Guard rejected that plan in a hurry. If they wanted to make the trip under the United States flag, the boat had to be towed to sea as a "barge." They were pleased, however, to hear about the Fulton Shipyard at Antioch, where she could be prepared for her ocean voyage. The yard was 18 miles east of the mothball fleet, near the confluence of the San Joaquin and Sacramento rivers, about 45 water miles northeast of San Francisco. When they got there, they discovered with delight that Les Fulton, the owner, was an old riverman who spoke their language.

On this first visit, Greene and Way also met the new owner of the *Delta King*, Mr. Chok na Roang, head of the Southeast Asia Importing & Exporting Co., who earlier had outbid Greene on the boat. Pleasant but in a state of shock, he had a problem with his purchase—he didn't want the *King!* He had bid sight unseen, under the impression the vessel was seaworthy and propeller-driven, capable of a voyage across the Pacific. Having no use for a paddlewheeler, he offered to sell it for payment of his expenses. Greene declined, realizing he had his hands full taking just *one* steamboat back to the Mississippi. Way, however, advised Greene to keep his eye on the *King* and to buy the boat later to prevent possible competition.

Getting the *Queen* ready for the ocean voyage became complicated immediately. Insurance companies and their various agents differed widely on how the vessel should be prepared. It wasn't every day that someone wanted to take a paddle-wheel steamboat to sea. Way traveled east and talked to a barge official with experience on the Gulf of Mexico. They came up with a plan: the boat "should be side-planked two decks high, the forecastle provided with a wooden 'cow catcher' to shed seas, and some appropriate shoring installed in the deckroom." This procedure sounded workable. Capt. Greene now chose to stay at Cincinnati and tend to business, letting Way execute the plan with two able associates sent by Greene to help him: Charles Dietz, steamboat engineer, and Bill Horn, ship carpenter.

By February 1947, it was time to remove the *Delta Queen* from the mothball fleet and tow her to Fulton's at Antioch. In a pea-soup tule fog, Way and his two assistants went aboard to await Les Fulton's tugboats. Three cold-and-dreary hours later, the tugs found the sternwheeler, after almost giving up in the fog. Finally, as Capt. Way reports in his book, "The moorings were cast off, and about 2:30 p.m. on that February 4, the Delta Queen commenced her first voyage under the banner of Greene Line Steamers." The *King,* still at anchor among the immense gray ships, sat alone now as the remaining *Delta* twin in the fog-shrouded ghost fleet.

"There was unquestioned thrill," Way continues, "in feeling the big boat in motion, and knowing a spark of life had been rekindled within. Thrill rapidly changed to chill. No water, no food, no bedding, and a cold wind blowing. Came darkness on the Sacramento, and a full moon, and a threat of more fog." But without incident, the *Queen* arrived and was tied up at Fulton's. The chilled men found refuge in a local hotel where they thawed out and spent the night.

In the days that followed, the crew at Fulton's prepared the big river steamer for her coming test. Workmen planked over the sides of the lower two decks, installed inside shoring, and dismantled the paddle wheel (which would only be a drag in the water). Because the *Queen* was to be towed on the open sea and would serve as home for Way and his two associates for several weeks, they carefully packed their food and water needs. They prepared for "the worst the sea has to offer" with life-raft rations, a portable foghorn and distress flares.

As work progressed, the three developed a certain resignation to shipwreck. "I don't think we felt this way at first," says Way, "but the idea grew little by little and settled down on us with a certain finality. We could mentally see the Delta Queen away out on the Pacific Ocean in the middle of a stormy night and then the fatal crash. Man the lifeboats!" He concludes, "If you think this vision overdrawn . . . you have not contracted to deliver a flat-bottomed steamboat from San Francisco to New Orleans via the Pacific Ocean."

One day in March, with work still under way, an unexpected but distinguished guest arrived. Jim Burns, who had supervised building the *Delta King* and *Delta Queen* in Stockton two decades before, came by to pay his respects to the *Queen* before she left California. One by one, the workers stopped their jobs and came over to meet and shake the hand of this patriarch of the river, now 84 years of age. Few knew him personally, but most knew of his fame and wanted to pay tribute. After the "receiving line," Way and Fulton invited him up to a stateroom on the *Queen* for lunch. Asked about the life expectancy of the boat, Burns

Capt. Fred Way (below left) with Jim Burns in 1947 at Fulton's Shipyard, Antioch, California, before the boarded-up Queen *(still showing YFB-56 from her Navy duty) is towed to New Orleans via the Panama Canal.*

answered quickly and prophetically, "She will last Capt. Greene through his lifetime and someone after him."

In the final stages of preparation, Way said the *Queen* "looked like a huge piano box, cased two decks high with unpainted lumber, some 50,000 board feet of it . . . Surmounting all was the tall gray smokestack and over it the tarpaulin to keep Charlie's [engineer Dietz's] boilers dry. A ladder built two decks high was the sole way of climbing aboard ship. . . ."

As the Marine Inspection Service required a crew of five men on what the agency termed a "sea-going barge," Tom Greene sent two additional men to make the historic trip. Now, with work on the boat complete and the crew ready, a contract for towage was made with the Portland (Oregon) Tug & Barge Co.

Just as it seemed the voyage was all set to begin, the sky fell in. A labor dispute hit the *Queen* and threatened to include the entire Fulton Shipyard. The unions called a meeting. Their spokesman told Capt. Way to send home Greene's Cincinnati crew and to use ten union men for the trip. When Way's lawyer objected that the United States government only required a crew of five, the answer came back that "even the government was capable of error." The unions outlined the needed crew: a master, a mate, and a second mate; a chief engineer, an assistant engineer, and a second assistant engineer; three seamen and a cook-steward. The master and the chief engineer, at $1,260 each, would be the highest paid; the total came to $8,310. Fred Way recalls the wry comment he made at the meeting:

> I questioned the generosity of providing our boat with $3,225 worth of engineering talent to propel a boat which had her machinery torn down, her boilers empty, and dead as a church on Monday morning. I was reminded we had a gasoline pump on board which engineers could conceivably engineer. This was a point to consider, for this pump had cost $56.35.

Capt. Way found little room to maneuver. Refusal to comply meant the tugboat could not tow the *Delta Queen*, and the tug was already waiting with crew aboard. Also passage had to be made within 30 days to avoid the dreaded winds off the Mexican coast at the Gulf of Tehuantepec and—once through the Panama Canal—to avoid hurricanes in the West Indies. The next day, Way gave in; he sent his Cincinnati crew home and signed with the unions.

The new captain assigned to ride on the *Queen* was Frederick Geller, born in Germany. Two of the seamen aboard would be Russians, another a Finn; the second mate, Chinese; the others were Americans. At 5 o'clock on the morning of Saturday, April 19, 1947, the new crew was aboard the steamboat and ready to shove off. Capt. Steve King, skipper of the tug *Osage,* hooked up the lines at 5:20.

With mixed emotions, Fred Way was left standing on the dock to view the *Queen*'s departure. He recalls, "The morning was chilly and calm and a beautiful sunrise spread pink and orange tints upriver over Sherman Island. Mooring lines were cast off at 6:10 and the *Osage,* her Fairbanks-Morse diesels chugging, drew the towering, inert, board-covered steamboat slowly out into the channel of the San Joaquin."

Because the *Queen,* being towed stern first, began swinging wildly from side to side, Capt. King unhitched and maneuvered around to tie onto her bow. While the *Queen* floated free for a moment, a slight breeze came up and pushed her into a mudflat. She stuck fast. In his book, Way describes the stir this caused:

A newspaper photographer was hovering overhead in an airplane and snapped a picture. In a matter of hours this photograph and an exciting news story was featured on the front page of the Oakland (Calif.) Tribune with the headline "Delta Queen Balks at Fate." The Delta Queen resented being "sold down the river," said the story. By sheer coincidence the Atlantic liner Queen Elizabeth also elected to go aground on a mud flat off Southampton, England, at this time. The two "queens" on mud flats appeared in pictures as far away as New York.

Within minutes, the *Osage* tied onto the *Queen*'s bow and, without further incident, proceeded to San Francisco Bay. At 1:52 p.m., the tug, with its "piano-box" tow, passed under the Golden Gate Bridge and into the swells of a gray-blue Pacific. At that moment, the *Delta King* became the lone survivor in California from the legendary era when the two riverboats made their nightly runs between San Francisco and Sacramento.

More than two days later, in the late evening of April 21, the tug towed the *Queen* past Catalina Island, just off the Southern California coast. Capt. Geller, in command of the inert steamboat, wrote in the official log: "Heavy rain, rough beam sea. Vessel laboring moderately, rolling heavily at times." This was the first mention in the log of rough sea conditions, but others followed. Early in the morning of May 3, off the coast of Mexico at the Gulf of Tehuantepec, Geller reported, "Vessel rolling and pounding heavily at times. Notified tug Osage that wind increasing and vessel laboring and straining. Advised he pull ashore and follow coast." At noon that day, the log noted: "Rough sea. Vessel shipping occasional seas over bow."

Later, Capt. Geller described his experience on the *Queen* during that big blow: "We hove to for about 12 hours and the crew became very anxious. At 3 a.m. I took the Second Mate and we inspected the whole vessel from bow to stern and found her tight and seaworthy, except that she was rolling from 28 to 30 degrees."

On May 10 the *Queen* arrived at Panama and became the first paddle-wheel steamboat to pass through the Panama Canal in the 33 years since its opening in 1914. The next week, in cruising north through the Caribbean and the Gulf of Mexico, the tug and its tow hit more rough weather. Log notations included "Vessel rolling heavily," "Rough seas," and "Vessel rolling and pitching." Finally, on May 18 at 2:10 in the afternoon, the *Osage* towed the steamer into calm water at the mouth of the Mississippi River. After covering 5,261 miles of open sea in 29 days, the *Delta Queen* had arrived in one piece.

At noon on May 19, the *Osage* departed and two new tugboats took over. They towed the *Queen* upriver and took her ashore opposite New Orleans at a repair yard operated by the Avondale Marine Ways. Tom Greene and Fred Way came to meet the boat. During the following two months, workmen uncrated the former pride of the Sacramento River, reinstalled the paddle wheel, shortened the smokestack to allow clearance under bridges, and put the machinery back into operating condition. On July 16, the Coast Guard issued a permit for the trip up the Mississippi and the Ohio.

When it came time to assemble a crew, getting volunteers posed no problem. In fact, dozens of men begged Greene to allow them to come along as deckhands on this historic voyage. In his good-humored fashion, Fred Way describes what this meant:

> As we proceeded up the Mississippi the calibre of my deckhand crew was augmented, at every landing it seemed, with fresh recruits from Cincinnati and Louisville, until the final stretch found the deck roster so loaded with Big Brass that a boiler explosion would have set the financial affairs of Cincinnati back on its heels for our generation. We had glass manufacturers, insurance executives, real estate magnates, oil corporation officers, manufacturers, and newspaper men. Once we had two prominent morticians aboard . . . when our paddlewheel broke down, I counted $5 million worth of talent scrambling around between the bucketplanks armed with nuts, bolts and wrenches.

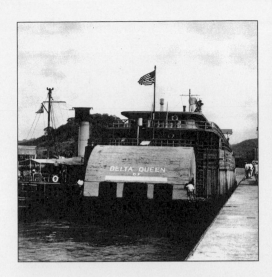

In May 1947, Delta Queen *becomes the first paddle-wheel riverboat to pass through the Panama Canal (above left). After layovers at New Orleans and Cincinnati, she was overhauled and remodeled at Dravo Marine Ways in Pittsburgh, beginning in September (above right). Six months later, the rejuvenated steamboat returned to Cincinnati and docked at Greene Line wharfboat.* Queen's *inaugural cruise on the Ohio: June 30, 1948.*

As the *Delta Queen* approached Cincinnati on the Ohio, the crew strung flags on her jackstaff, one for each nation she had passed: the United States, Mexico, Guatemala, El Salvador, Honduras, Nicaragua, Costa Rica, and Panama. With her conglomeration of businessmen-deckhands and an assortment of volunteer pilots and other crew, the *Queen* arrived at Cincinnati on July 27. As Capt. Way landed her, she was greeted by a throng of steamboat buffs and other well-wishers on the Greene Line wharfboat. She tied up there for almost two weeks.

Then, with Fred Way as captain and Jesse P. Hughes as pilot, assisted by C.W. Stoll as steersman, the *Queen* steamed up the Ohio to Pittsburgh. Completing a 7,309-mile voyage from California, she tied up at the Dravo Corporation facility on Neville Island. There, she would undergo a major overhaul. Dravo, the only shipyard on the upper Ohio big enough to drydock the 285-foot steamboat, hauled the *Queen* onto the marine ways on September 8, 1947.

But before ever getting onto the ways, the *Queen* nearly sank in a little-known incident. Fred Way III, son of Capt. Way, tells of his experience as night watchman on the vessel: "Having been instructed to be on the lookout for fire, I diligently watched for fire but ignored the sound of running water. Next day my father noticed the *Queen* was sitting extremely low in the water. It seems someone had left a valve open in the hull, and water was filling her hold. Within minutes,

---

And on to Pittsburgh

According to Fred Way's daughter Bee Rutter, the *Queen*'s trip from Cincinnati to Dravo Marine Ways was an odd mixture of adventure and discomfort. She recalls a dreary boat painted battleship gray inside and out. At the time, she wondered how Dravo could ever "pretty up such a strange looking craft" enough that passengers would *pay* to ride. "It was hot and dirty. The air-cooling system didn't work, water was available only in the rest rooms and galley, food was minimal, passengers slept on army cots, all the plumbing wasn't hooked up, and an unpleasant smell permeated the boat. We spent a lot of time in the pilothouse with the windows open."

The *Queen* carried only a handful of crew and passengers. In addition to the threesome who did the piloting—Fred Way, Jesse Hughes, and C.W. Stoll—those aboard included Capt. Way's son Jim Way, who served as watchman; Andy Lodder, long-time river buff and friend of the Greene's; Bill Horn, ship carpenter and mate; Charlie Dietz, engineer, and his wife Hazel who did the cooking.

Also aboard for all or part of the trip to Pittsburgh were Capt. Stoll's wife Marijane and a few other river buffs and friends of the Greenes including J. Mack Gamble, Bee and "Woody" Rutter, Carl Hatley, and Marion Frommel, plus Tom and Letha Greene and their two sons, Gordon and Tom, Jr.

water outside the boat would have reached a row of open portholes and poured into the hold." (Yes, the *Queen* originally had portholes, which were removed in the renovation). Quick action saved the day.

Historical footnote: That September, soon after the *Delta Queen* was hauled onto the ways, the Sons and Daughters of Pioneer Rivermen held their annual meeting aboard the boat. According to S & D president J.W. "Woody" Rutter, that was the last meeting of their organization at a location other than Marietta, Ohio.

Before the work was started and actual costs known, Tom Greene became worried that the overhaul would turn out to be more costly than originally anticipated. It was then that he and Letha offered to sell the *Queen* to the owner of the *Island Queen,* after that steamboat exploded and burned at Pittsburgh. But the offer was declined.

So it was full speed ahead with the project. As he had done in California, Greene put Fred Way in charge at Dravo. The *Queen* needed many changes. Because her builders hadn't planned for subfreezing temperatures, workmen brought exposed water pipes inside or covered them, and they removed the paddle-wheel cover to avoid icing problems. They also enlarged fuel bunkers and fresh-water tanks for Cincinnati-New Orleans trips. Technicians altered the air-cooling system; the original, an evaporative type, passed air through pads wet with river water. Now, in some areas, that would have brought foul odors into the boat. Also the original system was designed for the dry air of California's interior rather than for a humid climate.

Greene ordered other changes: The dining room was moved below to the former freight deck, allowing more space for dining and dancing. Two forward decks were elongated to give extra room for passengers to sit or stand while outside. And there was the major job of removing the Navy's gray paint from the entire wooden superstructure and applying several coats of white paint and varnish. The landing stage or swinging gangplank at the bow was added later at Cincinnati.

The time and money spent at the shipyard were prodigious. Each day the *Delta Queen* sat on the marine ways, it cost about $1,200. As unforeseen problems arose, quick decisions were needed to keep the job moving and costs down. Capt. Way's grandson Dick Rutter tells of hearing his grandfather talk about his frustration with the many delays while Tom Greene, who had been so decisive in buying the *Queen,* now wrestled with his options. As Way put it, Greene "played The Thinker while the taxi meter ticked." According to Letha Greene in her book *Long*

Live the Delta Queen, while their friends at the bank came to the rescue in financing work on the boat, the resulting mortgage burdened the company for many years.

Fred Way suggests that anyone who has built a new house or remodeled an old one would understand—the work at Dravo took much longer and cost much more than anyone had guessed. But finally the job was finished, and it was done well. He comments:

> We were in the repair yard for a few days over six months, and that was then a record long stay at Dravo, and I think it still is. The Delta Queen went to Dravo's very much of a question mark and she emerged every inch a steamboat.

The *Delta Queen* took a trial run on February 27, 1948. The next day, she left Pittsburgh for Cincinnati with Captains Way and Hughes taking turns at piloting. She arrived at the wharfboat in Cincinnati on the morning of March 1. At that point, Fred Way's job was over. As he put it, Greene Line had absorbed the new luxury liner into its operation.

In the following months, Tom and Letha Greene furnished the cabins in anticipation of the *Queen*'s inaugural passenger cruise on the Ohio. They scheduled it for the month of June—21 years after the *Queen*'s historic maiden voyage on the Sacramento, which also took place in June.

The California boat had found a new home.

11

The Landlocking of a King

In Cincinnati, as the Greenes prepared the *Delta Queen* for her first passenger cruise on the Ohio, the future looked bright. But, in California, the future for her twin appeared bleak indeed. The headline that met the eyes of *San Francisco Chronicle* readers on March 30, 1948, announced: "Delta King Faces Death by Scrapping."

The newspaper reported: "For the fourth time since the war, the once-proud Sacramento River steamer Delta King is being offered for sale by the Maritime Commission, either for operation or scrapping." The story told about the earlier winning bid by "Chinese interests" who didn't realize the boat was a paddlewheeler and had abandoned the deal. Then it described how the Commission had put the boat up for sale two additional times but had rejected bids both times for being too low. The River Lines had bid highest one of those times, a junk dealer the other time.

The article concluded, "While this pulling and hauling has been going on, the Delta King has deteriorated steadily. Her wooden decks and superstructure are warped and leaky . . . When bids are opened April 20 in Washington, they feel there's a good chance the Delta King will be sold for scrap."

This time, The River Lines came out high bidder at $17,552. Norvin Fay, president of the firm, said his company planned to put the vessel back into service in the Sacramento area. But the Commission again rejected the bid as too low. Four auctions and still no sale. The *King* continued to sit in the mothball fleet at Benicia.

In the fall of 1948, the Commission tried once more and received four bids.

When they were opened in September, high bid of $24,000 came from L.G. Wingard of Seattle and his partners. Newspapers reported that the high bidders planned to put the steamboat into sight-seeing excursion service on Puget Sound. But according to Wingard's widow, Mary Lou Wingard (interviewed recently), they planned to use the vessel as a floating fish cannery on Alaska's Bristol Bay. Other bids received: $20,000 by the Asia Development Corporation of Shanghai, $10,575 by The River Lines, and $5,777 by J. R. Bundesen of Pittsburg, California (the latter bidding for scrap). Would the Commission accept the high bid this, the fifth time?

The suspense ended two months later, when the Maritime Commission accepted the Wingard offer. Four partners shared ownership: L.G. Wingard and his wife, plus Jack Salmon and Les Fulton. On November 17, the new owners towed the *King* from the mothball fleet to Fulton's Shipyard at Antioch in preparation for the trip north. But, once the boat tied up at Fulton's, their plans faltered and came to a standstill.

Days passed without any work being done. Days turned into weeks, weeks into months. Over a year went by. The *King* sat in a state of disrepair, no maintenance performed since the boat's Navy service. Plans to take the vessel north had run into financial snags.

The *Delta Queen* had made a name for herself when she left the West Coast for the Mississippi and the Ohio. But the *Delta King* was fast reaching obscurity in the postwar period. First, anchored at the mothball fleet for more than two years—then tucked away at Fulton's—the *King* was nearly forgotten by the busy world of California in the late Forties.

And a busy world it was—a far cry from the Depression years. Thousands of returning servicemen went back to school or bought homes; subdivisions grew up almost overnight; city boundaries extended in every direction. Between 1940 and 1950 the state population increased by 50 percent. Proud owners of "giant" new 12-inch TVs invited friends over to watch Ed Sullivan and Milton Berle in black and white. It was a time of promise but also a time of uncertainty. The Berlin blockade in 1948 and the Russian atomic-bomb explosions in 1949 reminded us that the world's problems were far from solved by the Allied victory in World War II. And the next year found the United States engaged in combat again in Korea.

An unheralded event—unrelated to the *King* or *Queen* but of interest to historians and steamboat buffs—took place in 1950. In August of that year, the little paddle-wheel steamer *Petaluma* made her final run down the Petaluma River to

San Francisco with a load of freight. That trip marked the end of 103 years of steamboating in California. An unexpected footnote came 35 years later in August 1985, when Hal Wilmunder began passenger day trips on the Sacramento with his newly-built paddlewheeler *Elizabeth Louise*. But with Capt. Wilmunder's sudden death in 2003, the future became unclear for his pride and joy—the only stern-wheel steamboat in recent years to offer commercial service west of the Rockies.

In May of 1950, a year and a half after Wingard and his partners bought the *Delta King*, they announced that they had given up plans to take the vessel north; it would be too expensive to convert the craft to a fish cannery. This news set off a flurry of activity by parties who saw the boat's potential for various uses. Barney Gould, San Francisco theatrical impresario, hoped to make the *King* into a show-boat; Jim Palmer of San Diego also envisioned the vessel as a showboat in his city's Mission Bay. And Libby, McNeill & Libby, commercial food canners, expressed an interest. But nothing came of these ideas, and the sternwheeler stayed at Fulton's another two years.

Finally, in early 1952, the owners sold the *King* to Kitimat Constructors, a company with an unusual plan for the historic boat. The vessel wouldn't be turned into an excursion boat or a showboat or made into a fish cannery—nor would the craft be scrapped. Instead, the new owners would tow the *King* to British Columbia and beach the vessel high and dry as a dormitory for construction workers at Kitimat, 100 miles south of the Alaskan Panhandle. As agents for Alcan (Aluminum Company of Canada, Ltd.), Kitimat Constructors' first task was to prepare the *King* at Fulton's for the open sea. Then would come the towing to Victoria, B.C., the conversion for housing, and finally the delivery to the head of Douglas Channel at Kitimat. There the boat would be set up as home for crews building a brand-new town in the wilderness, with the giant new Alcan aluminum smelter as centerpiece.

Workmen at Fulton's removed the *Delta King*'s steam engines, machinery, and paddle wheel and stored them at the shipyard. But they left the boilers and generators on the boat to provide heat and electricity at Kitimat. Renovation of the vessel included a bright new coat of white paint with green trim, a pleasing change from wartime gray. In final preparation for the sea voyage, carpenters installed plywood sheathing on heavy timbers around the forward portion and lower decks. Doors and windows that might be smashed by ocean waves were also covered. In early April, workers completed the job, and the *Delta King* awaited its Canadian adventure.

Just after midnight on April 15, two Fulton tugboats, *Bear Flag* and *Mr. Thomas,* pulled the *King* away from the dock. With a security crew of two aboard, the flotilla went on an outgoing tide down the San Joaquin River. Arriving on San Francisco Bay, they stopped at the Standard Oil Long Wharf at Richmond. Fulton's tugs then returned to Antioch. Next day after dark, the seagoing tug *Navigator,* of the Island Tug & Barge Company, tied onto the *King* and chugged across the bay to the Golden Gate.

At the moment the *Delta King* slipped under the bridge and disappeared into the blackness of the Pacific swells, an era passed into history. For the first time since the mid-1920s, neither the *King* nor the *Queen* floated on California's inland waters. A quarter of a century after their maiden voyages, only memories of the legendary sternwheelers remained in the state where they were born.

The *Navigator* proceeded up the coast with the boarded-up craft and made its first stop at Victoria. There, workmen outfitted the *King* for a new life as workmen's dormitory and prepared the vessel for the final leg of the voyage to Kitimat. Reportedly, the boat's purchase and its conversion to crew quarters cost half as much as it would have cost to build temporary housing from scratch. When the work was finished, the tug pulled its tow from the harbor at Victoria and headed north for the remaining 450 miles of the saltwater journey.

On May 8, the 1,500-mile trip nearly complete, tug and tow reached the opening of Douglas Channel and turned into that fiord-like waterway leading 40 miles inland to Kitimat. Later in the day, the *King* arrived at the end of the channel, where the former pride of the Sacramento River would play a valuable role in the new community.

Douglas Channel experiences extremely high tides, occasionally as much as 39 feet. Knowing this, workmen created a long, narrow cofferdam on the shoreline and excavated a trench behind it slightly larger than the hull of the *King*. They left an opening on one end. Then at high tide on May 15, 1952, they floated the riverboat in, closed the opening with a bulldozer, and pumped the water out. The *Delta King* now rested on solid ground, landlocked in Canada for the next seven years.

T.W. Paterson, writing in the *Daily Colonist* of Victoria reported the recollections of Hugh Parmiter, a banker at Kitimat:

A level bed had been bulldozed out for the King on the shore . . . and all awaited the big day of the highest tide in May when it could be floated

In 1952, Delta King *was towed to Canada along route shown on map. Aerial photo shows tugboat pulling with long tow line. Bottom left: view from tug as the* King *wallows in Pacific swells. Bottom right: stopover at Victoria, B.C. (note Navy's YFB-55 identification still visible near bow).*

into position. The tide elected to arrive at the unseemly hour of 2 a.m. and few saw the fevered activity, the pushing of tugs, aided with cable winches positioned along the upper shore like artillery pieces. It was an education to hear the screams and shouts and orders given at one end of the boat and promptly countermanded by another authority at the other end . . . to see the flashing arc lights on shore and the boat searchlights on deck.

Ironically, the sternwheeler, after surviving the dangers of the open sea, almost passed into oblivion within weeks of arrival. According to Paterson, the *King's* boiler room caught fire: "Volunteer firefighters unthinkingly attacked the oil blaze with water! Miraculously, the results were not disastrous." Another time the vessel found itself temporarily in jeopardy, when an exceptionally high tide came over the earthen barrier, refloated the boat, and broke the connections to water mains and sewers.

In the years at Kitimat, a multiracial potpourri of construction crews, land clearers, and laborers called the *Delta King* "home." Not only did the boat serve as bunkhouse for more than 200 Alcan employees, but its boilers provided heat for the hospital, school, recreation hall, cafe, and smelter, as well as for its own cabins.

However welcome this heating arrangement may have been to its users, it proved troublesome for neighbors living downwind. Hugh Parmiter says the boilers consumed about 1,200 gallons of oil daily and, until workmen finally made adjustments, much of the oil poured into the air as smoke. He reports:

> Half of this [oil] flew out of the smokestack in waves reminiscent of a ship laying a smokescreen, and our office, directly downwind, was the immediate beneficiary. Each member of our staff carried a duster permanently in the left hand, to wipe a clean spot on which to work, and nary a letter was sent out that was not generously smeared with blots of oily soot.

At Kitimat, Alcan had undertaken a venture of monumental proportions, the largest project (to that time) ever undertaken by a private company. It dammed a river, ran the stream backwards through a mountain, dropped it down a man-made waterfall 16 times higher than Niagara, ran it through turbines, and then released it into the Pacific. The company did all this to produce electricity. Production of aluminum requires cheap power in steady, enormous quantities.

With a power source assured, Alcan set out to build its aluminum smelter, as well as to construct housing for thousands of workmen and buildings to provide goods and services—in effect, to create an entire new community. The company needed lumberjacks and bulldozer operators to clear the forests; carpenters, electricians, plumbers, and machinists to build the new plant and the many other buildings. Getting the necessary manpower was crucial, and it wasn't easy in such an isolated location. The Canadian government cooperated by encouraging a large number of immigrants to come to the country.

Herb Thompson, a machinist at Kitimat living aboard the *Delta King* in 1953-54, tells of the "DPs" (displaced persons) and others who came there: "The Germans worked mostly in the mechanical trades and the Portuguese mainly in the smelter pot lines."

Paul Aha, an operating engineer from Germany, began living on the *King* in 1954. He calls the project "an unbelievable undertaking done with private money" and says production of aluminum began the year he arrived.

Tony Rigoni, who lived aboard the *King* in 1956-57, read about the need for workers in the Italian edition of *Reader's Digest* and migrated to Canada from his hometown of Asiago in northern Italy. He was only 19, couldn't speak English, and had never been away from home before. But jobs were scarce in his country, and he felt he had no other satisfactory choice. He was a carpenter by trade, but until he learned to speak English, he worked as a laborer at Alcan; later he operated a bulldozer. Rigoni tearfully recalls, "Those first years were the hardest and loneliest of my life. I was a kid away from home and family, didn't have anyone to talk to. My roommate was Norwegian—he couldn't speak my language and I couldn't speak his. Neither of us spoke English. All we knew how to say to each other was, 'Good morning!'"

Rigoni reports that 47 nationalities were represented at Kitimat and, due to language differences, little communication took place. He says, "Many of the workers were really rough—they had nothing to do in their off hours but drink and fight. I was scared to death of their violence and cruelty; sometimes I'd take refuge in my room on the *Delta King*."

Alcan had its own security crew, Rigoni says, so the Royal Canadian Mounted Police only came into the picture if more serious crimes were committed. In case of damage to Alcan property, the company had an ace in the hole: it simply deducted the cost from the violator's next paycheck. Alcan overlooked gambling by employees, for years a favorite pastime on the *King*. Some men lost as much as $5,000 in one night.

With 14,000 young men mostly between 20 and 30—some of whom hadn't seen a woman in years—it was inevitable that someone would introduce prostitution. According to Rigoni, two enterprising entrepreneurs went down to Vancouver, hired four women, and brought them to the *Delta King*. Word got around fast. In no time about 3,000 eager men formed a line leading up to the riverboat. "Price of admission" was $200, big money in those days. But at Kitimat there were few ways to spend a paycheck, and almost everyone had money saved.

At first, Alcan security didn't realize what was going on. The operation continued unabated for two or three hours. Then came the crackdown. The prostitutes, the entrepreneurs, and the first ten men in line were taken into custody. They had violated Canadian law. A few days later in court, one of the would-be customers waxed indignant—he said he paid his money but had received nothing. And now, adding insult to injury, the judge was fining him $2 plus 50 cents in court costs. Although he had only minimal command of the English language, he managed to convey his feelings to the judge about the injustice of it all. He said, "Mr. Police—me no play, me no pay."

By late 1958 Alcan had built additional housing and announced that, early the following year, it would no longer need the *Delta King*. Since the boat could be refloated and used elsewhere, the company offered the landlocked riverboat for sale and began negotiations with interested parties.

In early January, the Chamber of Commerce in Stockton, where the *King* and *Queen* had been built, started a drive to acquire the vessel as a local monument and theater-restaurant. At the request of chamber directors, State Senator Alan Short planned to introduce emergency legislation to unfreeze $175,000 in state beaches and parks funds to buy, transport, and remodel the boat.

But first, a chamber delegation went to Sacramento to seek approval by the State Beaches and Parks Commission. In spite of letters of endorsement from the state historian, the San Francisco Maritime Museum, and the president of College of the Pacific at Stockton (now UOP), the Commission turned down the appeal, citing other projects with higher priority. And what about the Stockton City Council? If the state purchased the *King*, would the city agree to manage it? When the City Council failed to resolve this issue, the matter dragged on.

Then on March 2, 1959, John Kessel, a Stockton real estate man and head of a local business group, announced purchase of the *King* from Alcan for $32,000. The Chamber of Commerce had acted as his purchasing agent. The boat would be a privately-owned attraction on the Stockton Channel, rather than a state-financed historical monument, and would feature a theater-restaurant, hotel, and museum.

Meanwhile, at Kitimat, the snow-covered *Delta King* awaited the dramatic day when it would be refloated and towed away to the city of its birth. On the night of March 27, work crews and a tugboat went into action. T.W. Paterson, writing in the *Daily Colonist,* reported Hugh Parmiter's observations:

> Crowds braved a midnight chill to watch the King's departure. . . . water was pumped in. Despite her years of inactivity and lack of maintenance, the old King floated slowly, steadily from the mud. Only her rudders had to be freed. When the dike was broken, the riverboat answered the tow-line demurely, floating into the channel at high tide.
>
> As the lines of her hull from midship to stern became visible for the first time, cheers went up from the crew, construction workers, and onlookers. Floodlights focused on the blistered paint . . . [and] were reflected in the three tiers of her stateroom windows. In darkness . . . she seemed a ghost ship as she slid gently across the calm surface of the channel. When Island Tug & Barge completed preparations for towing the King southward to Victoria, the only passengers still aboard were a watchman and a fat tabby cat.

Tony Rigoni says the *Delta King* had provided the first home for a lot of men at Kitimat, and he estimates that 2,000 turned out to see the refloating and to bid the craft farewell. He recalls his sadness on seeing the *King* leave and describes his last view of the riverboat: "They opened up the dirt barrier and waited for high tide. Once the tide was in, the water was very calm. The boat began to float—they pulled with lines from a tug. Within moments the *King* just disappeared into the darkness."

Memory of the old riverboat was kept alive for years by an annual celebration at Kitimat that had a raft race, dances, casinos, food, and entertainment. The event was called "Delta King Days."

At the Victoria stopover, shipyard workers reportedly installed wood sheathing on the foredeck and sides of the California-bound vessel (though minimal boarding-up shows in news photos). Then the Island Tug & Barge's *Lloyd B. Gore* traveled with its tow down the Pacific coast. *Harbour & Shipping*, a trade paper published in Vancouver, reported, "Nothing could stop the doughty four-decker from completing that trip. Three storms tried, storms that sent green water over the cabin house of Island Tug's *Lloyd B. Gore*. But the *Delta King*, despite her flat-

Landlocked for seven years, Delta King serves as dormitory for smelter workers at Kitimat, B.C. In 1959, unkempt King slips under Golden Gate Bridge on voyage to Stockton.

bottomed hull, no keel, and 50 feet of superstructure, wallowed tenaciously south-
ward to a royal welcome from her beloved San Francisco as she entered the Bay."

The long-awaited arrival took place at 5 p.m. on April 28, 1959. The *San
Francisco Chronicle* reported the event:

> The old Delta King, her lower windows boarded over and her green and
> white paint peeled half off, was towed through the Golden Gate late yes-
> terday afternoon. She was creaking, in the words of Robert MacDonald,
> one of her two crew members, "like Boris Karloff's living room." Donald
> House, who sailed on the 285-foot craft seven years ago, said the four-
> day voyage from Victoria, B.C., provided him with a shocked look at an
> old friend. "It was like having a date with a girl you thought looked pret-
> ty sweet 20 years ago," he declared. . . .
>
> A joyful, noisy greeting was planned for the Delta King's arrival from
> British Columbia. . . . But the Prowler, loaded with newspapermen,
> radio announcers, television cameramen, and business and civic notables
> . . . did not arrive until long after the Delta King had been anchored off
> Treasure Island. She was greeted, instead, at the Golden Gate by a small
> flotilla—Ellis Brooks' yacht Sea Brooks and a medium-sized white
> whale, which swam alongside and spouted gently.

After passing under the Golden Gate Bridge for the second time in its career,
the proud-but-aging riverboat settled down to rest overnight on the familiar waters
of San Francisco Bay. The next day would see the sternwheeler heading back to its
birthplace on the Stockton Channel.

ON PACIFIC AVE.
STOCKTON
HOWARD 6-0211

HURRY — HURRY
LEAVES SOON

FILMED IN STOCKTON

A WONDERFUL WORLD OF EXCITEMENT!

METRO-GOLDWYN-MAYER
Presents

SAMUEL GOLDWYN, JR.'S.
Production of

MARK TWAIN'S
The Adventures of Huckleberry Finn

In CinemaScope And METROCOLOR   Starring **TONY RANDALL**

Co-Starring **PATTY McCORMACK · NEVILLE BRAND**

MICKEY   JUDY   ANDY   BUSTER
SHAUGHNESSY · CANOVA · DEVINE · KEATON

with FINLAY CURRIE · STERLING HOLLOWAY

Presenting as "JIM"   And Also Starring as "Huckleberry Finn"
ARCHIE MOORE · EDDIE HODGES

Screen Play by JAMES LEE · Directed by MICHAEL CURTIZ

TODAY AND SUNDAY AT 1:35-3:39-5:40-7:45-9:47

Soon after returning to Stockton, Delta King performs in movie filmed on San Joaquin River. Disguised as a Mississippi riverboat, the King is pushed by tugboat on side away from movie camera.

Two false smokestacks belch black smoke to simulate an operative steamboat. Only a bit part for the King—but a brief moment of glory.

12

"Double, Double Toil and Trouble"

It's morning on April 29, 1959—time for the last leg of the *Delta King*'s trip to Stockton. By 10 o'clock everything is ready, and the tug begins to tow the *King* north on San Francisco Bay. The *Prowler,* flagship of the Stockton Inland Port Fleet with Commodore Jack Benton aboard, escorts the flotilla from the bay and accompanies it during the 14-hour trip.

Word of the *King*'s voyage gets around fast. By the time the vessel reaches the Carquinez Strait, hundreds of people line the shores to see the famed riverboat "on its way home." Here, workers from the C & H Sugar refinery temporarily leave their jobs. They join others watching, as the *King* passes under the same Carquinez Bridge the craft had passed under so many times in its youth. As the sternwheeler and tug move past Vallejo, Crockett, and towns along Suisun Bay—and start up the San Joaquin River at Antioch—dozens of small craft form a parade of boats that remain with the *King* until dark.

Despite the late hour of the *Delta King*'s after-midnight arrival at Stockton, a crowd of 200 riverboat fans, supporters, and the just-plain curious turn out to welcome the historic vessel back from Canada. They want to celebrate the craft's return to the place where it all began more than three decades before. Little do they know what bizarre times lie ahead at Stockton over the next decade.

On April 30, the *Stockton Record* headlined: "Delta King Back Home Again Minus Paddle Wheel, Paint" with the subhead "Once Pride of River." The following day, the paper ran an editorial, "Welcome to the Delta King":

Memories of when the Delta King was built and launched in Stockton, or of its majestic steaming through the Delta, evoke from old-timers a warm welcome for the vessel as it returns to a dock near its birthplace. But old-timers are not alone in their fascination with the return of the King and with what the future holds for this craft once accurately described as palatial . . .

There will be considerable public interest in the restoration of the Delta King and in fitting and decorating it in an approximation of its former glory.

The good feelings and exhilaration lasted less than a month. On May 27, Barney Gould, who had wanted to buy the boat seven years before and expected to buy it in 1959, filed a $1.5 million damage suit, claiming the sternwheeler had been snatched from under his nose. The suit claimed he had an option to buy the vessel from the Aluminum Company of Canada and that the firm had breached the option and "wrongfully sold" it to the Stockton Chamber of Commerce and John Kessel. Gould charged that the company was "induced" by the San Francisco Maritime Museum Association and Stanley Dollar, Jr., its former president, not to enter into a contract with him. Defendants—in addition to Alcan—included the Stockton Chamber, the Museum Association, Dollar, and Kessel, plus the manager of the Chamber and the surplus disposal officer for Alcan.

Behind the scenes, trouble was brewing, too. To Kessel, it seemed his "backers" were dissolving into thin air. In his eyes, not only had the Stockton Chamber acted as his agent in purchasing the *Delta King,* but without its promises to back him up and find investors for the project he never would have gotten involved. Years later, Kessel-estate executor Evelyn Madrid summed up how Mr. Kessel saw the situation: "As soon as the *King* got to Stockton, he felt they dropped it like a hot potato."

In the fall of 1959, however, the tired old riverboat achieved a brief moment of glory and a kind of immortality. Disguised as a nineteenth-century Mississippi River steamboat, the *King* played a part in the MGM film, *The Adventures of Huckleberry Finn.*

The movie—starring Tony Randall, Judy Canova, Andy Devine, Buster Keaton, Archie Moore as "Jim," and Eddie Hodges as "Huck"—was filmed on the San Joaquin River. So that no one could see the paddle wheel was missing, the *King* was shown mostly at a distance and from the front. A tugboat, on the side away from the camera, provided movement, while two dummy smokestacks belched black smoke from two smoke pots. The real stack, between the two phony stacks, was rendered virtually invisible with sky-blue paint. The film, produced by Sam Goldwyn, Jr., also included a few interior shots. To be sure, the *King* had played only a bit part, but the vessel enjoyed more glamour and excitement in those brief scenes than it had experienced in many years.

Then, for the *King*, it was back from the "reel world" of Hollywood to the real world of Stockton. Yet the events ahead might just as well have been plotted by a Hollywood screenwriter. From day to day, you scarcely knew whether you were watching a John Wayne western, a Perry Mason mystery, or a Laurel and Hardy comedy. The decade at Stockton would bring forth a tangle of events and activities, financial headaches, ownership puzzles, government interventions, and legal snarls. It was hard to tell the guys wearing the white hats from those wearing black hats without a program. And there was no program.

"Actors" in the drama proliferated; at times, events seemed to unleash the proverbial cast of thousands. Stars would include famed trial-lawyer Melvin Belli of San Francisco, the flamboyant and self-styled "King of Torts"; retired Air Force colonel Max Mortensen, flier of 200 missions and holder of the Silver Star and 20 air medals; the disillusioned Stockton developer John Kessel, who thought he had bought the *King* with the Chamber's full support; and, of course, the star-crossed *Delta King*, last of the historic passenger and freight riverboats in California.

Also having "star" status: Barney Gould, theatrical producer and publicist whose lifelong dream of owning a showboat in San Francisco kept eluding him, and Tom Horton, satirical columnist at the *Sacramento Union*, who criticized his city for neglecting its own waterfront.

Supporting actors would include Grogan Plumbing & Heating Co., a contracting firm that had done extensive work on the *King*; J. Edward Ogden, alleged owner of a strip of land known as Kessel Cove, where the vessel was moored; and Gene Detgen, mysterious Southern Californian, who suddenly claimed ownership of the boat. Grandiose predictions of success were made; lawsuits were filed; the craft changed hands more than once; auctions of the boat were scheduled and then canceled. Sixty-eight ill-conceived windows were cut in the hull, setting the scene for big trouble in later years. "Scouts" from Sacramento, with piracy in mind, stalked the vessel. The story line, sometimes exciting but often repetitious, provided an interesting topic of conversation for those on the sidelines. But it proved an ordeal for the participants. And all the while, the *King* sat on the Stockton Channel deteriorating, month by month and year by year.

During the decade at Stockton, at least six potential buyers negotiated or received options to buy the boat. Owners and would-be owners considered several locations other than Stockton, ranging from the Berkeley Yacht Harbor on San Francisco Bay to the Hawaiian Islands. Other possibilities envisioned: the San Francisco waterfront, Moss Landing (down the coast), Los Angeles, and Seattle.

Almost every year from 1959 to 1966, potential buyers hired naval architects and marine engineers to do surveys on the *King* to determine its current condition and to assess possibilities for various uses. Uniformly, these expensive surveys reported that the steam engines and paddle wheel had been removed; the hull was in good condition; the superstructure and decks were structurally sound, though in need of repair. The first two surveys found the two boilers and auxiliary equipment still in place; the following ones said these items were missing (no notations about when or by whom removed). The only people who seemed to profit from these inspections were the architects and engineers.

On November 1, 1959, the *Modesto Bee* told of John Kessel's plans for a 100-unit *Delta King* lodge, swimming pool, ice rink, and shopping center with the vessel as "heart and soul" of the project. He hired a hostess for the boat, and, reportedly, Art Linkletter, radio and television personality, would emcee the grand opening in January 1960. But in late January, when only preliminary work had been completed, Barney Gould reported that the boat was for sale. He said he had made Kessel an offer and understood others were also negotiating. The only comment reporters could get from Kessel was "No comment."

In March, Kessel obtained a marine survey that said the *King* could easily be powered by a diesel engine, which would operate either a propeller or paddle wheel. This indicated new thinking on the owner's part, but it didn't provide a solution to the problems at hand. In June, the *Sacramento Union* ran a story about Barney Gould that—while not full of hard news—may have set a record for alliteration in headlines: "Busy Barney Battles Businessmen to Buy Bigger Boat." The text said Gould "hopes to buy or battle his way to ownership of the old *Delta King*." The word "bigger" in the headline referred to his having owned the two smaller predecessors to the *King* and *Queen*, sternwheelers he had hoped to make into showboats. His plans had gone awry when the *Port of Stockton* (formerly *Capital City*) sank in 1952 and the *Fort Sutter* burned in 1959, just two days after the *King* returned to Stockton.

Finally, in August 1960, John Kessel ended his silence. He announced that plans to convert his boat into a floating museum and entertainment center had collapsed for lack of financial backing. Kessel said a group of backers withdrew,

New exterior paint job at Stockton gives boat new cared-for look after seven years of harsh weather and poor upkeep in Canada.

While optimism for successful venture at Stockton still runs high, owner John Kessel poses with associates in front of "world famous" Delta King.

because they doubted it could be a success in a community the size of Stockton.

In February 1961, the *Oakland Tribune* ran a story that described the polarities and hard feelings at Stockton: "Once the vessel was back and the citizens were through shouting, 'The King is home, long live the King,' the businessman [Kessel] found that civic leaders had abandoned ship." For a contrary view, the article quoted James Sommers of the Stockton Chamber, who said the organization had given Kessel no assurance of aid: "We ran a promotion that brought the King back, and that's all. The whole trouble is that nobody is willing to invest in a restaurant."

Curious about what was going on at Stockton and wanting to see the boat, I drove there from the Bay Area on a cold and dreary day in early 1962. A stark, lonely scene met my eyes. The *Delta King*—nestled up to its moorings amid stalks of cane growing from the muddy shore—appeared deserted. Green paint from the vessel's Kitimat days peeled on its hull; a solitary light burned on an upper deck. Soft rain fell as I snapped a picture and hurried back to my car with thoughts of returning another day.

Kessel tried again for the brass ring on July 15, 1963, when he and six partners, all from Stockton, filed incorporation papers for Delta King, Inc. The new group, with the partners as directors, planned to sell stock to raise money for converting the boat to motel and night-club use. Apparently, the new corporation failed, because in February 1965 it filed new articles of incorporation, using the same corporate name but with none of the original six partners on the board of directors. The new board consisted of only three members, all from Southern California. Again—failure.

The plot thickens when famed San Francisco attorney Melvin Belli enters the picture. Having made headlines the year before as Jack Ruby's defense lawyer in Dallas, Belli would soon be making headlines as co-owner of the *Delta King* in Stockton. On July 14, 1965, John Kessel signed a bill of sale transferring ownership of the vessel to Belli and Max Mortensen, general manager of Delta King, Inc. Then the two signed a promissory note to John Kessel for $247,683 plus interest, to be paid back in six yearly payments.

They immediately announced plans to open the riverboat in September as a restaurant, hotel, and entertainment center at Stockton. But these plans fell through, as had others before them. The next news came in February 1966 when Mel Belli reported that he'd found a home for the *King* on the San Francisco waterfront. He described plans for a "floating Ghirardelli Square" with restaurants, night clubs, and shops. That scheme never materialized, either.

A month later, Grogan Plumbing & Heating Co., a contracting firm that had worked on the *King*, filed a suit for $51,423 against Belli and Mortensen to collect unpaid plumbing bills. The U.S. government placed the boat in custody, and the *Stockton Record* reported the seizure on March 10:

> As Jimmy Durante would say: "It's downright humiliat'n'!" In this case, he'd be referring to Stockton's own Delta King, that once plush riverboat. The King is "under arrest" and in "protective custody" under the watchful eye of a deputy U.S. Marshal.

After a trial that aborted erroneously due to a false report the case had been settled out of court, the marshal announced he would sell the *King* at public auction on October 21 to satisfy the contractor's lien. But when bidders and spectators assembled—with only five minutes to go until auction time—the judge canceled the sale and rescheduled it to allow Belli extra time to arrange a loan. Werner Busch, who had ridden on the *King* many years before, was in the crowd that had gathered to witness the auction. He commented, "I certainly hope that old vessel finds a home. Cost only $3 for a cabin, maybe a little more for the honeymoon suite. You know, a lot of Californians were conceived on that boat."

The postponed auction never took place, as Belli came up with a check to satisfy the judgment. According to him, the door now opened for a new *Delta King* location—the Berkeley Yacht Harbor. There, he said, the boat would sit landlocked on a concrete foundation, surrounded by a moat to give the illusion of being afloat.

In this period, Erle Stanley Gardner wrote *Gypsy Days on the Delta*, in which he referred to "my friend, Melvin Belli" and told of plans for the Berkeley location. Gardner said:

> Melvin Belli, who never does things by halves, is having one of the spacious staterooms fitted up as his own "Admiral's Room" and is looking forward to spending much of his time living aboard. Belli's exuberant personality, his drive, his fertile imagination, and his love of California history guarantee that there are new days in store for the majestic Delta King.

In an interview years later, Mr. Belli said, "I've always liked boats." He confirmed to me that he would have lived aboard had plans worked out for a Bay Area location. But it was not to be.

Before *Gypsy Days* could hit bookstore shelves, the government seized the *King* again. A new $2,100 lien had been filed by Grogan Plumbing; it stated that this figure represented the costs resulting from the auction postponement. Smarting from this latest blow, Belli vowed to file a counter suit against Grogan, charging harassment.

Now, let's run our film "fast forward." Berkeley didn't get the *King;* the boat wasn't put up for auction again; and there's no record of a Belli suit charging harassment. But several legal maneuvers took place in quick succession, including a bill of sale executed in December 1966 transferring Belli's interest to Max Mortensen and Richard F. Gerry (the latter a defense attorney for Belli and Mortensen)—and another bill of sale in January 1967 in which Gerry transferred his interest to Mortensen. Now, supposedly, Mortensen owned the *King* outright.

Aside from that change of ownership, little of importance took place during the year. So fast forward again—this time to September 1968, when cries of "fraud" and "usury" were heard coming from a Stockton courtroom. Belli and Mortensen were battling J. Edward Ogden and his wife over ownership of Kessel Cove, where the *King* was moored. Ogden's alleged ownership of that property would play an important part in later developments. So keep his name in mind.

Then, in December, San Joaquin County scheduled an auction of the *King* to satisfy claims of more than eleven thousand dollars plus over two thousand dollars in delinquent property taxes and penalties. Again, a last-minute cancellation of the auction—this time due to a surprise development. An unknown Southern Californian by the name of Gene Detgen had filed a third-party claim, claiming he bought the boat from Mortensen on August 15, 1968. Detgen—another name to keep in mind. He plays a vital role again later in our drama.

During the late 1960s, while the pot alternately simmered and boiled in Stockton, something big was cooking 45 miles to the north that would ultimately affect the *King*. In December 1966, after plans had been announced for the boat's Berkeley location, *Sacramento Union* columnist Tom Horton bemoaned the loss of both the *King* and the *Queen* to the area years before. He also ridiculed his city's current lack of foresight on its waterfront:

> It should come as no great surprise to you, if you have resided in our town longer than two weeks, that Sacramento was not even in the bidding for the Delta King. If somebody brought the Delta King back to

Sacramento, where it belongs, and pumped new life into the erstwhile pleasure cruiser, it would be the biggest upset since David and Goliath.

Whether or not the Delta King would prove economically feasible on the Sacramento River . . . is not really the point. Its move from Stockton, where it languished near death, to Berkeley, which many regard as a fate worse than death, strikes me as symbolic of Sacramento's stagnant attitude toward its own waterfront.

Then fast forward just over two years to February 1969, when Tom Horton wrote: "The Delta Queen and the Delta King plied the Sacramento River—they are in every respect Sacramento boats—and their removal to foreign waters will forever befoul the history of the Capital City."

A short time later, a Horton column printed a letter from Jerry Vorpahl, a young transplant from St. Paul who said his hometown used to hold four-day celebrations upon arrival of the *Delta Queen*. Vorpahl suggested that Sacramento find a way to buy the *Queen*, which had been offered for sale recently, he said, due to new restrictive, maritime-safety laws (which threatened to end her career as an overnight boat). He asked, "Why can't we get something off the ground, or into the water, in this town? . . . So let's get us a riverboat for Old Sacramento or else let's quit talking and cover the river with concrete for a parking lot. . . . "

In May 1969, the Sacramento Jaycees (Junior Chamber of Commerce) asked columnist Horton to suggest a community service project for their organization. His answer: "A riverboat." Later Horton noted that Jaycee president Robert Luther "took to his suggestion like Huck Finn to a dead cat." Robbie Van Vorn—a colorful riverboat booster who wore a business suit with cowboy hat and imported Spanish boots and who owned a print shop—turned out bumper stickers promoting the idea. Within days, they appeared on bumpers around town with the slogan: "Riverboat's Comin'!"

But where would the riverboat come from? Jerry Vorpahl's idea for obtaining the *Delta Queen,* even if she were available, wasn't practical; she probably would cost millions. More and more, eyes were turning toward Stockton and the *Delta King,* the steamboat that had been a familiar sight at Sacramento 30 years before. Most knew the boat had been stuck for years in a legal and financial quagmire. But no one knew if the vessel was for sale—or even who owned it at the moment. It was general knowledge that the old steamer had deteriorated over the years and that ownership was clouded. Word came back from Stockton that the *King* had been unattended for long periods of time and that souvenir hunters and other trespassers had gone aboard.

Ironically, although Horton had suggested a riverboat for Sacramento as a Jaycee project, plans were being made by a group of seven or eight people who mostly were *not* members of the Junior Chamber. A prominent exception was Jim McMullen, insurance sales manager, who was a Jaycee and probably the only one in the group who had seen and been aboard the *King*. Once, on a scouting mission to Stockton, McMullen had even been stranded aboard when the gangplank fell off. The real spark plug of the early movement, however, was Robbie Van Vorn, who was not a Jaycee member.

The group had searched in Southern California and the Northwest for a boat; they had consulted with riverboat aficionado Barney Gould. Up to late spring it was a fruitless quest. But as the summer of 1969 approached, in meetings and over late-night beers, they talked increasingly of the *King*. It seems they'd found the riverboat Sacramento needed.

There was no denying it—a conspiracy was brewing. It wasn't a malicious plot for personal gain but rather a secret plan fueled primarily by civic pride and the desire to bring publicity to the city. As a bonus, those involved would have themselves a rousing bit of adventure. Historic preservation of the boat, at least in the early discussions, was only a secondary motivation. The contemplated scheme, when discovered, would receive nationwide news coverage, including an account on television's *Huntley-Brinkley Report*.

Whatever label you might put on the planned action, and whatever the participants' reasons for attempting it, they were thinking of doing the unthinkable. When the time was right, they would just go down to Stockton and bring the *Delta King* back to Sacramento where it belonged.

13

The Paddle–Wheel Pirates

Attempting a riverboat heist might not be the wisest thing in the world. But the Sacramentans planning to "liberate" the *Delta King* weren't stupid, and they weren't naive. In the spring of 1969, as the scheme gained momentum, members of the loose-knit group showed the good sense to seek legal advice before executing their plan. Tom Horton, who worked on the fringes of the group and who wrote his daily column in the *Sacramento Union* pumping up enthusiasm for a riverboat, had an inspiration. He invited Geoffrey Wong, a young lawyer just three months past his bar exam, to attend one of their meetings.

Wong attended, got involved, and soon became *pro bono* legal counsel for the group. He suggested a two-part plan that might at least cushion the blow when their actions were discovered. First—before attempting to move the *King*—he advised them to purchase one of the liens that had been placed against the boat. This could give their group a small but important connection to the vessel. At the very least, it would muddy the legal waters and make prosecution by the owners (whoever they might be) less likely. Secondly, he advised that they incorporate as a nonprofit organization dedicated to the furtherance of local steamboat history.

To accomplish one of those ends, Wong negotiated with J. Edward Ogden, apparent owner of the riverfront property in Stockton where the *King* was moored, for the purchase of a $14,000 wharfage lien Ogden held on the boat. At well under face value, the riverboat group bought the lien and obtained a letter from Ogden requesting removal of the vessel from his property. A week later, on July 18, 1969, the group incorporated as a nonprofit corporation under the name "Riverboat's Comin'!, Inc."

The organization had already contracted with Lauritzen River & Bay Towing of Antioch for two tugboats to tow the *King* to Sacramento—one from Lauritzen, the other subcontracted from Sanders Towboat Service of San Francisco. Members of the newly-formed cabal were now ready to execute their secret escapade.

On the morning of Saturday, July 19, a work party of about a dozen volunteers, mostly Sacramento Jaycees, arrived on the bank of the Stockton Channel near the *Delta King*. Feeling a mixture of enthusiasm, curiosity, and trepidation, they observed that everything was quiet and there appeared to be no security—and that a plank led invitingly onto the boat. They went aboard and began their work to prepare the *King* for the voyage planned for that evening.

To prevent the vessel from taking on water while under way, Jim McMullen had prepared pieces of plywood the right size to board up 68 windows that Belli and Mortensen had cut in the steel hull just above the waterline. It was tough, dirty work down in the hold, and the day was hot. By late afternoon, sweaty and tired, workers finished the job. Most headed home. Ben Brewer, prominent member of the Sacramento Yacht Club, and Michael Fitch, bank officer, were among the few who remained to see the *King* leave on its trip to the capital city.

Jerry Vorpahl, one of the early voices saying that Sacramento needed a riverboat, drove to Stockton for the afternoon. On weekdays, Vorpahl worked with the California Chamber of Commerce; on weekends, he volunteered in "The Seven Steps" rehabilitation program to help parolees from state prison get started again in the outside world. Accompanying him that day driving to Stockton was a parolee who asked, "Is what you're planning for tonight a caper?" (the crime world's term for a venture involving theft). Vorpahl paused, took a deep breath, and said, "Well, I guess there might be those who'd call it a caper." Then he added, "In any case, it's a caper for a good cause."

Geoff Wong, the legal brains behind the group, arrived last, after having shown his versatility that day in Sacramento. He had won the city's first Frisbee championship and had driven down in the afternoon. Five others would join Wong on board the *Delta King* for the evening's clandestine river adventure: Tom Horton, newspaperman; Gordon McDonald, stockbroker; Justus Ghormley, state Transportation Department; Dee Heaberlin, engineer; and Dan Clarke, real estate salesman (the only Jaycee on board). Together the six would ride the *King* to glory or defeat, while Robbie Van Vorn, the nonprofit group's chairman of the board, would man the command post in Sacramento.

Years later Wong recalled the anxiety he began to feel by early evening when the tugboats failed to arrive at the appointed hour. "We were all ready to go, but the tugs weren't there. I was getting concerned that someone would report our activity to the police and that we all might be busted before we could get the *King* away from the shore. Finally, the tugs arrived about 9 o'clock."

News of the voyage, soon to break in newspapers and on radio and television, would have other big news to compete with. On the following day, *Apollo 11* astronaut Neil Armstrong would walk on the surface of the moon, taking "one giant leap for mankind."

In a column headlined "A Ghost Comes Back Big as Life" and datelined, "Aboard the Delta King, July 19-20," Tom Horton described the experience of six men still on earth:

That morning under a hot sun she had seemed a hopeless derelict, but now it was dark and suddenly she seemed a brooding duchess, gray and ghostlike under a summer sky . . .

An orange crescent moon rose off her stern, and the knowledge that men were circling it this very moment, and tomorrow would walk its face sharpened our appreciation of the contrast. Nothing we hoped to do would ever change the world, but nothing they would ever do in space would make us forget what we were doing tonight.

We were riding the King back home . . .

At 10:30, all but six were put ashore . . . We moved about her with flashlights and lanterns and held our breath while others climbed to her highest extended points and placed small lights at the four most notice-able spots. Now, more than ever, she had the look of a ghost ship . . .

We were ready to cast off . . . "All clear!" Dee called to the [tugboat] Eddie Foy. We felt her move. I marked the time. Seven to 11. The shore-line began receding in the dark . . .

It was, without exaggeration, a ghostlike ride. As the hour neared midnight, she slipped silently and almost unnoticed out of the Stockton channel and into the San Joaquin River to begin the strangest voyage of her strange life. The first of a night made for chilling sights came when we stood on the bow, looked up and saw a light in the wheelhouse. It was Gordon McDonald with a lantern.

We climbed to the wheelhouse and out onto the top deck where the air was warm and the stars appeared as they never appear among city lights. We wondered how it must have been when she was alive with dancing and dining, drinking and music and laughter, and then shortly we fell silent. The quiet purr of the Eddie Foy, the crickets and the faintest ripple of water were the only sounds in the night.

Shadowy figures moved about tiny campfires doting the shoreline, and once a shout was heard. "That the Queen?" "No, the King." "Where you taking her?" "Sacramento." "Good luck!"

Then . . . we crawled into sleeping bags and tried to sleep on a cement floor off the stern, much like troops slept aboard her during the war . . . At 3 a.m. we thought we were in a storm or on an ocean [actually, a windy unprotected stretch of river]. Waves crashing against the stern sounded like thunderclaps and everybody's mind raced to the plywood in the hold. We left the sleeping bags and looked outside at a vast expanse of black water that gave us the feeling of drifting through phantom seas. But Dee appeared and said, "She ain't takin' enough water to brush your teeth with.". . .

At this point, it may help to know that from Stockton the *King* was towed down the San Joaquin to where it joins the Sacramento River, then upstream on the Sacramento past Rio Vista. The rest of the voyage took place on the Sacramento Deep Water Ship Channel, a timesaving shortcut (opened in 1963) that bypasses the winding river once used by the *King* and *Queen*. To complete the trip, the strange flotilla had to pass through a lock to return to the main river at Sacramento.

Horton continues his description of the trip:

We awoke to a blistering morning sun and in time to see the Rio Vista bridge sliding straight up between its twin towers, like a giant guillotine. . . . Cars slowed or stopped on the levee roads and people on the banks stared in disbelief. A man banged on the door of his camper: "Alice! Get up! Get up, Alice, and look at this!". . .

We walked her decks, admiring the gracefully curving stairway from the dining room to the bar. Some of the stained glass remains, traces of finely carved woodwork are there . . . But she's a colossal mess from top to bottom and the misbegotten efforts to remake her have only served to further clutter her . . .

People began to appear on the banks with cameras, more people saw her through the locks and she reappeared at the bend of Miller Park [in Sacramento] like a long-missing celebrity . . . Cruisers and outboards escorted her to the Tower Bridge and the Sacramento Yacht Club greeted her with horns and whistles, even applause. At twenty minutes to one, she was secured at the wharf where she once arrived every other morning and departed every other evening, all in regal river splendor.

Sacramento Awaits King's Homecoming

By TOM HORTON
Sacramento Union Staff Writer

ABOARD THE DELTA KING—The mighty King is coming home.

The last of the great California river steamers and the one-time monarch of the Sacramento River, its paddlewheel stilled and its smoke stack silenced since World War II, was towed quietly away from its berth in the Stockton channel Saturday night and began floating toward a new home on the Sacramento waterfront.

An audacious group of Sacramentans, acting with all the raw nerve of riverboat gamblers, claim this is where the Delta King belongs.

Limping out of the Port of Stockton like a sick whale, nudged along by tugboats fore and aft, the 43-year-old steamer began a dramatic journey through the Delta waterways to Rio Vista, up the Sacramento deep water channel to a berth just below the Tower Bridge and, hopefully, a more promising future.

When the still-majestic King rounds the bend at Miller Park later today, it will climax one of the most daring river maneuvers ever seen on the historic inland waterways, and may touch off one of the

See Page 2, Col. 1

July 20, 1969: As the King is towed up the deepwater channel instead of the river, boat and tug must pass through a lock (above left) before getting onto main river at Sacramento.

Sacramento Union readers were alerted to arrival by Tom Horton's scoop; he was one of six who rode the King from Stockton.

Back home again in Sacramento, the King is greeted at old River Lines dock by pleasure boats on the river and a crowd on Tower Bridge.

The Old Delta King Comes Back Home

By TOM HORTON
Sacramento Union Staff Writer

The Delta King, plying the Sacramento River for the first time in some 30 years, returned Sunday to the waterfront where she once boarded passengers for moonlight trips to San Francisco.

It was by the light of that same moon, which like the King has changed a great deal in 30 years, that the ghost-like paddlewheeler was slipped out of the Stockton channel an hour before midnight Saturday and sent on a quiet 13-hour voyage to Sacramento.

There was nothing quiet about the King's reception.

By the time she was secured at the old River Lines dock in the southern shadows of the Tower Bridge, near tidal waves of reaction were being felt from Sacramento to San Francisco. Depending on who you talked to, the handful of Sacramento men who returned the gallant King to its home port should be considered:

1—Riverboat saviors.

...reached Sacra-

Touches of elegance remain . . .

Attorneys Steam Up Over Boat

By TOM HORTON
Sacramento Union Staff Writer

The famous trial lawyer charged piracy on the low seas, and the rookie attorney defiantly returned the challenge as the Delta King threatened Tuesday to spark one of the strangest legal confrontations since Daniel Webster argued with the devil.

This one matches San Francisco's Melvin Belli — the "King of Torts" — against Sacramento's Geoffrey Wong, the "Sultan of Yanuca."

Belli says Sacramento took the Delta King from Stockton in an "act of piracy." Wong says it was an "act of love."

Contacted at the Brown Palace Hotel in Denver, where he is conducting the 20th annual Belli Seminar, the flamboyant Belli paid grudging tribute to Sacramento's riverboat captors while labeling them pirates.

"This restores my faith in the terrestrial imagination of mankind," Belli told The Sacramento Union. "It was a complete act of piracy. I don't believe in capital punishment, but I think at least

GEOFFREY WONG

MELVIN BELLI

Trouble brewing!
Sacramento Union *stories:*
July 21 and July 23, 1969.

They say it was piracy. But she was dying an inelegant death in Stockton, and that was the real crime.

The above firsthand report by Tom Horton appeared in the *Sacramento Union* a few days after the *King* arrived. A firsthand report was something Horton's newspaper had that the rival *Sacramento Bee* didn't have.

What's more, the first news of the adventure—a scoop by Horton and the *Union*—had come in the Sunday, July 20 edition, which was on press while the *King* was en route to Sacramento. How was Horton able to write a news story about an event before it even took place? The answer is simple. He knew the riverboat group's secret plans and wrote the story beforehand. He gambled the affair would go according to plan, and luck was with him. He also hedged his bets by having his wife witness the *King*'s departure at Stockton. After the vessel left, she called the newspaper to confirm that the trip had started. The facts of the story held up—he reported that the boat left Stockton on Saturday night and would arrive in Sacramento on Sunday for its "homecoming." When *Union* readers opened their Sunday papers, here's what they saw:

> The mighty King is coming home. . . .
>
> When the still-majestic King rounds the bend at Miller Park later today, it will climax one of the most daring river maneuvers ever seen on the historic inland waterways, and may touch off one of the biggest riverboat battles since paddle-wheelers first began carrying men and supplies from San Francisco to Sacramento.
>
> Riverboat's Comin'! Inc., a nonprofit group which became incorporated only last Friday, didn't exactly purchase the Delta King, but they didn't exactly steal it, either.
>
> They simply went down and got it.
>
> The next sound heard on the river may be that of Melvin Belli, flamboyant San Francisco attorney who was one of the last alleged owners of the King. In recent years, however, ownership of the King has been more muddied than the Sacramento River it once ruled in the 1920's and 30's, in concert with its more famous sister ship, the Delta Queen. . . .
>
> Geoffrey P. Wong, legal counsel for the riverboaters, said he felt they were fully justified in taking possession. "What we're doing is trying to save the King," Wong said. "The King was lying neglected and unattended in the Port of Stockton. Riverboat's Comin'! is preventing the deterioration and probable loss of an invaluable—and irreplaceable—historical monument."

Local media weren't the only ones to report the *King*'s unconventional voyage. Both Associated Press and United Press International distributed the news. Newspapers from Atlanta to Seattle, Los Angeles to New York, ran wire stories. UPI referred to the perpetrators as "liberators" and reported Wong's remarks that ownership was "clouded" and that "We have rumors of various transactions and hear there are all sorts of back taxes and liens against the boat." Newspapers played with words: "Liberation or Larceny?"

The story of the "piracy" had such appeal in its sheer audacity that television's *Huntley-Brinkley Report* aired it right after the news of the moon landing. Historical trivia buffs take note: The *Delta King* "pirates" landed their vessel at Sacramento 38 minutes before Neil Armstrong and Ed Aldrin landed their lunar module on the surface of the moon (the *Eagle* landed at 1:18 p.m. PDT on July 20, 1969).

On Monday morning, Riverboat's Comin' named C.A. Lauritzen, Jr. "Honorary Admiral" of the *Delta King* for his role as captain of the *Eddie Foy*, one of two tugboats that did the towing. Two generations of Lauritzens had been aboard for the memorable voyage: C.A. Jr. and his son, C.A. III. The eldest family member, 87-year-old Christian A. "Chris" Lauritzen, stayed home. But this did not prevent the "dean of the Delta" and original owner of Fulton's Shipyard from heartily wishing his son, his grandson, and his favorite riverboat a successful trip.

In a Monday news story, Tom Horton referred to a quiet 13-hour voyage to Sacramento but then quickly added:

> There was nothing quiet about the King's reception. By the time she was secured at the old River Lines dock in the southern shadows of the Tower Bridge, near tidal waves of reaction were being felt from Sacramento to San Francisco. Depending on who you talked to, the handful of Sacramento men who returned the gallant King to its home port should be considered: 1—Riverboat saviors. 2—Pirates.

Writing in the *San Francisco Chronicle*, reporter George Murphy quoted Geoff Wong that an official celebration and rechristening would be held on Friday with "beautiful girls, bands, and dignitaries." The article reported that Wong cheerfully admitted there was some question about who owned the *King*. The *Chronicle* writer then commented: "Melvin Belli, the shy, retiring San Francisco barrister, maintains he has 'an interest' in the boat." Wong was quoted again: "We're not claiming ownership—we're just acting as caretakers." When asked if the group hadn't violated one or more sections of the penal code, Wong replied: "Oh, no. You have to show criminal intent. We had no criminal intent. All we want to do is preserve what is a historical monument for Sacramento."

The *Chronicle* added, "Besides, piracy can only be committed on the high seas, a San Francisco legal expert said." The article then concluded: "Grand theft? Well, that's something else again."

In the week before the rechristening celebration, Wong gave himself a crash course on admiralty law. And Robbie Van Vorn, chairman of Riverboat's Comin', announced that housewives, Boy Scouts, businessmen, students, retired people, and skilled craftsmen were volunteering to assist in cleanup and restoration. He said others were pledging money and materials. But legal and oratorical skirmishes took the spotlight. Under a *Sacramento Union* headline, "Attorneys Steam Up Over Boat," Tom Horton wrote:

> The famous trial lawyer charged piracy on the low seas, and the rookie attorney defiantly returned the challenge as the Delta King threatened Tuesday to spark one of the strangest legal confrontations since Daniel Webster argued with the devil.
>
> This one matches San Francisco's Melvin Belli—the "King of Torts"—against Sacramento's Geoffrey Wong, the "Sultan of Yanuca." Belli says Sacramento took the Delta King from Stockton in an "act of piracy." Wong says it was an "act of love."
>
> Contacted . . . in Denver . . . the flamboyant Belli paid grudging tribute to Sacramento's riverboat captors while labeling them pirates. "This restores my faith in the terrestrial imagination of mankind," Belli told The Sacramento Union. "It was a complete act of piracy. I don't believe in capital punishment, but I think at least the pirates should be made to walk the plank and fall into a polluted slough.". . .
>
> Wong . . . dispatched the following telegram to Belli . . ."If our act of love be piracy, then we proudly dare to stride the plank of justice."
>
> "Who is this Chinese pirate?" demanded the 61-year-old Belli, who has been married four times and makes as much news outside the courtroom as he does inside. "Undoubtedly, this guy (Wong) has got too much imagination to be a member of the American Bar Association," said Belli, whose run-ins with the bar have been well-publicized.
>
> "I don't know whether to take that as a compliment or an insult," responded the 28-year-old Wong, who has never been married, became an attorney only six months ago and last year made headlines by winning a San Francisco newspaper contest that sent him to the Fiji Islands

Riverboat's Comin', Inc. Invites You
to the
OFFICIAL RE-CHRISTENING
of the
DELTA KING
— SACRAMENTO —

Friday, July 25, 1969, 5:00 P.M.
Tower Bridge, South Rail

Ration of Grog to follow
Sacramento Union's Mark Twain Lobby
301 Capitol Mall

Sacramento Union *photo shows addition of "armament" on board the* King, *as riverboat group prepares to hold big welcome-home party. Handbill invites the public to attend.*

Sacramento Mayor Richard Marriott speaks at festivities. At right, a U.S. marshal is arresting Geoff Wong and Delta King. Below, the Sacramento Union *reports abrupt end to party.*

Bumper sticker created by Riverboat's Comin'!, Inc.

SAVE THE KING

RIVERBOAT'S COMIN'!, INC., 455 Capitol Mall, Sacramento, Calif.

U.S. Marshal John Begovich takes charge of the King.

Band Plays On

Delta King Seized at Party

Continued From Page 1

hard-nosed characters from the U.S. Marshal's office, and a hippie-looking associate from the firm of San Francisco attorney Melvin Belli, the self-proclaimed "King of Torts."

More than 1,800 onlookers lined the Tower Bridge, near which the famous Sacramento riverboat is parked.

The warrant of arrest for the vessel — "her engines , boilers, tackle, apparel, appurtenances, motors, furniture, etc.;" and for "Riverboat's Comin! Inc., Geoffrey D. Wong, Robert Van Vorn" personally

The Delta King was claimed in the suit to be the property of "Gene Detgen," a Los Angeles resident who is reportedly a piano repairman and who allegedly has invested $125,000 in its purchase five years ago, and $100,000 in its refurbishing in the past two years.

On hand for the rededication Friday were Sacramento Union columnist Tom Horton, who first decided that Sacramento needed a riverboat; Mayor Richard Marriott; a handful of city councilmen; the Tower Bridge bystanders; two dozen private ships, which circled the giant riverboat like gnats; the Sacramento City-County Chamber of Commerce; the entire Sacramento Banjo Band and others.

What Begovich did was arrest the boat itself. It is a curiousity of Admiralty Law, under which questions of piracy fall.

A partner of Belli's, claiming to be attorney for the King's owner, said it was a choice between the legal action or "Belli would've come up in a frigate and seized the ship himself."

But such action, he said, "would've been the same self-help approach that these people (RCI) used.

"They found our boat and decided for reasons best known to them that they should pirate it (from Stockton where it was assembled and launched in 1925.

"We decided instead on legal means. It's not as dramatic, but equally effective."

Friday's rededication ceremony was at times interrupted by outcries from Belli's associate for Begovich to "Throw these people off — this is weird."

The day ended with the prospect of a legal free-for-all in a reception in the Mark Twain Lobby of The Sacramento Union, as riverboat aficionados pledged their lives, fortunes and sacred honor to the preservation of the Delta King—no matter where it came from — in Sacramento.

to reign for one week as the "Sultan of Yanuca."

[Belli said] They . . . have absolutely no title to the Delta King. I told Max [Mortensen] to go to the U.S. attorney and file piracy charges."

"Our corporation dares him to do just that," Wong said. "Mr. Belli has never officially established his title to the Delta King and we feel it is incumbent upon him or any other alleged owners to do so before they can prove such rash charges as piracy."

Belli said he is eager to do anything that will save the King from total deterioration, including restoration on the Sacramento waterfront. "I'm a reasonable man," he said. "If someone steals all my chickens and makes them healthier than when I had them, I'm happy. I can deal with a pirate just as well as a banker, if not better."

On the day of the big celebration, Friday, July 25, 1969, Tom Horton wrote a news story headlined "Riverboat 'Rescuers' To Crown King Today" with the subhead "Cannon Law?":

> While rumors spread that Melvin Belli was mounting a Montgomery Street armada, Sacramentans put a small cannon on the bow of the captured Delta King and prepared for today's boisterous rechristening and welcome home party. . .
>
> Belli was reported planning to hire a frigate, sail to Sacramento with a boarding party and tow the Delta King to San Francisco. The Sacramentans, who contend they "liberated the King from the clutches of neglect," appeared unbothered by the threatening legal storm.
>
> Gerald E. Vorpahl, a trustee of the riverboat corporation, said some 300 invitations were mailed for today's welcome-home festivities. . . . The rechristening will feature a vintage bottle of champagne that will slide down a wire from the bridge and, it is hoped, will shatter on the steel bow of the King.

The champagne had been selected with care—a bottling from 1927, the year the *King* and *Queen* began service on the river. But when festivities began and the bottle failed to break, it was an omen for a late afternoon of bizarre events. Acting without warning, two celebration-happy members of E Clampus Vitus (historical and social group) grabbed Sacramento Mayor Richard Marriott by the ankles, turned him upside down, and held him over the side while he broke the bottle against the hull. Meanwhile, Geoff Wong, who was supposed to be part of the ceremonies at the bow, instead was starring in a rough-and-tumble scene in other parts of the boat.

Racing from deck to deck and from bow to stern, Wong was trying to escape a process server in close pursuit. Both he and his pursuer, Vasilios B. Choulos from Belli's office, wore suits and ties, which was not the ideal attire for a chase in the Keystone Kops tradition—especially on a hot day, well over 100 degrees. Finally, Wong bowed to the inevitable and accepted service of the legal papers, which brought an admiralty suit against Riverboat's Comin', Van Vorn, and Wong. But he accepted only after delaying long enough to allow completion of most of the ceremonies on the bow.

The Riverboat's Comin' group, their guests of honor, and spectators on the Tower Bridge then received a rude awakening. Paul Merz, writing in the *Union*, described what happened next:

> Looking for all the world like a pudgy Matt Dillon, U.S. Marshal John Begovich took his stand Friday night on the second deck of the Delta King. Stetson firmly planted, guns drawn, the ex-senator seemed in grim earnest as he proclaimed: "This ship is hereby seized by the United States government.". . .
>
> The warrant of arrest for the vessel—"her engines, boilers, tackle, apparel, appurtenances, motors, furniture, etc.;" and for "Riverboat's Comin'! Inc., Geoffrey P. Wong, Robert Van Vorn" personally. The Delta King was claimed . . . to be the property of "Gene Detgen," a Los Angeles resident who is reportedly a piano repairman and who allegedly has invested $125,000 in its purchase five years ago, and $100,000 in its refurbishing in the past two years. . . .
>
> The day ended with the prospect of a legal free-for-all . . . as riverboat aficionados pledged their lives, fortunes and sacred honor to the preservation of the Delta King . . . in Sacramento.

By the time the sun set that evening on the Sacramento waterfront, the U.S. Marshal and his men had entrenched themselves on the aging riverboat. As observed by the *San Francisco Chronicle,* "If, as sailormen believe, all ships have souls, one can conceive of the Delta King's soul considering these machinations and just sighing, softly."

Dixieland jazz festivals turn the King into a lively place. The fans at top are enjoying a 1969 program at the old River Lines dock. The jazz group above performed in 1971 at a different location—on Yolo County side of the river, across from original site at Sacramento (visible at right).

14

And All That Jazz

Although Riverboat's Comin' no longer had possession of the *Delta King* and was not allowed aboard, the organization continued with optimism and boundless enthusiasm at other locations. Viewing the government seizure as only a temporary setback, its members assumed they could buy the boat if they collected enough money. They tirelessly answered phones, accepted donations, and took the names of those offering to work on the vessel when it was available.

Having succumbed to the seductive charms of the *Delta King* despite the craft's decrepit condition, dozens of volunteers worked long hours to further the cause of the beleaguered riverboat. Seeking contributions and aiming high, they offered the title of "Commodore" for $1,000 or "Vice Commodore" for $500. Most donations came at the lower end of the scale: for $50, a supporter could become a "Second Mate"; for $10, a "Crew Member"; anything less than that, he or she became a "Deckhand." Collected funds were placed in trust pending clarification of the boat's ownership.

Volunteers created miniature replicas of the *King's* smokestack for use in stores, restaurants, and other businesses to collect small-change donations from customers. They also organized a group of young women called "Riverboat Belles" to raise funds and, later, to act as hostesses for events on the boat. In a special fundraising effort, Sacramento's popular Music Circus declared the final August performance of *Show Boat* to be "Delta King Night," all proceeds going to the vessel's new fund. Because Jerome Kern's musical involves riverboats and had originally opened in 1927, the same year the *King* and *Queen* began service on the river, the tie-in was a natural.

On August 7, 1969, less than two weeks after the aborted rechristening cele-bration, RCI (Riverboat's Comin'!, Inc.) went back on board the *King*. By court order, the U.S. Marshal released the vessel, since the "owner" had defaulted on payments of more than $100 per day to keep deputy marshals aboard. As the mar-shals moved off, the riverboat volunteers moved back on with their own 24-hour security officers and a guard dog.

That same day, RCI paid San Joaquin County $4,808 for tax liens on the *King*. Geoff Wong explained that the liens were "purchased" to protect the boat from any unscrupulous third party who might pay them and then force it to be auctioned off for salvage purposes.

The next day, the long-awaited Mel Belli arrived at Sacramento to the delight of a swarm of radio, television, and print reporters. He had made recent headlines as defense lawyer for Winnie Ruth Judd, the so-called "Trunk Murderess," who had been captured after her seventh escape from a mental institution. Now, he would be making headlines because of his connection to the *Delta King*.

Belli's request to board the vessel was refused politely but firmly by a private security guard. Angry, Belli faced the hovering news people and blasted Riverboat's Comin'. The *Sacramento Bee* reported his harangue: "It's very cute for this Chinese lawyer to have a group come down and steal the boat. They think—your chamber of commerce included—it is humorous . . . and [they] welcome back someone with stolen property. That man should be concerned about his status with the bar." In response to the question of just what Belli's claim was to the vessel, he snapped, "Nothing, other than I own it."

The *Sacramento Union* also described his visit: "Attorney Melvin Belli, his Rolls Royce plastered with 'Save the King' stickers, drove to the Sacramento river-front . . . [He] adopted the alleged pirates' slogan with the explanation he thought it referred to him, the self-proclaimed 'King of Torts.'" Asked if he planned to meet with members of RCI, he answered, "I don't do business with thieves."

Belli was approached by a Riverboat Belle, who asked for a contribution to the "Save the King" campaign. "I'm a volunteer for the *Delta King*," she said. Belli replied, "I've never heard of it" and turned away. He then amended his comment: "I should have said 'I *wish* I'd never heard of it.'" Repenting, he stuck a dollar's worth of small change into the little smokestack canister.

On August 17, the Sacramento Banjo Band, featuring banjo artists Jack and Val Heathcote, performed on the bow of the King—the first in a series of free early-evening Sunday concerts. Because the boat wasn't yet ready to handle a concert crowd on board, the audience had to listen from the railing of the Tower Bridge. That same day, volunteers had conducted the first public tours of the boat. They announced that, so far, people had contributed more than $3,000 to the campaign and had pledged another $6,000.

In late August, Sacramento City Councilman Tony Stathos recommended that the city support the campaign to save the *King*. The council refused to become financially involved in the restoration. But it adopted a resolution, by Councilman James Fuller, endorsing the goals of RCI. The resolution ended with a whimsical warning of another potential piracy: "The *Queen Mary* may be next."

The nonprofit group came up with a surprise for Belli and his associate Max Mortensen when, on October 3, it filed suit for $250,000 on behalf of "all the citizens of the State of California." The suit alleged that the two men were willfully negligent in allowing the "valuable historical boat to rot for several years in the Port of Stockton." Less than three months later, a judge dismissed the suit, ruling that RCI failed to establish why it had any duty to protect the boat.

The high point of fall 1969 came on October 12, when a thunderous crowd climbed aboard the *Delta King* for Sacramento's first Dixieland Jazz Festival. For 50 cents, people could listen and watch on the bow or the stern. Ten different groups from Sacramento, Stockton, and the Bay Area carried their drums, clarinets, saxophones, and even two pianos aboard to provide continuous entertainment. Riverboat's Comin' co-sponsored the festival with the New Sacramento Traditional Jazz Society. Jerry Vorpahl performed multiple roles—as member of the society, trustee of RCI, organizer of the festival, and drummer of no small ability. And although no one knew it at the time, fans were witnessing the birth of the present-day Sacramento Jazz Jubilee, now an internationally renowned event.

A few days before the festival, Tom Horton previewed it in his *Sacramento Union* column. He finished with these words: "Sunday afternoon on the river. Drinking beer and watching the sun go down while the saints are marching in. The Delta King full of people and music. If that ain't a winning combination, God didn't make little green apples."

After the weekend, in a column titled "Da Levee's Swingin' at Last," Horton described the event:

Vorpahl filled the old paddlewheeler with 75 musicians from the New Sacramento Traditional Jazz Society, hauled on two pianos and 50 cases of Lucky draft and crossed his fingers.

*Volunteers, known as
Riverboat Belles, raised
funds for "Save the King"
fund. Above, a Belle
demonstrates folding
money contribution.*

*Mel Belli (right) assents
to making coin donation.*

*Map shows where the King
docked on the Sacramento.*

TOWER BRIDGE
YOLO DOCK   **RIVER LINES
                        DOCK**

**O STREET
DOCK**

YOLO
COUNTY

Sacramento River

SACRAMENTO
COUNTY

Lock to Port
of Sacramento
and Deep Water
Channel

"If the weather is good, we should have at least a thousand people," he said. By 2 p.m., the start of the festival, there were that many people already on board. By the time the first strains of "Yellow Dog" had sounded, Vorpahl had raced up to the wheelhouse and was standing there with eyes of the size of banjos.

"This is the way it should be on the river!" he exclaimed. "You can actually feel the old King vibrating."

It vibrated like that until 8 p.m. as almost 4,000 persons went down to the levee.

They sat in the sun on the bow of the King and hung from the railings of the second and third decks and clustered around the piano on the second deck, aft, and whistled and shouted and sang along . . .

Flushed with success, Riverboat's Comin' and the jazz group immediately planned a second festival for November 9. Although they increased the donation to one dollar, the price still seemed reasonable and a good crowd attended.

Jumping with activity, the *Delta King* hosted a seemingly endless stream of events in the fall of 1969: a Halloween party, wine tasting, a third jazz festival, flea markets, press parties, arts and crafts sales, dances, and public tours on weekends.

By December, Chairman Robbie Van Vorn estimated that more than 24,000 people had been aboard. The first two jazz festivals alone brought about 7,000 people aboard. And 9,000 came to a two-day river market sponsored by the Multiple Sclerosis Society, when all cabins, as well as the first passenger deck and freight deck, offered art and antiques. The Boy Scouts, 4-H Club, and retired teachers also held fund-raisers. From these activities and from donations, the non-profit group had collected some $11,000 for the "Save the King" fund. And while raising the money, volunteers had transformed the boat from a somber hulk into a lively place full of people and laughter.

Hundreds of people volunteered to work on restoring the *Delta King*, while donations of paint, lumber, and building materials poured in from stores and other businesses. Energetic work parties cleaned up the dirt and grime that had accumulated over the years. They scrubbed floors, pounded nails, and repaired windows to make the weathered craft usable by the public. Volunteers sanded and painted, installed lighting and replaced roofing. The boat hummed with activity.

In November, the City of Sacramento ordered the *King* moved for safety reasons. With winter approaching, the city was concerned that high water on the river might endanger the vessel along with the adjoining dock and warehouse (the boat was tied to pilings that held up the warehouse). The City Council gave the group permission to use the city's dock at the foot of O Street during the winter months. So, in mid-December, RCI towed the *King* from the Tower Bridge downriver two blocks to the new location.

Just three days later, on December 18, the City Council dropped a bombshell. Without warning, the council rescinded the docking permit it had issued a month before. The city engineer called the vessel a fire hazard and said the group had failed to meet conditions of the permit. As a result, three holiday parties had to be cancelled, and all future fund-raising events on the boat were jeopardized. No more public functions, no more revenue, no more progress on the "Save the King" campaign.

Seeming to confirm the notion that trouble comes in bunches, the next day—cold, wet, and windy—brought near disaster. During a special noon meeting of RCI to discuss the permit cancellation, the Coast Guard called with frightening news: The *Delta King* had broken one of its mooring lines—the boat was trying to take off on its own! Members rushed to the river and were astounded at what they saw. The stern line had given way, and a strong south wind was blowing the vessel upriver. Only a thin bow line held the craft. The *King* had been moored parallel to the shore pointing upstream; now the wind had turned it around until its bow was facing downstream. At times, the boat swung halfway across the river.

The *Sacramento Union* suggested the reason: "The defiant Delta King, apparently reacting to a stern City Council edict to 'shape up,' Friday made an unsuccessful attempt to 'ship out' for calmer waters. Sacramento's adopted riverboat grunted, strained and with the help of a strong tailwind broke part of its moorings . . . and headed upstream!" When the vessel moved out to a 90-degree angle to the shore, City Engineer J. Carl Jennings remarked, "It looked as if the boat was coming right up O Street."

In the middle of the afternoon, RCI member Milt Lane, operating his small work boat, tried to move the *King* back into position. But the strong wind foiled his efforts. Time and again, his boat got the *King* almost turned around and docked. Then a gust of wind would catch the high superstructure like a kite and undo all progress; the challenge would start all over again. The battle with the elements continued for almost six hours, long into the night. Finally, a tugboat, commissioned from the lower Delta, chugged upriver and came to the rescue. The two boats, working together, managed to get the old steamer back to the dock.

RCI volunteers breathed a collective sigh of relief but shuddered when they realized what *could* have happened. If the *King* had broken completely loose, it could have crashed into a bridge or a marina causing hundreds of thousands of dollars worth of damage. It also could have sunk to the bottom, with the strong likelihood of prosecution by the Coast Guard or the Army Corps of Engineers for blocking the channel—as well as legal action by the "owner" for loss of the riverboat. What's more, such a catastrophe would have meant the end for the last great, historic sternwheeler in California. Years later, Wong confided that this was the scariest part of the whole *Delta King* episode in Sacramento, Mel Belli and his lawsuits notwithstanding.

Reeling from the events of December 1969, early in the new year officers and members of RCI tried to assess the future. They had a riverboat they loved but didn't own, a vessel they had possession of but couldn't use. Compliance with all city regulations was impossible. For example, cabin ceilings were less than the minimum height allowed by city code, and the mandated plumbing and electrical work would be expensive. The volunteer group neither had the money to do the work nor did they think it wise to start a costly renovation until ownership was established.

RCI members were faced with a dilemma. Not only would it be hard to conduct their "Save the King" campaign without a place to hold fund-raising events, but it would also be difficult to maintain the present momentum and enthusiasm. Thus, in an effort to keep interest alive, seek new ideas for saving the boat, get new workers, and solicit donations, the group held support rallies at a local restaurant in February and March. They also entered a float in the Saint Patrick's Day parade, an entry judged the best in depicting the "Luck of the Irish." In the light of their recent troubles, one might wonder what kind of luck RCI had in mind.

Riverboat's Comin' continued with a few brave attempts at fund-raising at locations away from the boat. Events, well publicized by volunteer Jane Pope, included a flea market in April and a street fair in June. But hard reality suggested that leaving the City of Sacramento provided the only practical alternative. Yolo County officials seemed receptive to the idea of docking across the river (the city and county of Sacramento occupy the east side, Yolo County the west bank). So, in the fall, the two parties began negotiating.

During this period the *Delta King* received additional exposure nationally when the October 1970 issue of *True* magazine came out with an article titled "Who Stole Melvin Belli's Boat?" *True* told of the early plans of Belli and Mortensen to make the *King* into a "floating pleasure palace" and then said that

170

People of Riverboat's Comin'!, Inc. pose on the boat. First board of trustees, starting clockwise: Janet Thompson (holding broom), Robert Van Vorn, Geoff Wong, Jack Heathcote, Marilyn Harris, Ben Brewer, Jerry Vorpahl, Justus Ghormley, and Gordon McDonald (not shown are James McMullen and Michael Fitch).

The volunteer group did its best to keep the King in Sacramento, holding fund-raisers, sponsoring work parties aboard, and offering tours of the old sternwheeler.

RIVERBOAT'S COMIN'!

WELCOME HOME
DELTA KING

JULY 20, 1969

SAVE
THE
KING!

DIXIELAND
Jazz Festival

on board the
DELTA KING

Sunday
Nov. 9
2 'til 8
pm

$1.00
children free

THE NEW SACRAMENTO TRADITIONAL JAZZ SOCIETY

presents its second All Day Dixieland JAZZ FESTIVAL on board the famous old sternwheeler, the DELTA KING . . . moored at the foot of the Tower Bridge. Over 4,000 people turned out last month to see and hear some of the finest Dixieland Jazz since Al Hirt and Louie Armstrong were adrift together in a dingy in the middle of the Sacramento River with no oars and only their horns.

As Tom Horton, famed columnist from Galt, put it: *"Sunday afternoon on the river. Drinking beer and watching the sun go down as the Saints go marching in. The DELTA KING full of people and music. - Now if that ain't a winning combination, God didn't make little green apples."*

Hey Man!
Bring your
Horn!

Because of the [...]
that a second rally should be [...] to step forward. The sec[...]
DELTA KING enthusiasts to City Hell where we will again ask for a [...]
prepare the path for a march to City Hall where we will again ask for a [...]
voice of support and cooperation from the City Council.

Every participant in the first rally will be back this Wednesday, March 4,
at 7:30 p.m.—and every riverboat lover in Northern California is
sincerely urged to join in.

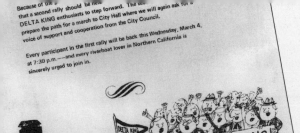

SAVE "OUR" KING!

WANNA BUY A FLEA?

SAVE THE KING
FLEA CIRCUS
SATURDAY & SUNDAY · APRIL 4 & 5 1970 · 11 am to 7 pm

...NATIONAL CUISINE
...SQUARE 5th & O
...ENTERTAINMENT

SAVE THE KING!

...RAMENTO...

...ON'T GIVE UP THE ~~last~~ SHIP!!!!

db associates

DELTA KING — SACRAMENTO
Honorary Boarding Pass

Name _____

Signature _____

Has boarded the Delta King on this date 4-3-71

Captain Morgan
Authorized Signature

DELTA KING CREW
Boarding Pass   1625

Name _____

Signature _____

Valid Until _____

Authorized Signature

RIVERBOAT'S COMIN', INC., 455 CAPITOL MALL, SACRAMENTO

RIVERBOAT'S COMIN', INC.   THE DELTA KING

Certificate of Accomplishment

This is to certify that

_____ has rendered important as well as valuable services toward the

preservation and restoration of Sacramento's proud riverboat the DELTA KING.

Sacramento, California

19____

Member, Board of Trustees   Member, Board of Trustees

171

for the past ten years the craft "had degenerated into what is kindly known as 'a piece of Americana.'" In discussing the magazine story in his column, Tom Horton noted that the article told more about Geoff Wong than about the legendary vessel; he said the boat was mentioned 22 times while Wong received 48 mentions. With tongue in cheek, Horton then cited a long list of assertions in the *True* article that weren't "true." His title for that day's column: "True Is All Wong."

Footnote to the ongoing Sacramento drama: While the *Delta King* faced myriad problems in California, on the other side of the Rockies the *Delta Queen* was fighting her own battle for survival. And she appeared to be losing. In October 1970, the *Queen* began her "final voyage" down the Ohio and Mississippi bound for New Orleans (more on this in later chapters). It seemed that she was about to be legislated off the inland waterways as an overnight passenger vessel.

RCI, after negotiating with Yolo County about moving the *King* across the river, received an okay in October. Geoff Wong, who a year later would be running for mayor of Sacramento, made this statement about the boat and his hometown: "When we returned the *King* to Sacramento, we explained we were liberating her from the clutches of neglect. We are now forced to move her away from Sacramento to escape the clutches of bureaucracy." To the waves of a crowd and the sound of banjo music, on November 19, the old sternwheeler—with 40 riders and a dozen news people aboard—was towed from the O Street dock. Twelve minutes later the *King* tied up at a private dock across the river.

There, the riverboat group would be able to offer public events again and raise money. But they hardly had time to take a deep breath and start planning for spring, when on February 4, 1971, a U.S. District Court judge ruled that Gene Detgen was the rightful owner of the boat. The ruling stated that the nonprofit organization "may well be right that the vessel is a historical monument, but if so, it still is a privately owned historical monument."

The ruling, which appeared to end the "Save the King" group, might have discouraged lesser folk. But Wong immediately talked of an appeal. And the trustees forged ahead, making plans for public functions in the spring. Detgen showed no signs of taking possession of the boat, and RCI proceeded almost as if nothing had happened. It seemed likely that, while Detgen had been declared owner of the vessel, he didn't know what to do with it.

One of the first events held at the new location was a rock concert in April. Then in June, and again in September, the group returned to the format that had been such a success the first year in Sacramento: Dixieland jazz. Again the sounds of jazz music and the cheers of a crowd, toes tapping and hands clapping, echoed up and down the river.

The New Sacramento Traditional Jazz Society reported that in the two short years since the festivals began on the decks of the *King* amid great publicity, the society's ranks had grown from 50 members to more than 600. And it had become one of California's better-known jazz clubs. Within the next decade, the jazz group would become one of the world's largest.

As if to make up for the lack of public activity the preceding year, during 1971 RCI brought forth a flurry of events on the boat. In addition to jazz concerts, the busy schedule included a musical comedy, folk dancing, and several wedding receptions. The *King* also hosted events for the two major political parties (at that time deeply involved with Vietnam war issues)—wine tasting for the Young Republicans and a fund-raiser for the Democrats with U.S. Senator John Tunney aboard.

Tours of the boat were conducted with enthusiasm, too. One couple, Edwin Morgan and his wife Bea, tirelessly trained guides and gave up every weekend to personally conduct tours. Ed Morgan, who had served on the boat back in its commercial and Navy days, also acted as vessel historian. He was devoted to it. In appreciation, RCI proclaimed him "Captain" of the *Delta King*. And Marilyn Harris, putting in long hours as co-chairman, social director, and tour guide was quoted as saying, "I must be the only woman in the world having an affair with a riverboat." Seems unlikely that statement bothered her husband; Dick Harris served as the 1971-72 chairman of RCI (following Van Vorn and Wong).

Work parties toiled at all hours, often under the direction of Jack Schwartz, a Sacramentan with diverse construction skills. Students, a department store employees group, and numerous individuals sanded, painted, and hammered. Volunteer union roofers installed a new roof. Workers on the boat even included several dozen members of the 87th Aerial Port Squadron at McClellan Air Force Base. But the biggest single group of volunteers ever to work on the *King* was a party of Boy and Girl Scouts, almost a hundred strong.

Joy and optimism prevailed. Then, out of the blue, on October 18, 1971, RCI and almost everyone involved since the group's beginning were served with legal papers. Gene Detgen had filed a new lawsuit against them—a blockbuster. The suit named the nonprofit organization, two tugboat companies, eighteen individuals by name, and 50 Jane and John Does as defendants. It asked damages for depriving the plaintiff of his possession and use of the boat, causing him great emotional and mental distress, and damages for malicious prosecution (referring to RCI's suit that was dismissed). It also called for punitive damages of $500,000.

In spite of the whopping new lawsuit, RCI, still in possession of the *King*, held a few functions in 1972. One was a March of Dimes benefit swim of 20 miles downriver starting from the vessel. Another was a wedding on the bow. Yet another was *Playboy* magazine's use of the *Delta King* as background for a photo session. Featured was Miki Garcia, an RCI volunteer who was winner of the Miss Sacramento bikini contest two years before. Miss Garcia had served as guest celebrity for "Save the King" fund-raising and as honorary chairperson for a number of events. Now she had been chosen as Playmate of the Month for the January 1973 issue of *Playboy*. But when the article appeared, none of the pictures taken aboard the craft were used. Had those photos appeared, the world might well have seen the historic steamboat in a new light.

RCI had fought the good fight, but its luck was running out. Even previously successful kinds of activities went sour. One night a drunken partygoer damaged railroad switches on nearby property. A few months later, a woman fell overboard. As time passed and enthusiasm waned, some of the old stalwart workers dropped out, leaving only a few people to handle the dwindling number of fund-raising events.

Eventually, the condition of the boat became an issue. In 1972, the state Fire Marshal shut down the vessel temporarily. And in 1973, Yolo County closed it to the public permanently, pending repairs. RCI said it couldn't do repairs because it didn't own the craft. This impasse finished the activities of the nonprofit organization. Those remaining in the group had little choice but to sit back and wait for the inevitable—Gene Detgen taking possession of the boat. And, at some unknown time in the future, they would have to deal with the legal charges hanging over their heads.

In the nearly five years the vessel sat at Sacramento, no one ever reported having seen Detgen in the area or having heard from him directly. In fact, none of the riverboat group even knew what he looked like (Max Mortensen always acted as his agent). So it was natural that some people thought Detgen's "ownership" of the *King* had been a sham all along, merely a paper arrangement to front for Mortensen, likely the real owner, and to provide protection against creditors. But this theory, even if true, wouldn't have helped with the group's legal problems, nor would it have prevented the boat from being taken away.

In early February 1974, the news media reported an announcement by "an agent of Gene Detgen" that the *King* would be moved to an undisclosed location in the Bay Area. On Saturday, February 16, as two tugboats tied onto the venerable paddlewheeler, only a handful of spectators assembled to watch and trade memories. The *Sacramento Union* interviewed Harold Scott, a Los Angeles advertising executive, who recalled making trips to Sacramento just to ride the *King:*

> We were a bunch of crazy kids at UCLA in the '30s . . . We used to cut class on Friday, all pile into a car, get 20 gallons of gas for a dollar, drive up here to catch a ride on the King to San Francisco. We'd let all the pretty secretaries from Sacramento buy us soft drinks and dance all night, sleep on the beach and come back on the King Saturday night . . . It was a beautiful boat. Those were the days, fun days.

Scott shook his head and stood there gazing at the departing hulk. In 1969, enthusiasm and fanfare had marked the boat's arrival at Sacramento. Now, almost five years later, there was nothing but quiet and sadness.

The *Delta King* had figuratively and literally run out of steam. The old riverboat's time at the capital city had ended—not with a bang but with a whimper—as the tugs towed the vessel downriver to an unknown destination.

176

San Francisco Chronicle 7
★ Mon., Feb. 25, 1974

A Riverboat's Pastoral Graveyard

Last Days of the Delta King

By Don Wegars
Chronicle Correspondent

Aboard the Delta King,
Solano county

The Delta King, one of the two great pre-World War II Sacramento riverboats, is tied up these days in a hidden channel cut deeply into the rolling farmland hills of the Sacramento-San Joaquin Delta.

The once-regal sternwheel steamboat came to this mysterious and pastoral anchorage in the early morning hours of February 17 after four unproductive and desultory years in Sacramento.

The sudden and basically unexplained move was in keeping with the King's wandering past, which has seen her all over the Bay and Delta, in British Columbia and — almost — on the Yangtze river in China.

"It's really a shame," Captain Dan Huff said, standing outside the pilot house. "All her machinery gone, the inside stripped."

Captain Huff, one of Southampton Towing Co.'s tugboat skippers, brought the ungainly 250-foot long vessel dowm the Sacramento in under 12 hours with two tugs and a crew of six.

"It was a little hairy," he recalled. "We were getting a stiff cross-wind and putting

Photos by Stephanie Maze

vated for a waterfront development somewhere. But it would take an awful lot."

Owner Detgen was unavailable to comment on his plans and Max Mortemson, a retired Air Force colonel who is Detgen's Bay Area associate, declined to talk, too.

The steamers Delta King and Delta Queen were built in Stockton in 1927 for the Sacramento - San Francisco run. They cost $1 million each and were said to be the finest riverboats ever to sail America's rivers.

During the 1930s, both made overnight cruises remarkable, passengers recalled, for drink, dalliance and general good times. The boats were done in by good roads and the Depression and stopped running on the Sacramento in 1940.

The Delta Queen went on to great things — she went to the Mississippi and is in service there, the overnight steamboat in the United States.

The King served as a Navy ship on San Francisco Bay during World War then was sold to a group Chinese businessmen on the Yangtze river the group backed off contemplated navig sternwheeler across cific.

*Newspapers imply end is near for the historic boat, with graveyard headline (*San Francisco Chronicle*) and cemetery cross photo (*Sacramento Bee*). During low tide at Collinsville (below), the King appears to be floating but actually sits on the muddy bottom.*

15

Riverboat Gamblers

A steamboat nearly as long as a football field isn't easy to hide. Yet, apparently, that's what Gene Detgen (or his "agent") thought he was doing when he had the *Delta King* towed away from Sacramento in February 1974. Unverified reports had circulated that the boat was bound for refurbishing in Oakland and a new career as a restaurant at Fisherman's Wharf in San Francisco. Quite possibly Detgen encouraged those rumors to throw everyone off the trail.

The *King* never got to San Francisco Bay. In fact, the craft, towed by tugboats from the Southampton Towing Co., went only half way. On February 21, the *Oakland Tribune* reported: "The mystery of the Delta King, the last of the Sacramento River passenger boats of pre-World War II vintage, continued today as the historic old riverboat lies inexplicably moored among the tules at Collinsville. . . . a once-thriving river town across the river from Antioch. The vessel was tied up, apparently untended."

Reportedly, Detgen tried to hide the *King* from public view to lessen vandalism of the unmanned vessel. Dan Huff, tugboat skipper on the trip downriver from Sacramento, commented many years later: "Trying to hide her was like trying to hide the Empire State Building." Capt. Huff felt a special attachment to the boat. In the early days of World War II, he had served aboard the twin steamer *Delta Queen* ferrying Pearl Harbor wounded from San Francisco piers to military hospitals around the bay.

On February 25, the *San Francisco Chronicle* ran a six-column news story, along with two big pictures of the *King*. The headline: "Last Days of the Delta King"; the subhead: "A Riverboat's Pastoral Graveyard." In the next few days, the

Sacramento Bee, the *River Times-Herald* of Rio Vista, and other papers published similar stories. Although they didn't specify the exact location or draw a map, they might just as well have done so. The secret was out.

The *Delta King* had been purposefully scheduled to arrive at Collinsville in the middle of the night to avoid curious eyes. Because there were no lights at the entrance to the small slough, Capt. Huff's wife Shirley used her car's headlights on the levee to guide the tugs and their tow into the narrow opening. The *Chronicle* gave Huff's description of bringing the *King* in: "It was a little hairy. We were getting a stiff cross wind . . . I was hitting the tules [large bulrushes] on both sides."

Reporting on the vessel's condition, made worse by vandals and neglect over the past two years, the *Chronicle* said, "The boat's engines are gone and so is her paddle wheel; the oak paneling in the cabins has been ripped out, windows are broken, the paint is flaking, railings are broken. Scrap, cans, paper and dog feces litter the decks and public rooms." About the latter, Huff commented, "They had a watchdog . . . I guess the feeling was that a trespasser would slip on the stuff and break his neck."

The story stated that the boat had been "slowly succumbing to time, weather, vandals, and curio hunters" and then quoted Capt. Huff again: "There's not much left to take. The Delta King is being hauled around like the moth-eaten corpse of some emperor. Maybe there ought to be something like maritime euthanasia."

Within a few days of the news stories, souvenir hunters and the just-plain curious were beginning to arrive in cars and boats. One of the visitors, in a category all by himself, was Barney Gould, who had long sought ownership of the *Delta King* for use as a showboat at San Francisco. Driving up in an old Studebaker, he walked aboard and was heard to mutter something about being deprived of his option to buy the vessel years before.

Three months later, on May 15, 1974, Gene Detgen transferred his ownership of the *King* to the Quimby Island Reclamation District, a planned $7-million recreation project in the Delta touted as "one of the most imaginative undertakings in Northern California history." Since Max Mortensen had masterminded that project and since Detgen was thought by some to be a "front" for Mortensen, it's not clear just what this transfer of ownership meant. Reportedly, Detgen now held a note secured by the *King,* much as a finance company holds the papers on a car until it's paid for.

Quimby Island developers promoted the historic steamboat as the centerpiece for their big new recreation area. They sent out a press release calling their plan "the first project of its type in the world . . . a vast combination of fish development and research, aquatic sports and recreation, public park areas and a huge private recreation club in a totally pollution-free area." The release said the *King* would "offer the public a living monument to California history. The riverboat will house an elegant restaurant, offer sleeping accommodations in spacious staterooms; the hull will be a huge entertainment center, a riverboat museum and, on the cargo level, a shopping area." The release also asserted that refurbishing the vessel would "help herald America's coming bicentennial," although it's unclear just what connection a 50-year-old California sternwheeler would have to the country's 200th anniversary celebration.

Those grandiose plans got off to a bad start in the early summer of 1974. Lack of attention to the *King's* mooring allowed the vessel to shift position in the small, shallow slough known as McDougal Cut. At a very low tide, the *King* came to rest on the muddy bottom. When the tide rose, the boat didn't rise with it. Suction of the mud held the craft down long enough to allow water to enter the hull through the windows cut near the waterline years before in Stockton. With its hold full of water, the boat lost all buoyancy and was inundated up to the freight deck. Most of the wooden superstructure remained dry.

In a photo taken for the July 20 *Sacramento Bee,* the *King* is shown from the vantage point of the Collinsville cemetery. A graveyard cross looms in the immediate foreground. The caption reads: "A cross in the cemetery may be symbolic for the Delta King, half-submerged in McDougal Slough." Kirk McBride writing in the *Sacramento Union* said, "It looks as though the riverboat Delta King is not long for this world."

Just weeks later, at the other side of the continent, an earthshaking event took place. As a result of the Watergate scandal, on August 9, 1974, Richard M. Nixon resigned as President of the United States. Thus the sinking of the *King* had been followed by the sinking of a president. Since the President's resignation received more press coverage than the predicament of the *King,* one playful observer couldn't resist saying, "It just goes to show, in our country, a president is more important than a king."

But all jokes aside, the *Delta King* was in trouble and needed help. Before the end of August, divers began working to refloat the old paddlewheeler. Art Helwig of Diver's Exchange in Alameda supervised the project, which involved wrapping a "girdle type device," made of black plastic, around the hull to seal the windows so the muddy water could be pumped out. When powerful pumps had removed enough water, buoyancy was restored and the boat rose to the surface.

Within a few days, the *King* was towed 15 miles up the river to Rio Vista and tied at a dredging yard among dredges and other equipment. There, in September 1974, the Quimby Island Reclamation District began to prepare the boat for its new role. Workmen started repairs. They also installed crayfish tanks on the freight deck along with equipment for processing and freezing fish.

Although company officials said the highly-touted recreation project would open in about a year, work on the vessel proceeded slowly, then finally stopped altogether. As had happened so many times in the *King*'s past, the developers had run out of money. They issued and attempted to sell a whopping $96 million in notes. Almost two years later, the reclamation district, in default on about $5 million, filed for bankruptcy. The district temporarily withdrew its bankruptcy petition in 1976, then filed again in 1977.

Worse yet, the federal Securities and Exchange Commission accused 21 defendants of fraud in the sale of $2.2 million in Quimby Island securities. While using the tax-exempt reclamation district as a vehicle for saving taxes on the project was legal, the statements allegedly made in connection with the sale of securities were not. Some investors reported that salesmen told them the bonds were backed by the State of California, when in fact securities were backed only by the district's farms and marshes. And the SEC couldn't get an accounting for much of the money received from investors. Reportedly, two of the sales outfits peddling the securities turned out to have questionable backgrounds, including employees with prior convictions for mail and wire fraud, conspiracy, and dealing in stolen securities. The *Delta King* continued to sit at Rio Vista.

Meanwhile, echoes of the past were heard from two legal cases with no connection to Quimby Island. The first case harked back to the abduction of the *King* from Stockton. When the vessel departed Sacramento in 1974, Geoff Wong, members of Riverboat's Comin', and two tugboat companies still faced a major lawsuit. On July 8, 1975, the suit was dismissed. Wong, who as a lawyer had spent hundreds of hours on the suit (mostly without compensation), theorized that Gene Detgen dismissed the suit because he finally decided he couldn't win on the basis of financial gain as a motive: All money collected had been put into the "Save the King" fund.

The other legal case proved much more complex. It went back a decade to 1965, when Mel Belli and Max Mortensen signed a promissory note to John

Kessel for purchase of the *King*. Reportedly, Belli and Mortensen had never made good on that note. Kessel had died, but his estate continued with a suit against Belli, Mortensen, and Richard F. Gerry. The case was heard in Superior Court at Stockton in the summer of 1975.

Complicating matters, Belli filed a cross complaint against several people including Kessel, Gerry, Mortensen, and J. Edward Ogden. And to further cloud the picture, complaints and cross complaints were filed by some dozen individuals who held claims of one sort or another against the *King* or property where it had been moored at Stockton. Belli, who told the court he had a "romantic and personal interest" in the riverboat, even entered his own counterclaim to get title to the vessel for himself. He also revealed that, at one point, there was an effort to get entertainer Danny Thomas as an investor.

Judge Chris Papas heard the case in lieu of a jury. After long hours spent in the courtroom and late nights studying evidence and arguments, he ruled in April 1976 that Belli and Mortensen were liable for payment of $247,683.76 to Kessel's estate plus $30,000 court costs. Judge Papas estimated that the two were now responsible for paying $500,000 when interest since 1965 was included. The "riverboat gamblers" had gambled and lost.

In a 40-page memorandum of opinion, Judge Papas revealed his thoughts about the tangled affairs of the legal case that kept nine attorneys arguing for five weeks in court:

> The facts and legal issues involved in this proceeding defy description. Seldom, if ever, in the history of Anglo-Saxon and American jurisprudence has there been a case in which a simple sale and purchase transaction turned into such a commercial and legal nightmare.
>
> Most, if not all, of the parties in this venture are brilliant in their own fields, but totally and completely ignorant and incompetent in matters unrelated to their particular expertise.

In this document, Judge Papas said, "Mortensen felt that Belli's reputation, notoriety, acquaintances, flamboyancy, and expertise would cause investors to come into the deal. . . . It is crystal clear that Mortensen was the engineer and architect of each of these transactions and Belli, the willing, naive follower, who was led into believing there was a pot of gold at the end of the rainbow."

Meanwhile, back at the "fish ranch," the *Delta King* sat in the limbo of Quimby Island's bankruptcy. In 1977 Assemblyman Vic Fazio and State Senator

JUDGE CHRIS PAPAS WITH THE DELTA KING FILE

Criminal and Civil Cases Overflowing In County's Courts

By Helen Flynn

"The facts and legal issues involved in this proceeding defy description," says Judge Chris Papas as he holds voluminous Delta King file. Case kept nine attorneys arguing for five weeks in court. Papas adds: "Seldom, if ever, in the history of Anglo-Saxon and American jurisprudence has there been a case in which a simple sale and purchase transaction turned into such a commercial and legal nightmare."

Top right, the King sits forsaken at the Rio Vista dredging yard where boat docked 1974-78. At left, Tom Fat has just made "the winning bid" on the vessel at 1978 auction in Rio Vista. Although Fat loses to another bidder at a court hearing a fortnight later, in the meantime he is invited on talk shows, receives numerous phone calls and two offers of marriage. Fat says, "They were the wildest two weeks I ever lived."

John Dunlap came out for state acquisition of the vessel. A representative from the state Department of Parks and Recreation inspected the craft, but the idea ended there. Because of that proposal, however, application had been made for inclusion in the National Register of Historic Places. The following year, the National Park Service accepted the *King* into its register. Now the riverboat held official historic status, an honor to be sure, but this didn't help the boat's cause. It can be noted that most of the cries of "Long live the King!" heard at that time referred to Elvis Presley, who had died in 1977, not to the California paddlewheeler.

Rescue of the *Delta King* seemed "so near, yet so far." Among those who wanted the riverboat saved, expectations ranged widely. The optimists thought the state might eventually acquire and restore the venerable old steamer, while the pessimists expected the craft to go to a buyer who already had plans to shear off the vessel's superstructure and make it into a barge. In July of 1977 the *Sacramento Bee* asked: "Is it any longer realistic to hope for restoration of the Delta King, given the legal entanglements, its fearsome state of disrepair and rehabilitation costs, estimated to run into the millions? Is it perhaps time to accept the possibility that rumors of its demise may not be grossly exaggerated?"

When asked to comment on the *Bee*'s questions above, Karl Kortum, Director of the San Francisco Maritime Museum (now the National Maritime Museum), took an optimistic stance. He said, "The *King* is eminently restorable, because it has a steel, not wooden, hull and therefore a solid foundation for building." Kortum thought it incredible that the vessel had not been restored for the waterfront at Old Sacramento. "It's the only boat that can properly fill that space."

Whatever the craft's potential may have been at that time, the Solano County tax collector held the trump card. Because of overdue tax liens, the county sheriff seized the *King* and announced an auction sale for August 3, 1977. But as the Quimby Island Reclamation District filed a bankruptcy petition (its second filing) almost simultaneously with the sheriff's announcement, he canceled the sale.

As if a bankruptcy filing and a canceled auction weren't enough excitement for one month, a group from Sacramento purchased Gene Detgen's interest in the *King*. Gus Skarakis, chief counsel for the state Department of Consumer Affairs, headed a group of four businessmen. He and three others joined together as creditors, holding a note on the vessel. The group told of its plans for riverboat restoration but was stymied by the bankruptcy filing. On August 9, the *Sacramento Bee* said, "Skarakis concedes the legal footing is so tenuous he could be left 'with just a piece of paper,' but he thinks that even an outside chance of returning the Delta

King to Sacramento is worth a riverboat gamble any day."

The *Bee* article concluded: "In the meantime, the beleaguered steamboat sits in ghostly silence on the banks of the Sacramento at Rio Vista. Some believe her legal and structural conditions are such that only God can save the King." A footnote: Scavenging of the boat continued at Rio Vista. The smokestack was removed and taken to the levee at Isleton to serve as a tool shed.

Finally, legalities were cleared for a sheriff's sale, set for January 27, 1978, at Rio Vista. The morning dawned cold and foggy. By auction time at 11 a.m., fog still hugged the riverbank. A crowd of nearly 200 showed up, including Barney Gould, who still had hopes of somehow turning the *King* into a showboat. But bidding wasn't in the script for this theatrical impresario and perennial riverboat devotee, who had neither the money nor the backers to buy the vessel.

Deputy J. Roger Wilson conducted the auction from the hood of a sheriff's car. He announced a minimum acceptable bid of $17,655.87 and asked for bids. "$18,000" came the immediate response from Tom Fat, the attorney son of Frank Fat, well-known Sacramento restaurant owner. Long silence. Then a voice called out "$19,000." It was Terry Black, young Sacramento entrepreneur. These two men, the only bidders, continued back and forth for several minutes through a total of 18 bids. Finally, after Fat bid $32,000, Black dropped out.

Tom Fat and his family now owned a riverboat—or almost owned it. A U.S. district court in San Francisco still needed to confirm the sale two weeks hence. At that time, the court would give other potential buyers an opportunity to bid, provided they offered at least ten percent more than Fat's bid.

At the confirmation hearing on February 10, a new bidder showed up. Harry Lee, representing Berkeley restaurant owner M.K. Sun, offered $35,200, the minimum amount necessary to overbid Tom Fat's offer at Rio Vista. Although Fat had a chance to raise the new bid, he said nothing and the auction was over. The *Delta King* now belonged to Sun, who had attended the hearing with his family wearing native Chinese garb. Approaching Sun, the ubiquitous Barney Gould immediately proposed a joint operation of the vessel between the two of them. But the idea didn't take hold.

Sun, who had served as a major general in Chiang Kai-shek's Nationalist Chinese army during World War II, said he had been assured of a waterfront site in San Francisco. He added that he and his family would operate a Chinese restaurant on one of the boat's five levels and lease space on other decks for cafes serving Mexican, French, and Italian foods.

Tom Fat, when questioned by newsmen about his reason for not bidding at the hearing, said it was because of the high cost of restoration. His fortnight's experience, however, did have merit. More than a decade later, Fat said, "I had the boat for two weeks—the wildest two weeks I ever lived. I received two offers of marriage, people were calling me from all over, I was on talk shows."

Six months after Sun bought the *Delta King*, he had it towed down to the bay. The vessel docked at the Red Rock Marina in Richmond, just north of the Richmond-San Rafael Bridge, where it was moored in an old ferry slip left from the days when ferries crossed the bay to Marin County. There it sat for the next two years mired in bureaucratic procedures, waiting for permits from various governmental agencies.

In 1980, Sun passed one hurdle when the Bay Conservation and Development Commission granted him permission to dock the *King* on the San Francisco waterfront. Also that year, he had the boat towed about six miles to Richmond's Inner Harbor and tied up on a small inlet called Lauritzen Channel. Offering better protection from wind and waves, the new location was near where Henry J. Kaiser built Liberty ships during World War II.

The next year proved tragic for both the Sun family and the *Delta King*. In early 1981, M.K. Sun died, leaving plans for restoration of the boat in question. And in the spring, an event took place that surpassed all the disasters and near-disasters of the *King's* past. The vessel was moored improperly, allowing the overhang of the freight deck to slip over the dock at high tide.

On the fateful night of April 3-4, when the tide started to fall, the port side hung up on the dock. As the water receded further, the *King* began a starboard list that increased until the windows in the hull on that side were at water level. What had taken place seven years earlier at Collinsville happened again at Richmond. But this time, it happened in spades—the water here was more than twice as deep.

We can imagine a quiet moment in the darkness; a single light shines overhead on the dock. With its port side caught, the boat has been tilting slowly away from the dock as the tide ebbs. Bay water has just reached the windows on the starboard side of the hull. Water begins to trickle into the hold.

The tide continues to fall. The list to starboard increases. The water flows faster, ever faster. Eventually, a virtual river pours through the misbegotten windows. The splash of rapids, the gurgles of air pockets surfacing. Now the towering superstructure tilts quickly, and there's a guttural moan from the port side as it slides from the dock. A shudder—then another shudder. The giant begins to go under. Water gushes through the doors and windows of the freight deck and above. Waves. Turbulence. Bubbles.

The *King* settles gently on the muddy bottom. Ripples radiate out across the channel. Silence.

As dawn breaks, workmen on the dock are shocked at what they see. Only the two top decks rise above the water at the starboard stern. The vessel rests on an uneven bottom in 20 to 30 feet of murky bay water with flooding of the hold, freight deck, and first passenger deck. The bow sits in a slightly shallower part of the channel. Thus the grand staircase, in the forward section, is spared. But as the tide rises, water comes right to the bottom of the first step.

It looks like the end. There seems little chance the *Delta King* will ever float again.

16

Come Hell or High Water

April 7, 1981—News item from the *San Francisco Chronicle:*

The historic riverboat Delta King, which has had nothing but bad luck
since the Sacramento River steamboat business folded up years ago, quietly sank at a dock in Richmond over the weekend.

April 23, 1982—An account based on the author's journal:

A year has gone by. The *Delta King* still sits on the muddy bottom. I step
onto the dock and approach the boat. Looking at the old paddlewheeler in the late afternoon light, I feel a sadness—a gut-level hopelessness.
I see no sign of life around the forsaken vessel, no one on board, no evidence of salvage work other than a few flotation bags piled on the dock.
The smell of bay mud fills the air.

Dirty green moss clings to the superstructure where wood siding
meets the murky bay water. The steel hull is not visible—it's all under
the water. Portions still above water show immense surfaces of gray,
weathered, splintering wood and scaling paint, broken windows, and
everywhere the evidence of years of neglect. A mournful, lonely scene.

It seems as if I can almost feel the *King's* suffering, the quiet despera-
tion and abandonment. The riverboat is huge and, in its heyday, had
been powerful. Yet there must be a limit to the amount of abuse this
crippled old steamer can take. The vessel has managed to keep alive a
touch of its original dignity with a stately pilothouse and the graceful
curve of its decks. But, realistically, how long can the boat be expected
to survive?

Listing to starboard and most-deeply submerged at the stern, historic Delta King
lies forlorn and deserted after sinking
at Richmond, California, in April 1981.
Near right, photo shows the stern as bay
water floods the hold, freight deck, and
first passenger deck. Far right, pumps
gush water in a failed refloating attempt.

The morning after the *Delta King* sank in April 1981, *San Francisco Chronicle* reporter Carl Nolte got wind of the sinking and drove to Richmond. Later—but before writing his news story—it became his role to break the news to the shocked owners. Within a few days, Randall Crane, attorney for the M.K. Sun family, said he thought his clients would try to raise the boat and continue with plans to restore it. He added, "Whatever it takes, they'll do it."

But refloating a deeply-submerged 285-foot steamboat is easier said than done. "Dead in the water" says it all. The problems in such operations are legion, the pitfalls mind-boggling, the costs enormous. The five surviving sons of M.K. Sun were not maritime people. Little did they realize what an uphill battle they faced. They asked many people for advice and got many opinions. One common theme in the answers: Whatever system they might use, there was no guarantee it would work. Raising the boat in water that deep would make the refloating job at Collinsville look like child's play.

Interviewed a decade after the sinking, eldest son Chant Sun recounted an early unsuccessful attempt, in which a salvage company got the *King* almost refloated. But it sank again, and his family gave up. Sun recalls receiving almost-daily phone calls from Barney Gould offering ideas for saving the craft. Following the riverboat aficionado's advice, on May 20 Sun went to San Francisco's Aquatic Park to see if the Golden Gate National Recreation Area might offer a solution. Gould had suggested that if Sun gave the *King* to the federal government, it would spend $2 million to restore the boat. But, in looking for the GGNRA office, Sun by accident got to the office of Karl Kortum, Chief Curator of the National Maritime Museum and founder of the historic ships project at the park.

"I hadn't come to work yet," says Kortum. "My assistant Mary Clark saved the day. She persuaded Sun to stay and seated him on a little tin stool at the head of the stairs. And there I found him, when I arrived. A later owner of the boat, when he heard the story, said, 'that stool should be in the *King*'s museum.'" Kortum was certain that Sun's appeal to GGNRA would be hopeless and would just waste valuable time. He knew the agency had rejected the idea two years before. Time was running out for the *Delta King*. As Kortum put it, "The last riverboat in California—last of some 283 sternwheelers and sidewheelers, and with her sister *the best* riverboat—was now an almost certain candidate for dynamite and the clamshell bucket."

Kortum was convinced the *King* could eventually be included in the fleet of historic ships at San Francisco's Aquatic Park. But he recognized that careful groundwork must be laid first. He told Sun he knew of only one man who could accomplish this: Robert Taylor of Vancouver, British Columbia. A lover of old ships, Taylor already had restored a small sternwheeler as a restaurant at Vancouver. And he possessed the necessary patience and diplomacy. Kortum knew that any time government is involved, the process is bound to be long and drawn out.

Two days later, as the result of Sun's visit with Kortum, Sun and Taylor talked by telephone. Kortum calls this the turning point: "In this chancy fashion started the most remarkable chapter in the ill-starred history of the *Delta King*." In July 1981, Taylor signed an option-to-buy agreement with Sun.

A coincidental footnote: That same month, fire destroyed buildings at the old River Lines wharf at Sacramento, where the *Delta King* and *Delta Queen* had docked from 1927 to 1940. While these facilities were no longer used and the blaze had no direct connection to the drama unfolding on the bay, the news reminded historians that remnants of the riverboat era were gradually disappearing from the California scene. But, in this case, as one relic vanished, the preservation of another was being planned.

Robert Taylor enjoyed the backing of Karl Kortum and the blessings of several National Park Service officials. But the GGNRA had no public money available. Taylor would have to find private financing. He estimated it would cost at least $10 million to refloat and restore the boat. Clearly, the project needed investors and a commercial aspect to make it feasible.

So Taylor headed for Chicago to present his ideas to executives of Resort & Urban Timeshares, Inc. (RUTI). According to Taylor, "These were powerful and influential men in the financial world, the venture-capital world, the legal world." Principal founder and chief executive was Ralph Wienshienk, a senior partner in a New York law firm and former chairman of McCall's Publishing. Bert Kantor, a Chicago lawyer, had raised millions for the motion-picture industry.

RUTI had just raised over $8 million cash in what was known as a blind pool. Taylor said, "Their names and reputations were good enough that they attracted this kind of money with no questions asked. They were in good financial shape and looking for projects, but that didn't prevent them from being very tough on me. I suppose it's understandable—this guy from out of the West with a sunken riverboat. Anyway, they put me through a wringer . . . Then they told me we had a deal." Taylor, who had hoped for a 50-50 split on profits, had to settle for 20%.

Back in the Bay Area, Taylor hired naval architect David Seymour to devise a plan for raising the boat. Soon after, he contracted with Podesta Divers, Inc., to handle the on-site work. Meanwhile, Taylor announced his plan to moor the *King* at San Francisco's Aquatic Park Lagoon as a classy addition to the historic ship collection at nearby Hyde Street Pier. A time-share arrangement for 45 staterooms or suites on the boat would finance the project. People buying one time-share unit would own the right to spend one week a year in their accommodations aboard. The public would be allowed to use the two lower decks, where a museum would feature California riverboat history. At the end of 50 years, title to the vessel would go to the National Park Service.

On January 22, 1982, the *San Francisco Examiner* outlined Taylor's plan and added this comment: "When the Delta King settled into the mud of the Richmond inner harbor last year, it looked as if the famed [boat] . . . had reached a pathetic end. But, to paraphrase Mark Twain, the reports of its watery demise are greatly exaggerated." Seemingly, with the proposed plan, everybody would win: The historic fleet would gain one irreplaceable vessel at no cost to the government; time-share owners would have a colorful and convenient place for a yearly vacation in San Francisco; the *Delta King* would be saved for posterity. "I don't see how anybody could be against it," Taylor said. "Everybody's a winner."

Problems, however, lay ahead. At a raucous hearing held at San Francisco's Fort Mason on March 17, the GGNRA Citizens Advisory Commission listened to the public's views on Taylor's plan to locate the *Delta King* at Aquatic Park. While the commission's final decision would not be binding on the GGNRA, its decisions were usually honored. The hearing room overflowed with 150 people, most of them wanting to speak, so individual time had to be cut severely. Barney Gould got up and said the boat would be an asset to the area but then became sidetracked with a tirade about vandals setting fire to his riverboat *Fort Sutter* 23 years before. I testified about the *King*'s historic value. A number of other preservationists and steamboat buffs urged the commission to accept the plan.

But opponents of the plan were numerous and vociferous. Primarily people from the high-rise Fontana apartments, the South End Rowing Club, and the Dolphin Club (all located at Aquatic Park), they protested strongly. Organized and outnumbering proponents two to one, the opponents warned of noise and trash, of views being blocked—and they suggested the boat might become an eyesore. They pointed out that giving title to the National Park Service after 50 years could well be saddling the agency with a white elephant. One Fontana resident presented petitions bearing the signatures of 115 fellow residents opposing the project. After several Dolphin Club members complained about the plan, Dave Hull,

Principal Librarian at the Maritime Museum and a club member himself, rose and said, "The *Delta King* certainly would add a great deal of vivid color and history to the park—more than the Dolphin Club does."

No one expected a decision by the commission at this hearing, and none was forthcoming. That would come later. But it was clear Taylor faced more than just the major challenge of refloating the *King*. The political snags and shoals ahead appeared more numerous than anyone had imagined.

Karl Kortum had long sought an authentic California riverboat for the Maritime Museum's collection of historic vessels. His thoughts on the museum's need for the *King* and the mooring controversy were simple: "The riverboat was a major factor in the development of California. . . . The *Delta King*, now wallowing in the mud in Richmond, is our last chance."

Years before, Kortum had fought a losing battle to protect waterfront views; he had opposed construction of the 17-story Fontana apartments. Now he was confronted by arguments from residents of those apartments about the size and looks of the *King*. He said the boat would occupy less than one percent of the space in Aquatic Park Lagoon. "Alongside the Fontana, the *Delta King* looks like a rowboat. . . . This is a big fuss about nothing."

Writing in the *San Francisco Chronicle*, columnist Herb Caen pointed out the irony of a protest that claimed the sternwheeler would be "highly detrimental" to the panorama from Fontana West, one of two high-rises on the northern waterfront. Caen said this building had blocked enough views to produce later passage of a 40-foot height limit. He concluded, "Which would you rather look at— Fontana West or a riverboat?"

In spite of the strong opposition at the hearing, Taylor continued with his plan to raise the craft. But realizing that public relations could make or break his project, he chartered the small bay cruise boat *Oakland Pilot*. He filled it with representatives of the news media, members of the Citizens Advisory Commission, historians and preservationists (Barney Gould among them) for a firsthand look at the *King*. With this group, I went aboard at San Francisco and crossed the bay to Richmond's Inner Harbor.

June 2, 1982—An account based on the author's journal:

Our charter boat enters the long, narrow Lauritzen Channel. In the distance, we spot an indistinct gray form we know must be the *Delta King*, sunken now for 14 months. As we draw closer, some on our boat begin to recognize the old sternwheeler. I can feel the excitement mount.

The *King*'s paddle wheel and smokestack are missing. The stern faces us, and only the top two decks clearly show above the water. At least half the venerable riverboat is submerged; the other half lies in shambles. As we approach in near silence, I hear faintly audible gasps. Shock, I believe, is the primary emotion, as we gaze at what used to be the pride of the river.

We tie up on the port side. As I go aboard, I feel as if I'm stepping into a ghost town. Everywhere I look, I see flaking paint, rust, broken windows. Driftwood and debris litter the deck. Dust or bay mud covers everything. Ravaged by vandals and souvenir hunters, weathered by the sun, rain, and tides, the *King* appears beyond repair. Almost four decades of carelessness and neglect have taken their toll. Yet, surprisingly, the deck feels solid under my feet. At least, the basic structure is sound—a powerful tribute to the designers and builders.

We enter the double doors into the former lobby. I note that the grand staircase has been spared a watery fate. But the fancy bronze filigree of the stair railing has long since been removed, as has the stained glass above the side windows. The deck tilts awkwardly to starboard and stern. Looking back from the staircase toward the old dining room, I see standing water. The smell of wet wood and bay water permeates the deserted rooms and passageways. Even the two dry upper decks give off a musty, dank odor.

It's a sorrowful sight. But there may be hope. Robert Taylor, Canadian businessman and would-be riverboat savior, says he plans to raise and restore it. He's very convincing. "The *Delta King* has the potential to be a beautiful boat again," he exclaims to the press and assembled dignitaries, "and a beautiful boat she shall be."

Our tour of inspection is over. We board our charter boat and return to San Francisco. Now I discover I've lost my camera case on the morning tour. I drive back to Richmond and obtain permission to board the *King* again to look for the missing item. Thus I get to inspect the boat again, this time without the busy activities of the morning. When I climb aboard, it's early afternoon and the tide is rising. In the morning, the bow had projected just above the water; now it's completely under.

As I wander the decks, I'm aware of a deep silence. I'm awed by the thought that, for the first time, I'm completely alone on the legendary *Delta King*. Here I am aboard the historic riverboat I've admired from afar for 30 years—now I have this long-lost twin of the *Delta Queen* all to myself, with the echoes of my footsteps the only sound.

In the quiet of the afternoon, I reflect on the old steamer's past. That history—for me previously plain and unadorned—now comes alive. Somehow, I feel as if I've gone back to the 1920s and '30s, when the *Delta King* and *Delta Queen* paddled nightly up and down the Sacramento. Through bay fog and valley heat, with deck lights ablaze and the sound of music and laughter wafting on still air, these boats touched the lives of many people. For a brief moment, I felt I had experienced that nearly-forgotten time.

That day, as we first approached the *King* on Taylor's charter boat, the salvage crew was pumping water out to demonstrate their plans for refloating. Once aboard the riverboat, we went on a tour led by National Park Service guides. Karl Kortum offered a brief history of California paddlewheelers, salvage foreman Orville Hanners appeared in his "hard hat diving suit," and Taylor gave a short but rousing talk describing his plans. In spite of the boat's poor condition, which Associated Press described as "half sunk and fully decrepit," most of our tour group seemed impressed with the potential of the *King*.

To raise a vessel the size of the *King,* in water of that depth, presented a formidable task. David Seymour and Podesta Divers studied seven possible ways; finally, they chose a flotation method using large air bags. They would pump the bags full of air inside the hull for lift. Then additional bags would be placed outside the boat, like water wings, to add stability. When pumps removed enough water, the old sternwheeler would rise to the surface—or so they hoped.

To their great dismay midway in the refloating operation, divers discovered that most of the air bags (which had been purchased secondhand) had leaks. Finally, the salvage company discarded the original plan. Instead, Seymour says, "They decided to make the hull itself into a floatable entity." In other words, both the steel hull and the wooden freight deck resting on it would be sealed to make the boat's hold into a giant air bag itself. He says they decided, "If we could make the hull reasonably watertight, pump most of the water out and stabilize her as she lifted, we stood a chance."

Using plywood and working underwater, divers began to patch what Seymour called "those silly window openings" in the steel hull. Divers also had to make the portholes watertight. But the hit-or-miss openings and cracks in the freight deck proved most difficult to seal. All work had to be done in dim or nonexistent light under many feet of murky water in unfamiliar territory—and without the benefit of boat plans. Orville Hanners, interviewed later, said, "Sometimes it got downright spooky down there."

Developer Robert Taylor poses by sunken Delta King *(note standing water inside). At right, bow soaks under water. Below, old dining room on first passenger deck is flooded.*

More than a week after refloating, the waterlogged boat still displays green strands of moss. Note watermark high on wall. Above right, mud, mussels, and barnacles cover nearly every surface after the vessel is raised. At left, salvage foreman Orville Hanners wears his hard-hat diving suit. Below, June 1982: the King floats for first time in nearly 15 months.

Finally, the great moment seemed at hand. A press release went to newspapers, radio and TV stations announcing that early on Monday morning, June 21—at low tide—the *Delta King* would be refloated. The news media were invited to come and witness what would be a dramatic event starting at 6 a.m.

At the appointed hour, Robert Taylor arrived in a little green Jaguar coupe. Journalists milled about the dock in the dim light and cool of the early dawn. Already big hoses were spouting bay water from the boat fore and aft. Generators, supplying power for the pumps, roared in the background.

Working at top speed for three hours, eight huge pumps discharged thousands of gallons of water per minute. They pumped—and they pumped. But by 9 o'clock, the *King* hadn't budged an inch. And the tide was rising. As fast as the water was pumped out, it was finding its way back in. Discouraged, the salvage crew turned off the pumps. They needed to plug the remaining leaks, and they would have to use more pumps. This meant extra work and another delay until the next favorable low tide.

Two days later, after Podesta Divers had patched additional cracks in the freight deck and added six more pumps, the bow suddenly rose up. In fact, the bow now stood much higher than normal, several feet out of the water. But the stern had sunk even deeper, where water now came up to the Observation Deck (next to top deck). And still there were leaks they hadn't found.

As I observed the crew working feverishly on that Wednesday afternoon with a sunken giant that seemed full of surprises, I felt as if I were watching a military operation. They had won a battle in raising the bow, but would they win the war? As Orville Hanners gave orders, young men in wetsuits ran back and forth on the dock, throwing lines and shouting to one another, while others scurried aboard the *King*. As generators roared and pumps gushed water, Taylor worked alongside the crew. The day teemed with drama and anticipation—the coming night would be pivotal.

During that frenzied struggle on Wednesday, Hanners had a hunch. He sent for 10 bales of shredded newspaper, thinking the material might plug a gap between the freight deck and the stern bulkhead, a place he suspected still harbored a major leak. In the middle of the night, divers dumped the shredded newspaper on the surface of the water inside the *King*. As soon as the paper got wet, it sank and was sucked into the cracks, slowing the flow—like hair in a bathtub drain. Now, finally, the pumps could gain in the battle against the bay.

To speed up the process, on Thursday about 3 a.m., Hanners went underwater inside the boat and applied oakum, a caulking agent, to the worst crack at the stern. Within minutes the *King* gave a shudder. As Hanners scrambled to safety, the stern suddenly rose up. Then the boat rolled toward the port side and sank part way again. This showed the instability of the lightened vessel, and it also demonstrated the value of the air bags attached to the sides—they had prevented the craft from turning over. The pumps continued another four hours, gradually gaining on the leak rate.

Finally, the moment they'd been waiting for arrived. The boat broke totally free from the muddy bottom and came to the surface on an even keel. It was 7 a.m. on Thursday, June 24, 1982. After six weeks of hard work, they had won the final battle and had rescued the venerable sternwheeler from its underwater grave. For the first time in nearly 15 months, the *Delta King* was afloat.

After what had been an around-the-clock 36-hour struggle, the salvage crew was exhausted but jubilant. Taylor left briefly and returned with eggs Benedict and several bottles of champagne. A bottle was broken over the bow for good luck. Then Taylor, Seymour, Hanners, and the crew toasted one another and the *King,* drank the rest of the champagne, and ate their gourmet breakfast on the dock.

The next day, Hanners confided to me, "At times during the final night, I had doubts we were going to make it" But in the end, they did. Their victory constituted an 11th-hour rescue.

Robert Taylor had provided the key to saving the boat. Had he not raised half a million dollars, taken charge, and refloated the vessel, the fate Karl Kortum described most likely would have come to pass—the *Delta King* would have succumbed to dynamite and the clamshell bucket.

California news media then would have reported on the demise of the last vintage paddle-wheel riverboat in the state. Elsewhere, a few brief obituaries might have appeared telling how the *Delta Queen*'s lesser-known twin had come to an untimely end in the Golden State.

After refloating, waterlogged Delta King *sits with giant air bags alongside. Note dark watermark across second deck.*

King *in drydock: In spite of 60 years exposure to fresh and salt water, to sand bars and dry land, the steel hull passes inspection.*

17

The Riverboat That Refused to Die

To go aboard the *Delta King* after the refloating and walk the lower decks was to experience a strange, surrealistic world. Outside on the first passenger deck, hundreds of barnacles were encrusted on the crumbling rail at the stern, while graceful garlands of olive-green moss hung from the water-soaked wood siding. Inside the boat, what once had been the finest of wood paneling was now reduced to a warped mass of mangled, separating layers. On the freight deck at the stern (the old engine room), mussels and barnacles had attached themselves to every inch of the walls and overhead—and the deck itself was ankle-deep in sticky bay mud.

Within a few days, the *King* appeared dry when viewed from shore. But on board, the dampness, mud, and smell belied the initial look. This was still a water-logged boat. In fact, more than a week after the refloating, the strands of moss hanging on the wood superstructure remained alive and green.

With the sternwheeler now safely floating on the channel and drying out day by day, the drama shifted elsewhere. In July of 1982, within a month of the refloating, RUTI (Resort & Urban Timeshares, Inc.) put additional money into the time-share project. But, by this time, Robert Taylor had begun to worry about the slow pace of the National Park Service in San Francisco. He feared that opposition by Fontana apartment residents and the rowing and swimming clubs was having an effect. Although initially showing support, park officials now seemed to Taylor to be dragging their feet, as if they had lost their nerve.

Karl Kortum still supported the project and suggested Taylor go to Washington, D.C., to visit Congressman Phil Burton, a powerful force with the National Park Service. During his tenure, Burton had almost doubled the size of the park system and was known as the man who created GGNRA. In fact, it had been said that, in a political sense, Phil Burton "owns" the National Park Service. In August, Taylor traveled to Washington with Dick Thorman, his time-share associate from RUTI. They planned to see Burton and make a presentation that would include a videotape of the refloating of the *Delta King*. After overcoming several obstacles at Burton's office, including having to rent and carry a VCR past House-office security checks, they were shocked to see that their film maker had sent the wrong tape. Burton thought the mishap was funny; Taylor and Thorman weren't amused but tried to make the best of it.

Back in San Francisco, Taylor grew increasingly unhappy with the progress of his plan. The GGNRA Citizens Advisory Commission held more hearings in September 1982 and in January and March 1983. In addition to his worries about the opposition, it seemed to Taylor that the stumbling blocks and red tape were increasing, too. At the hearings, commission members suggested studies of alternate mooring sites, questioned environmental impact statements, and brought up concerns about National Park Service liability. They kept raising new issues until it seemed to Taylor the process might go on forever.

Looking back from a 1983 vantage point, it could be seen that the previous summer's visit with Congressman Burton and the videotape fiasco had little significance. Much bigger factors had come into play. Burton, who had appeared to favor the project, suddenly died in April of 1983. And soon after that, RUTI pulled the plug on Taylor, withdrawing financial support. Less than a year later, RUTI went bankrupt. Without his backers, Taylor looked for other financial help but was not successful. To save on moorage costs, the boat was moved from Richmond to the Alameda Gateway Marine Basin, site of the old Todd shipyard on the Oakland Estuary.

One night in early March 1984, Taylor made a telephone call that would change the fate of the *Delta King*. From his home in British Columbia, he called Walter Merrill Harvey, a Sacramento architect who had inquired about the vessel some months before. Taylor asked, "How would you like to buy a famous riverboat?" When Harvey showed interest, Taylor suggested the boat be taken to Sacramento, or at least removed from its Alameda dock, by the end of the week. Harvey replied that he needed more time and that he wanted to talk with someone about the possibility of a joint venture. He said some fast work would also be needed to pave the way with the city of Sacramento. They finally agreed that Taylor would send a letter authorizing Harvey to move the craft and renovate it.

But Taylor would remain in Canada.

Harvey discussed the availability of the *Delta King* with Edmund Coyne, a real estate developer from Marin County who had done riverfront development in Sacramento. He suggested they look at the boat in Alameda. Although they knew the *King* was in disrepair, they were shocked when they saw it. But they could envision possibilities for restoration of the vessel as a commercial venture at Sacramento. Coyne, who had done his college thesis on Mark Twain, saw grace and beauty amid the ruins. He says, "I'd heard about the *Delta King* and *Queen* from my parents and aunts and uncles as I was growing up. The Twain romance—it all came alive for me."

Deciding to take a first step, the two consulted with naval architect David Seymour, who knew the *King* well. Seymour told them the structural integrity of the steel hull was in its favor. Harvey then returned to Sacramento to drum up support from the city. At a meeting on March 20, council members unanimously passed a resolution supporting the idea of a restored *Delta King* on the city's waterfront but gave no specific approval for the plan. And they stressed that the city would provide no financial assistance—the project would have to be done solely with private money. A week later, the Sacramento County Board of Supervisors also endorsed the concept.

But in early April, Coyne and Harvey received a jolt—they discovered they weren't the only ones with plans for the boat. Quite by accident, on a trip to see the *King,* Harvey ran into Geoff Deuel, a Sausalito entrepreneur, who said he had plans to restore the vessel and dock it in San Francisco. Deuel claimed he had worked briefly as Taylor's agent in the Bay Area but had quit because Taylor hadn't paid him. He said he then began helping Chant Sun repossess the craft. According to a *Sacramento Union* account on April 16, Sun and Deuel stated that Taylor never paid anything after agreeing to buy the sternwheeler and that his option-to-buy had expired on March 31. Deuel said he would start the restoration just as soon as ownership legalities were straightened out. He warned Harvey that anyone who tried to move the vessel would be arrested by federal officers. "I have somebody watching the boat," Deuel said. "I'll know the minute it's moved, and I'll nail him."

So it seemed that Taylor—in spite of his heroic efforts to save the *King*—did not have the right to pass ownership. It was a confusing picture: Taylor supposedly not a player any more; Deuel claiming "first dibs" on restoring the boat; Sun attempting to get clear title again; Coyne and Harvey waiting in the wings. But not to be deterred, the latter two turned their attention to Chant Sun. Finally, Sun agreed that, once the title was cleared, he would enter into a joint venture with Coyne and his family, who would supply the financing. Coyne, in turn, offered Harvey a future percentage of the project in exchange for his architectural services.

Sun repossessed the *King* in May. But joint title between Coyne and Sun wouldn't be established until after the hull was inspected in drydock. Coyne was gambling an initial $10,000 in drydocking costs that the hull would pass muster. If it did, they would proceed with needed hull repairs. If it didn't, the deal was off.

In early June 1984, two tugboats towed the *Delta King* to Pacific Dry Dock & Repair, an operation owned by Crowley Maritime Corp., on the Oakland shore just a short way east and across the estuary from the Alameda moorage. In drydock, marine engineers soon confirmed that, despite the condition of the rest of the vessel, the hull was basically sound. Hull repair could begin. Title to the boat was then divided. Thirty percent went to Delta King Enterprises, Inc., which represented Chant Sun, his mother, a brother and other relatives. Seventy percent went to Coyne and Company, Inc., representing four brothers and one sister: Edmund, Michael, Charles, Christopher, and Jeanne.

Overseeing the repair work, Mike Coyne spent long days at the drydock. "After workmen sandblasted the hull down to bare metal," he says, "we happily discovered that more than 50 percent of the original galvanizing from the 1920s was still intact." Welders added small steel patches in the hull's thin spots. And they sealed the infamous windows in the hull that had caused so much grief; to close them, welders installed sections of steel bent to the same curvature. Finally, work crews added a thick coating of coal-tar epoxy to the exterior of the hull, a protective layer that reportedly would last 50 to 100 years in fresh water. By the time the vessel was floated back onto the estuary, the Coynes had spent approximately $140,000 for hull inspection and repairs. Forty years after its last major overhaul and nearly 60 years after launching at Stockton, the *Delta King* was ready to start a comeback.

But the course ahead gave no promise of clear sailing. Sacramento officials had not yet given assurance that the boat could be moored at Old Sacramento, a restored section of town by the river and the location preferred by the partners. Nor had the city actually agreed that the craft could be moored *anywhere* on the city's waterfront. Officials were reluctant to allow even temporary docking of the *King* with a superstructure still in shambles. Memories of the long drawn-out affair at Sacramento just a decade before were still fresh enough in their minds to make them wary. They would have welcomed a completely restored craft but were hesitant to accept a boat that might become an eyesore.

Coyne and Harvey knew that the cost of restoration would be less in Sacramento. And they felt sure they needed public exposure there to win community support. So they decided on a bold move. Regardless of governmental thinking, they would take the *King* to Sacramento. Harvey asked the California Rice Growers Association for permission to use its dock on the Yolo County side of the river, across from Sacramento and beyond jurisdiction of the city. When Coyne and Harvey received an okay, they were ready to take their gamble.

"The Last Voyage," as they called it, began shortly after 11 p.m. on the bright and clear evening of Thursday, July 26, 1984. A Crowley tug pulled the *Delta King* from Pacific Dry Dock along the estuary and onto the bay, where it soon became evident a second tugboat would be needed. So another was added, and the trip continued— one tug at the bow, the other at the stern. About 30 people, known as the "work crew," rode aboard the *King*. In addition to Ed Coyne and Walt Harvey, passengers included Mike Coyne, Joanna Walker (soon to be Harvey's wife), Delta journalist Hal Schell, and Barney Gould. This was Gould, whose near-lifelong quest to own a showboat seemed an impossible dream that always eluded him.

Ed Coyne says, "The night was crystal clear—the bay was smooth and glassy. We had a fantastic view of San Francisco, all the sparkling lights in the city, the bridges, Treasure Island. It was absolutely beautiful!" He recalls next morning in the bright sunshine at Rio

At top, bound for Sacramento on "Last voyage" are (left to right) Walt Harvey, Mike Coyne, Barney Gould, and Ed Coyne. At bottom, before arrival, Ed and Walt watch flag raising on the **King.**

Vista seeing people running from house to house, knocking on neighbors' doors and pointing to the *King* passing by. From there, the tugs and their historic tow headed up the Sacramento Deep Water Ship Channel, the same waterway the sternwheeler had traveled in quite different circumstances 15 years before (almost to the day) in the famous "piracy" of 1969.

They stopped momentarily at the Port of Sacramento to await the opening of a lock. From there, they would move onto the Sacramento River and to the *King*'s temporary dock. Within minutes, those on the boat expected to be at the center of a joyous homecoming celebration. The *King* arrived at the Port just after 11 a.m.—12 hours after leaving Oakland. The day was hot and growing hotter, without the semblance of a breeze. But in a short while, it would be time to party.

Tragedy struck, however, as they waited for the lock to open, precluding any idea of a celebration. Without warning, one of the passengers announced, "I'm hot, and I'm going swimming." With that comment, Edward Galardo—despite efforts to stop him—climbed onto the railing of the third deck and dived into the water. Soon it became evident this was more than a harmless antic—Galardo was in trouble. Trying to save him, passengers threw cushions and lifejackets, but he disappeared under the surface. In an instant, Ed and Mike Coyne dove from the boat and made repeated attempts to swim down and locate him in the 20 feet of murky water. But to no avail.

Later, onlookers watched in stunned silence as a scuba diver found Galardo and brought him to the surface—and paramedics tried resuscitation. Coroner's deputies said the 34-year-old man died at 12:50 p.m in a local hospital. Grim-faced passengers from the *King* quietly rolled up their sleeping bags and left in waiting cars and station wagons.

When the postponed reception and dedication were held the following week, more than 50 people gathered on the bow of the *King* and tried to forget the tragic happening of a few days before. While the Red Hot Peppers jazz band played, dignitaries and members of the press enjoyed champagne and hors d'oeuvres in the lengthening afternoon shadows of the California Rice Growers' dock. Coyne, Harvey, and Sun spoke of a promising new future for the vintage boat. To conclude the ceremonies, as photographers hovered, Sacramento county supervisor Sandy Smoley broke a bottle of champagne over the iron capstan on the bow and welcomed the *Delta King* back to Sacramento.

Soon the vessel's owners faced a new reality: While the Rice Growers' dock had provided a welcome haven for a first stop on the way to their hoped-for moor-

I ST. BRIDGE

OLD SACRAMENTO DOCK

TOWER BRIDGE

RIVER LINES DOCK

RICE GROWERS' DOCK

Sacramento River

PIONEER BRIDGE

Lock to Port of Sacramento and Deep Water Channel

At top, tugboat begins towing the King *upriver from Rice Growers' dock. Above left, tug and tow near destination at old River Lines dock by Tower Bridge. Drinking a toast to the Delta King:* Chant Sun, Walter Harvey, and Ed Coyne.

age at Old Sacramento, it didn't offer good access for restoration work. And this location, on the Yolo side of the river just north of the Pioneer Bridge, was remote and not highly visible to the people of Sacramento. Within a short time, the partners had their eye on a better location for the long renovation ahead. In fact, the spot seemed like a natural—the old River Lines dock at Sacramento, where the *King* and *Queen* had tied up after their nightly runs from San Francisco a half century before. True, it wasn't at Old Sacramento. But, situated just below the Tower Bridge, it was right next door.

On September 4, Coyne and Harvey made a successful appeal to the state Lands Commission for permission to use that dock, which had been unused and without buildings since the fire three years before. Then, on the evening of September 25, they received the other important approval they needed: permission from the Sacramento City Council. Along with this came a lease agreement that, although not promising a spot at Old Sacramento, did indicate the city's desire to keep the boat somewhere within the city limits. Why was the city more receptive now toward the project? Assistant City Manager "Doc" Wisham explained: "Our change in attitude comes simply because we've seen some performance" (presumably referring to drydock repairs and resolution of title issues).

Coyne, Harvey, and Sun wasted no time. Early next morning, on September 26, 1984, they had the boat ready for the short trip upriver and to the other side. Having gone aboard the night before and slept on the deck in a sleeping bag, I awakened in time to see the eastern sky turn from pink to tones of gold as the sun rose over the water. The air was still, the river's surface glassy smooth. Off the *King*'s stern, the little tugboat *Prospect Island* warmed up for its morning's task, then chugged to the riverboat's bow. By 8 o'clock, the lines were secured. The tug's engines roared as the tow line pulled taut. We felt the *King* begin to move, ever so gradually at first, and within minutes we were under way on our trip north to the Tower Bridge, less than a mile away.

When we arrived at the old River Lines dock, workers tied the *King* to pilings in the shadows of the wharf it had shared with the *Queen* so many years before. Above us loomed the vintage elevator that had loaded cars of the 1920s and '30s onto the vessels. Immediately upriver sat the Tower Bridge that, during its noisy construction in 1935, had provided a cacophonous lullaby for the crews trying to sleep after their long night's work was complete.

The *Delta King* had come home.

18

Still the King!

Within minutes of the *Delta King*'s arrival at the old River Lines dock, workers installed ramps and scurried about preparing for the restoration. First, they had to remove tons of dried mud and debris from the hold and freight deck, a job that took several weeks. Because of its inaccessibility, the material had to be carried by hand in five-gallon buckets. Workers filled nearly 40 room-size dumpsters.

In spite of skeptics who said it couldn't be done "because the vessel is too far gone," Coyne and Harvey forged ahead with the restoration. They spoke of their plans to return the *Delta King* to its former glory, saying they would strive, as much as possible, for historical accuracy. Although the steam engine and boilers were long gone, much of the rest of the craft would be returned to the elegant feel of the original. The restored *King* would be a stationary-but-floating hotel with bed and breakfast (initially, plans were to lease it out; later they decided to run it themselves). The operation would feature restaurants, bars, night club, theater, shops, banquet and conference rooms. Throughout the boat, staterooms would be enlarged to double the original size and would number 44. The owners told of their search for financing and said they needed to borrow $3 million for the restoration alone, estimated to cost roughly $5 million when completed. Later plans to furnish and operate the facilities would push the total higher.

Soon Coyne and Harvey discovered a basic truth: Not only is riverboat restoration more expensive than restoring a building, but it has the proclivity to drive otherwise sane people crazy. It takes a carpenter with steady nerves to handle it. The curving lines of the decks—fore and aft (sheer), port and starboard (crown)—may be graceful, but they mean that few if any 90-degree angles exist.

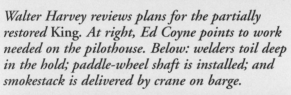

Walter Harvey reviews plans for the partially restored King. At right, Ed Coyne points to work needed on the pilothouse. Below: welders toil deep in the hold; paddle-wheel shaft is installed; and smokestack is delivered by crane on barge.

Almost nothing is square or level. The foremen and project planners had fun with an initiation rite for new crafts-people coming to work. They would ask to see the new person's tools. Then they'd select out the carpenter's square and toss it in the river, saying, "You won't have any use for *that* on this boat."

Walt Harvey took time out from the restoration on December 6, 1984, to marry his long-time friend Joanna Walker on the *Delta King*. Ed Coyne was best man. The ceremony was held in the captain's quarters, under the pilothouse, in what was the first wedding aboard the boat since it was docked at Sacramento in the 1970s. Joanna, with an Environmental Design degree, soon became the designer for the vessel's interiors, handling architectural drafting and giving other architectural assistance. After the wedding, the couple quipped, "We were married *on* the boat—and married *to* the boat."

Good news came early in 1985, when Sacramento's Housing and Redevelopment Agency released a proposed plan for the Old Sacramento waterfront that put the *Delta King* in a top-priority category. Originally, the agency planned to restrict the vintages of vessels docked there to the period from the Gold Rush to 1875. But because no authentic older craft were available, the agency adopted a bird-in-the-hand approach and recommended accepting the paddlewheeler built in the 1920s. While this action didn't guarantee a permanent berth for the *King* at Old Sacramento, the door was opening wider all the time.

In February, the project received a boost from Bruce Pierini, chairman of the Sacramento Museum and History Commission. Writing in the *Sacramento Bee* about the city's waterfront, Pierini said, "The Delta King is a good example of how the river will be put back in River City. The King promises to coax people to the river with its architecture, history, commercial enterprises and that intangible but nonetheless powerful magnet—ambiance."

In marked contrast to the attempts at volunteer restoration of the boat 15 years before at Sacramento, the new effort would require large sums of money. And financing was difficult. It's said that nightclubs, restaurants, hotels, and boats make up the highest category of loan risk. Unfortunately, the proposed plan for the *King* fit all four descriptions. Earlier, the restoration had been approved for financing with tax-free bonds, but the Tax Reform Act of 1985 removed that possibility. The Coynes continued to fund the project to keep it moving. And, in July 1985, when Sun chose not to add to his investment, the Coynes bought out Sun's interest for $300,000. Coyne and Harvey formed a new corporation: Riverboat Delta King, Inc. The Coyne family owned 70 percent, Walter and Joanna Harvey

30 percent.

Negotiations with the city about docking at Old Sacramento slowed, then temporarily stalled, when discussion turned to the design of ramp and wharf improvements. It was reported that, at one point, Coyne and Harvey even talked of taking the boat to San Francisco instead. Finally, the major issues were resolved, and the logjam was broken. The *Delta King* was assured of a berth at the long-hoped-for site.

Over the July Fourth weekend in 1985, the *King* moved to Old Sacramento—but only temporarily—to allow the Sacramento Water Festival to hold boat races south of the Tower Bridge. The *King's* exterior, though not finished, by then had been painted a sparkling white. And, with a shiny black hull, colorful pennants strung from pilothouse to bow, and passengers waving from its decks, the old paddlewheeler made an impressive show in its first appearance north of the bridge.

That day, as a tug towed the *King* to the temporary moorage, I took pictures from a small boat nearby. Without warning, I felt a chill run up my spine: The sight and sound of a vintage train from the California State Railroad Museum had suddenly emerged as a nostalgic backdrop, just behind the slowly-moving riverboat. Chugging along the levee, the steam engine spewed clouds of black smoke, while its whistle wailed a long and mournful note. Sternwheeler and steam train—a momentary scene from the past.

Originally, the partners had hoped to open the *King* for business in 1985, but that proved unrealistic. The restoration's pace was slow due to lack of outside financing. For a time, they aimed at 1986, then 1987. But, early that year, fate intervened. A popping sound and the grinding noise of concrete breaking woke the *King's* night watchman at 7 a.m. on February 7. Undermined by recent flood levels, the old concrete river wall at the dock had collapsed. This opened up a 250-foot-long crack in the concrete slab that had provided the working surface at the wharf. The crack grew larger and deeper until the dock began to buckle and sink into the crevasse created by the collapse. To avoid damage to the boat, Harvey quickly moved it 100 yards downstream.

It was obvious the old River Lines wharf had been completely destroyed and could no longer serve as a work site. Four days after the cave-in, Harvey had the *King* towed north of the bridge to the courtesy boat landing in Old Sacramento. There, the craft could tie up temporarily until crews could complete a special dock one hundred yards farther north at the foot of K Street. That berth had been set aside for the *King* and was scheduled for completion in May, but it was far from finished. Work to complete it was speeded up. In the meantime, all restoration ceased, as the temporary location had neither electrical connections nor convenient access for workers and materials.

Five weeks later, although the new berth had not been finished, Harvey and Coyne decided to take the boat there so that restoration work could resume. The move was scheduled for Saturday morning, when the public could see the event. Plans called for colorful flags flying on the *King*, with dignitaries aboard and a welcoming party on the dock. Dedication ceremonies would follow.

But the day before, forecasts predicted a major rainstorm with high winds. In a last-minute decision, Harvey rescheduled the move for Friday afternoon to beat the storm: He wanted to avoid the frightening possibility of wind overpowering the tugboat. Instead of the planned group of dignitaries, the riverboat now would carry only a small "crew," including Walt Harvey, Mike Coyne, and a few others (I felt privileged to be aboard on this short but significant trip). Not a conventional tug, the boat that towed the *King* on that last hundred yards was a surplus landing craft that had found use as a work boat on the river. It seemed minuscule alongside the *King*. But any doubts about its ability to pull the heavy vessel were soon dispelled. Its diesel engine roared and the riverboat began to move upstream on the *last* "last voyage." Soon the trip ended, and lines were made fast to the pilings of the partially-finished dock.

At 4:15 on the afternoon of March 20, 1987, the *Delta King* had arrived at the long-awaited mooring site in Old Sacramento. In tying up at its own dock, the venerable California steamer had concluded forty years of searching for a home and ended up where the famous *Chrysopolis* and *Yosemite* regularly docked more than a hundred years before.

Saturday morning dawned with occasional gusty winds, beautiful clouds, spells of sunshine, and no rain—a dramatic setting for the dedication party. Dignitaries, reporters, and photographers gathered on the bow. City Councilman David Shore and Carl Amundson of the Sacramento Housing and Redevelopment Commission each said a few words. Reporters interviewed Walt and Joanna Harvey, and the champagne flowed. To climax the celebration, Joanna broke a bottle of champagne on the boat's capstan.

By July, the developers had given up hope for a late 1987 opening. According to Harvey, the *King* could not open as a floating hotel that year, because collapse of the river wall had caused suspension of the restoration for four months. Clearly, the lack of outside financing was another factor in the delay. But whatever the reason, the *Delta King*'s fortunes changed for the better in early 1988. After a long search, the owners came up with a loan of $4 million from Home Federal Savings of San Diego. Until then, the Coynes had supplied all funds for the restoration. With the new financing in place, it was full speed ahead. Work on the boat started in earnest now, with Mike Coyne as project manager, Patrick Reilley as project administrator, and Coy Wallace as construction foreman. Coyne and Harvey continued their close involvement with day-to-day details. Electricians, plumbers, carpenters, and other crafts-people came aboard in growing numbers. The partners predicted a December 1988 opening.

For many of its derelict years, the *King* had been an anomaly—a steamboat without a smokestack, a sternwheeler without a paddle wheel. In May a massive steel paddle-wheel shaft, much like the original, came by barge and was installed in the old bearing supports on the fantail. Over the next few months, wooden arms and bucket planks were added until the boat proudly exhibited a bright red paddle wheel (purposely without a cover so people could see the wheel). In July, the barge returned to bring a shiny, new, black smokestack and install it, by means of a crane, high atop the boat behind the pilothouse. Later, eight lifeboat replicas completed the look—three on each side of the Observation Deck and two on the bow house.

Probably the most difficult part of the entire project was restoration of the vessel with historical accuracy, while adhering to modern standards and safety codes. The partners tried to preserve as much of the original historic fabric of the boat as possible—disassembling wood paneling, stripping and refinishing it, then reinstalling it over new electrical, heating, air conditioning, and plumbing lines. By any measure, it was a painstaking task.

While Coyne and Harvey didn't have the *King* ready that winter, at the beginning of 1989 they announced a grand opening of the hotel for May 20—the 62nd anniversary of the dedication of the *Delta King* and *Delta Queen* at Stockton in 1927. And they planned a low-profile "soft opening" to take place a few weeks before, to work out bugs in the operation and to start generating needed revenue. Little did they realize how extremely tight the schedule would turn out to be.

The pace of the restoration accelerated. Workers swarmed aboard, at times almost to the point of tripping over one another. 110 people were on payroll with another 30 coming aboard as subcontractors. By March of 1989, much had been accomplished. Then fate intervened again. Two events took place—one minor and one major—that made the homestretch even more difficult.

On March 20, the paddle-wheel shaft broke at the port side connection, leaving the giant paddle wheel tilted at an awkward 15-degree angle. Fixing it would take time and money. Just two days later, a nightmare was narrowly averted when those aboard were jolted by the unmistakable smell of smoke and a shout of "Fire!" A blaze had broken out in a third deck stateroom. It had been started by a plumber's acetylene torch earlier in the day and had smoldered in the wall until it suddenly flared up. Before it was extinguished, the blaze burned out two staterooms and caused smoke and water damage in four others. A fire at any time would have been bad news—but with rooms nearly finished and fully booked for opening weekend just weeks away, it was doubly hard.

In the final month before the soft opening in April, there seemed to be more jobs than would be humanly possible to finish. As pressure mounted, the work tempo reached white-hot intensity. Many of the crew worked overtime, some even nights and weekends. Faces were taut, tempers short.

Missing the deadline would mean bad publicity and loss of revenue on staterooms already reserved for opening weekend. What's more, a big wedding and reception scheduled for that weekend couldn't be canceled. Adding extra pressure, the hotel staff was already hired, trained, on payroll, and waiting to work. Yet no one knew if the boat could be finished in time. Owners pushed the foreman; the foreman pushed the crafts-people. Jobs were done and redone. Workers were taken from one job to another and back again. There appeared to be too many bosses. Some workers complained that their instructions were verbal and given to them day by day—that they hadn't seen plans on paper for months. Perhaps this could be considered a throwback to the last century when, according to folklore, some riverboat builders designed their craft using only a sharp stick in the river sand.

On the morning of the soft opening, April 28, it seemed as if the combined efforts of owners, foreman, and work crew still wouldn't be enough. Many of the crafts-people and most of management had been up all night, and the day was a mad scramble. At midday, furniture for the staterooms and restaurants was still being uncrated and assembled on the dock. Carpenters and plumbers bumped into hotel workers as they each hustled at their jobs. Kitchen help rushed supplies aboard, while painters touched up woodwork in the dining room. Chaos reigned. At 4:30 p.m., the city building inspector made his final inspection, while owners and office staff frantically hung pictures in the dining room and lobby. The first hotel guests were due at 5.

Grand opening, May 20, 1989: One thousand colorful balloons are released after the dedication ceremonies. During the evening celebration, a Roaring Twenties flapper descends the grand staircase, while fireworks explode over the restored paddlewheeler. Below, here's how the Delta King *looked that day from the river.*

Young waiters and waitresses, sharply decked out in black and white, received their last-minute instructions. As I observed their anxious-but-eager anticipation, I felt as if I were watching performers backstage just before curtain on opening night. In fact, the metaphor of live theater applied to the whole boat that afternoon. There was uncertainty up until the last second. But when the "curtain went up," everything happened much as it should.

The first guest aboard the *Delta King*, Carol Neyens of Yuba City, California, was welcomed aboard by the hotel manager and interviewed by a TV reporter. Crisply-dressed bellboys picked up luggage by the hotel desk, where fish had swum seven years before. Guests chatted in the lobby and eventually went sightseeing around the vessel or retired to their rooms. Some stopped for a drink at the Delta Lounge, while others went directly to the beautifully restored dining room. Fine wood paneling and shiny brass hardware recalled the boat's earlier years. Colorful flower arrangements were everywhere. Many an "ooh" and "aah" were heard throughout the evening.

During the first three weeks of May, work continued at a frenetic pace on the remaining unfinished areas, including the Delta King Theatre and Captain's Quarters (the pilothouse and adjoining rooms). Again the schedule was tight right up to the last minute. When they finished the restoration, Coyne and Harvey found the final price tag had risen to $10.5 million—more than they had ever imagined at the beginning. But they had a beauty on their hands.

May 20, 1989, dawned clear and warm for the grand opening. An occasion many of us had dreamed about for years, it seemed a perfect day to celebrate the return of the sternwheeler to its former elegance. Red, white, and blue bunting hung from railings of the three passenger decks and from the pilothouse. In the early afternoon, as bands played on the dock, attention turned to the river. Sacramento's Sea Ray Boat Club, with balloons and pennants adorning its members' craft, presented a colorful boat parade alongside the *King*.

Just before 2 p.m., the official rechristening ceremonies began. To honor the Scotch origin of the *King's* steel hull, a lone bagpiper stood on the top deck at the bow and played "Amazing Grace." Next came the benediction by Father Richard Dwyer, whose family had been one of three owners of the River Lines in the 1930s. Then it was time to break the traditional bottle over the *King's* bow, with champagne sent courtesy of The Delta Queen Steamboat Co. of New Orleans. As Joanna Harvey, Jeanne Coyne, and a trio of Coyne wives—Jane, Leanne, and Terry—smashed the champagne bottle, one thousand red, white, and blue balloons were released from the top deck. The crowd cheered; the balloons soared; confetti and streamers flew in all directions.

Simultaneously at the stern, a U.S. Navy honor guard raised the American flag, while veterans who had served on the *King* and *Queen* almost half a century before, saluted. A crescendo of sound came next. Bands played while the sternwheeler was given a 21-gun salute; a steam engine blew its whistle; a cannon was fired; boats on the river sounded their whistles and horns. It was a tribute befitting the return of royalty.

"Roaring Twenties Night on the River," arranged as a benefit for the Sacramento Opera Association on the *Delta King,* offered a gala extension of the daytime festivities. Party guests at the sold-out event wore 1920s attire. Women became flappers for the evening, strutting down the grand staircase wearing colorful beads, headbands, feather boas, and short dresses with fringes. Men played their roles as dashing Twenties heroes in Great Gatsby outfits or as gun-toting gangsters in double-breasted pinstriped suits. Following dinner aboard, guests moved to the outer decks in the gathering darkness to witness a return visit of the boat club with its Parade of Lights, a sparkling procession of small craft with lights reflecting in the river. When it was pitch-dark, fireworks exploded over the Tower Bridge, providing a spectacular finale to the outdoor entertainment.

But the evening was yet young for those aboard. Guests could enjoy a musical in the Delta King Theatre or dance the night away in the Paddlewheel Saloon. Or they could try their luck in the Mark Twain Salon, where the Casino Monte Carlo offered "gaming tables" and where an hors d'oeuvres table displayed a stately ice sculpture of the *Delta King*.

Indeed, the old paddlewheeler had come a long way.

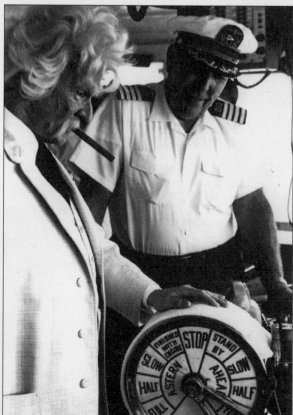

The Delta Queen *departs on another trip. Below, a southern farewell on the lower Mississippi. Left, Capt. Ernest Wagner receives "help" from an old river hand.*

19

A Queen's Life in Peril

On the day of the big celebration at Sacramento for the *Delta King,* May 20, 1989, the vessel's famous twin, the *Delta Queen,* steamed on the lower Mississippi headed for New Orleans. The *Queen* tied up for a few hours at White Castle, Louisiana, to let her passengers tour Nottoway Plantation, a National Landmark touted as the largest plantation in the South. She then headed downriver on her last leg of a 12-night cruise from Cincinnati. Next morning, passengers disembarked at New Orleans.

At the end of the following month, the *Delta Queen* passed another milestone in her history: 41 years as an overnight passenger steamboat on waters of the Mississippi River system. It was on June 30, 1948, that the *Queen,* with Tom Greene as captain and Jesse P. Hughes as pilot, had left Cincinnati on her inaugural passenger cruise down the Ohio. Also aboard was Mary B. Greene, Tom's mother and one of the rare women steamboat captains in the country.

In the decades of service after leaving California, the *Queen* didn't suffer the kind of physical abuse experienced by the *King.* Yet the *Queen*'s life turned out to be anything but easy. She may have seemed the pampered twin in terms of care and maintenance, but she and her owners encountered their share of drama, suspense, and hard knocks. According to Tom Greene's wife Letha in her book *Long Live the Delta Queen,* the first cruise under the Greene Line banner and many of the following trips ran into trouble. The tiller line—a steel-wire cable that connected the pilot wheel to the rudders and steered the boat—broke frequently and caused many a fright.

Robert Lodder, a passenger on the *Queen* when she broke her tiller line above

Brochure advertises inaugural passenger cruise of Delta Queen *from Cincinnati. After a postponement, trip began June 30, 1948.*

the Greenville Bridge on the Mississippi, recalls the hair-raising experience: "The river was flowing high and fast. Without the ability to steer, the only way left to maneuver the boat was by running the paddle wheel forward or astern. This the crew managed to do, as the *Queen* sped under the bridge—sideways." A hydraulic system later solved that problem. The oil burners under the boilers also caused concern; they produced excessive smoke until the company installed new ones. "In fact," Mrs. Greene says, "the first few years were very nearly a continuous shakedown until we finally got things in fine shape—after we really got acquainted with the *Queen*."

Two deaths in the family during the first two years of operation caused sadness and hardship. Capt. Tom's mother had come to live on the *Queen* but died in 1949, just a year after the inaugural voyage. The next year, Tom Greene passed away at age 46, leaving his wife with all the burdens of operating the vessel. As a people-oriented person, Tom had provided the lubrication that kept things running smoothly. He was greeter and musician, occasional cook or steward, mate or pilot, but always captain and general manager. Big shoes for Letha to fill. She describes the challenge: "The *Delta Queen* presented the problems of a ship, a restaurant, a night club, a motel, and government rules and regulations done up in a neat wrapping of wind, fog and rain, tied with a fancy wide bow of fun, romance, pleasure and restful vacations for thousands of river travelers."

Greene Line Steamers carried a heavy burden of debt from its original purchase of the *Queen* and her ocean voyage from California, but especially from the expensive repairs and remodeling completed in 1948 at the Dravo shipyard in Pittsburgh. The company found itself vulnerable to unexpected costs or sudden loss of passenger revenue. So the future looked grim in 1954, when the steamboat "ran through herself" on the Mississippi River near Rock Island, Illinois. A piston rod had broken in the high-pressure cylinder of the steam engine, and a damaged piston stuck fast in the cylinder. The crippled boat got to shore but was stranded with 190 passengers aboard. If the engine couldn't be repaired within a few days, Greene Line would be forced to cancel a three-week New Orleans trip. And this might put an end to the company—finances were that tight. Letha Greene visualized "going out of business with the bank mortgage still unpaid."

Fortunately, Andy Lodder, an officer of the company, recalled that the *Delta King*'s machinery had been removed before that vessel went to Canada. Last anyone had heard, Fulton's Shipyard had kept the parts, identical to the *Queen*'s, stored at its facility in California. A quick phone call disclosed that luck was with the *Queen:* Fulton's had the needed parts. Within hours, the *King*'s piston and rod were loaded onto a Flying Tiger cargo plane that arrived at the Quad City airport next morning. Mechanics and the boat's engineers made repairs in time to finish the trip and get the *Queen* off to New Orleans on schedule. Ironically, the *Delta King,* though landlocked in British Columbia with myriad problems of its own, had come to the rescue.

Years later the *King* came to the rescue again, when the *Queen* broke her steel paddle-wheel shaft on the Ohio River below Louisville in 1980. Because Greene Line had obtained the rest of the *King*'s parts from Fulton's after the Rock Island incident, the company had a replacement shaft available. So repairs could start immediately. During the time it took to change the shaft and rebuild the wood portion of the wheel, the *Queen* continued her regularly-scheduled cruises—minus her paddle wheel but with the assistance of a towboat alongside. Thus today's *Delta Queen* cruises with the original shaft from the *Delta King.*

With the near disaster at Rock Island in 1954, the firm had escaped financial ruin. But the specter of bankruptcy always lurked in the shadows. Letha Greene says they never failed to make interest payments on their loan, but getting the principal paid off proved tediously slow. She describes the years following:

Finances were growing worse and worse. How much longer we could continue in the struggle to keep the boat going was questionable. January first of each year found us scrounging around to pay bills, keep our feet dry from flood waters, and get out on the first trips of the season—to New Orleans and Mardi Gras . . .

The high cost of drydocking for the 1957-58 layover nearly finished the Greene Line. With big bills to pay and no money to advertise the coming season, a dismal future loomed ahead. Letha Greene decided to quit. She began to receive offers for the boat, including one for $5,000 from a man who wanted to moor the *Queen* as a restaurant in Cincinnati. But then help came from an unexpected source. A California family had enjoyed a trip on the steamboat in 1957; now the father, Richard Simonton, sent his check to reserve a cruise for the coming season. Mrs. Greene returned his check, explaining that the company had ceased operation. Simonton, a major player in the fields of radio, television, and Muzak, called her and suggested a plan to save the *Delta Queen*. He invited her to his home in North Hollywood to discuss details. She flew west.

Within a few days, they struck a deal. According to Bern Keating's *The Legend of the Delta Queen,* Simonton assumed $70,000 of outstanding debt and loaned the company $25,000 for operating capital. With another $25,000, he acquired enough stock to become majority stockholder. Letha Greene remained as president, while E. Jay Quinby, a friend of Simonton's from New Jersey, became chairman of the board with the duty of publicizing the boat.

Simonton and Quinby had a hidden agenda for gaining control of the *Queen*. As pipe-organ enthusiasts, they envisioned the boat as a perfect place for a calliope. One problem, though—they didn't own a calliope, and few were available. But through tenacious detective work, Quinby ran down an old one. He traced its path from a sunken showboat to a circus and then to a collector who didn't want to sell. But dogged persistence paid off. Quinby bought the calliope and installed it at the stern of the *Queen*'s Sun Deck with a row of colored lights under the steam whistles. After dark, the lights tinted the plumes of steam in delightful colors of the rainbow. Quinby was also the one who invented an electronic keyboard for the calliope. Passengers, who have since played the *Queen*'s calliope, can be grateful for this innovation that prevented live steam from burning their fingers.

Performing his job as publicist with flair and flamboyance, Quinby enjoyed himself immensely. Dressed in Prince Albert coat and top hat, carrying a silver-headed cane, he went ahead of the *Queen* as advance man, distributing vintage-style handbills and giving interviews. On board the boat, he sat at the calliope pumping out old favorites, the shrill notes echoing for miles up and down the river. Passenger bookings improved dramatically. In 1960, Greene Line paid off its mortgage, and by 1962 it had settled all its other debts as well.

That year the company hired Betty Blake, a public relations expert who proved to be a dynamo in promoting the *Queen*. Keating says, "Betty touched off a public relations blitz the length and breadth of the Mississippi River basin. She shuttled between 20 major cities talking to travel agents, bewitching travel editors, enchanting talk-show hosts. She discovered, to her delight, that most folk along the rivers were as fascinated by the old boats as she was." In 1963, Betty Blake revived the custom of steamboat racing, pitting the *Delta Queen* against the *Belle of Louisville*. With a touch of genius, she planned the race at Louisville during Kentucky Derby week. An outstanding success, the race, which was covered nationally by all three TV networks, became an annual tradition that continues to this day. In later years, Blake arranged races between the *Queen* and three other steamboats: the *Natchez,* the *Julia Belle Swain,* and the *Mississippi Queen*.

Bad news shattered the Greene Line's newfound peace and prosperity in 1966. Word came that Congress was about to pass a law that would be disastrous to the *Queen*'s future. Because of her wooden superstructure, the legislation would end her passenger cruises. Called the Safety of Life at Sea Law, it would outlaw wooden superstructures on vessels carrying 50 or more overnight passengers. Intending to reduce the risk of a dangerous fire at sea, the legislation targeted ocean-going passenger ships. But its broad language also included boats cruising on rivers—even the *Delta Queen* with sprinklers and other safety equipment—vessels never far from shore and not subject to the hazards of saltwater travel.

Letha Greene called Dick Simonton for help. He, in turn, summoned Jay Quinby and the general manager of his California business, William Muster. The three of them flew to Washington, D.C., to argue against applying the law to the *Queen*. Bill Muster stayed up all night writing a speech for Quinby to deliver at the hearing the next day. Muster's speech and Quinby's style charmed the senators. But the pair failed to achieve the desired result—an exemption from the law for the *Queen*. Instead, the senators compromised and gave all vessels, foreign and domestic, an extension for two years. After that, all would have to comply. A reprieve for the *Queen*—but only a short one.

Next, a supposedly routine Coast Guard inspection of the steamboat in late 1966 turned out anything but routine and nearly finished the *Queen*'s career. Coast Guard rules called for replacement of any hull plate that has lost more than 25 percent of its original thickness. Inspectors found plate after plate that would have to be replaced, signifying an immense and costly repair job. Then—after an agonizing delay—the inspectors discovered they had used an incorrect figure as their original-thickness guide (the boat had been built with three-eighth-inch hull plates, not half-inch as they had assumed). Using the correct figure, they passed the vessel with only a few required changes.

So the *Delta Queen* had survived another crisis. But by then it was time to consider her extension to operate, which was expiring soon. Betty Blake and Bill Muster went to Washington and lobbied. With the help of Representative Leonor Sullivan of Missouri and Senator E.L. Bartlett of Alaska, bills were introduced, passed by Congress, and signed by President Lyndon Johnson extending the boat's life again. But this extension covered only until November 2, 1970, a date that would take on an air of foreboding as it approached.

Because of the uncertainty of getting continued extensions to operate the overnight vessel, Muster pushed for an all-steel replacement for the *Queen*. But due to the high cost of building a new steamboat, he had to scout the country for investment capital. Finally, G.F. Steedman Hinckley of Overseas National Airways came forward in 1969; after negotiations, his company bought Greene Line. He proceeded with plans to build the new paddlewheeler.

Letha Greene stepped down as president, and Bill Muster took over. As she left the firm, she noted the irony that the older, slower mode of travel had become a subsidiary of the fastest. She said others would now carry on the tradition and added: "Many will yet be able to enjoy the pleasures of a river cruise and experience the thrill of a balmy moonlight night on peaceful river waters, the hypnotic swish of the paddle wheel, and the beauty of color-splashed sunsets, when the air is heavy with silence." Thus ended the Greene family's connection to the company that Tom Greene's father, Capt. Gordon C. Greene, had founded in 1890 when he had saved enough money to buy his first boat.

In the months before the *Queen*'s extension ran out in November 1970, it appeared she finally would be forced into retirement. One particular congressman, Representative Edward Garmatz of Maryland, adamantly opposed further extensions. As powerful chairman of the House Merchant Marine and Fisheries Committee, Garmatz made sure no such bills could get to the House floor. He steadfastly said, "No more extensions!" And no amount of argument that the *Queen* was fireproofed and safe—or that an extension should be granted until a new boat could be built—would convince him.

But Betty Blake and Bill Muster didn't give up. By June of 1970, they got the *Queen* listed on the National Register of Historic Places (years later she was also listed as a National Historic Landmark). They put on a whirlwind campaign to convince the country that the boat was a priceless gem that should be preserved.

They talked to the Society of American Travel Writers and pointed out that the Safety of Life at Sea Law was meant for ocean-going ships—that the *Delta Queen* never traveled out of sight of land. They showed that for 60 years riverboats had enjoyed a perfect safety record—not a single death of a passenger by fire. Capt. Clarke "Doc" Hawley, alternate master of the *Queen,* said the craft always cruised within four minutes of land and could be disembarking her passengers faster than ships at sea could get theirs into lifeboats.

Blake brought Vic Tooker, the *Queen*'s riverboat musician extraordinaire, with her to Washington where he played impromptu banjo concerts at the capital's restaurants. She lined up 13 governors and dozens of congressmen behind her crusade and got thousands of names on "Save the Queen" petitions. Letters poured in to representatives, senators, and the President—according to one estimate, more than a quarter million. Twenty-five separate bills were introduced to save the *Queen*, most of them granting her a permanent exemption. But they all ran up against a stone wall in committee chairman Garmatz. No matter how many congressmen, constituents, and newspaper editorials supported the historic steamboat, he was unmoved.

Sadly but proudly, as the November 2, 1970, deadline approached, Blake and Muster planned a "Farewell Forever" trip. On October 12, the *Queen* left Cincinnati for St. Paul. Two days later, Johnny Cash paid a tribute to the beloved steamboat on ABC Television, when he sang a song ending with the words: "So long, Delta Queen."

On October 21, with Capt. Ernest Wagner in command, the venerable old paddlewheeler left St. Paul and began her final cruise down the Mississippi River to New Orleans. Don Deming, cruise director on the trip, comforted grieving *Delta Queen* fans as best he could. He recalls, "The steamboat buffs were feeling a great loss; they talked of 'a steamboat that's dying.' Tearfully, they pondered the *Queen*'s future: Where would she go? Would she be drydocked? Would she be used as a museum or as a park? By day, they took pictures of each other for posterity in every conceivable place on the boat. In the evening, they drank champagne and listened to Vic Tooker's songs, which were real tear jerkers."

Working ahead of the boat along the river, Blake and Muster managed to bring out unprecedented crowds to meet the *Queen* at every stop. Deming says that, typically, the mayor of the town and the high school band would appear— children would sing "Swanee River" and people would hold up signs such as "God Bless the Queen." Writing about the trip, Bern Keating says:

Flourish for a Queen

An era, of sorts, ended yesterday when the paddlewheeler Delta Queen churned into New to keep the imposing wooden vessel from continuing her moonlight cruises. As the or

DELTA QUEEN   YOU'RE TOO

Sailing to the Unknown

The Delta Queen, ... the very few surv... s of the once-mig... eet of Mis ... sternwheel passenger ... essels, left Cincinnati ... ship's lasts ...

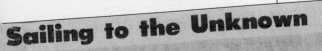

Tom Horton

...o Save a Regal Lady

We are aware of your efforts and ...astic response toward saving the ...of the Ki... er ship, the Delta ... in a fe... ...rame... ...ng e...

...s a... ...or... of...

the importance of riverboats to California history, as well as reminders of the Mississippi's past. The same men who sailed around the horn in wooden ships took wooden riverboats from San Francisco to Sacramento in 1849. You know what happened after that.

Frankly, Mr. President, I get the impression that ...re a few things which you like about Ameri... ...our understudy — the name es... ...to see that the good gets ...mov...

Delta Queen's Death Sentence Mourned by Puzzled Captain

DELTA QUEEN

The Delta Queen Sails Monday Into The Pages Of History

Sad days for the Delta Queen *as papers across the country report on "Farewell Forever" voyage. At left, Vic Tooker performs on landing stage. Bottom left, the* Queen *stops at Burlington, Iowa. Below, congressmen display "Save the Queen" petitions.*

Run Aground on Sea Law

By David Hunter

WHAT'S WRONG with a wooden riverboat? Supporters of the steamboat Delta Queen say the 1966 Safety at Sea Law is a good one but should not be applied to America's last steamboat because it never goes to sea.

What is unsafe at sea, they contend, is not necessarily unsafe on the river.

The 1966 law was enacted after the Yarmouth Castle fire between Miami and the Bahamas in 1964, a disaster that claimed 80 lives. It effectively forced American safety standards on ships at sea, regardless of flag, by denying unsafe junkers access to United States ports.

• • •

The Delta Queen, which uses inland ports, was caught by a provision requiring vessels built before 1936 to be made of incombustible materials. The Queen was built in 1926 and has a wood superstructure atop a steel hull.

Because of the boat's his-...e and social value as ...operating...

These Delta Que... ...Congress to exempt the last of ...n the Safety at Sea Law. If atte... ...ve to go out

3,000 Say Farewell to Delta Queen

Special Correspondence
...Crosse, Wis. — An esti-
...persons bade fare-
...e Delta Queen on
...ably was its last vis-
...esday afternoon.
...ived about 5:30 a.m.
...own river, docked at
...de Park and then left
...12:45 p.m. heading for
...ul while a circus calliope
...hore played "Auld Lang
...

...he 200 passenger excursion
...t that has been operating
... 45 years, 24 of them on the
...ississippi River, has fallen
...ictim to federal safety laws.
The laws now require a steel
...superstructure on all boats
...

Pictures on Page 4, Part 2

...carrying more than 50 passen...
...The Delta Queen is most...

Queen makes her last trip

Delta Queen, last paddlewheeler to carry overnight passengers on the Mississippi River and its
tributaries, arrives in St. Paul on her final voyage on the Mississippi. About 190 passengers
from the U.S. and Canada were aboard from Cin-

cinnati. The Queen, built in 1926, has been traveling mostly on the Mississippi and the Ohio
since 1948 and has been designated as a historic
place by the U.S. Department of the Interior. She
is only vessel thus designated.

UPI TELEPHOTO

Mobs poured out to greet the boat. Towns with a thousand people lined up 5,000 spectators to cheer the *Queen* . . . From Baton Rouge downstream, seagoing vessels blew whistles in salute . . . Towboats, excursion vessels, pleasure boats ran alongside, their crews and passengers cheering the gallant old steamboat.

Approaching the final stop at New Orleans, Tooker blasted out a greeting on the calliope. Fireboats saluted the steamboat with plumes of water. On the dock, the city's jazz greats had gathered, including the famed Olympia Brass Band, to give the *Delta Queen* a jazz funeral.

Once he had tied up, Capt. Wagner wrote in his log, "November 2, 1970: *Delta Queen* docked in high winds at the Bienville Street Dock, French Quarter." And he added the valedictory words . . ."End of Log."

Tooker played taps on his trumpet, passengers milled around saying tearful goodbyes, and crew members began the sad work of packing their belongings. The *Delta Queen* had come to the end of the line. Or so it seemed.

But several weeks later, it appeared a miracle was about to happen. The U.S. Senate had passed and sent to the House a little-noticed private bill to reimburse a former postal employee. Tacked onto that legislation was an amendment granting the *Queen* another extension. This bill didn't have to go past the unmovable Garmatz. Rather, it would go through the House Judiciary Committee, which included Congressman William McCulloch of Ohio, a prime *Delta Queen* supporter, and Emanuel Celler of New York, chairman of the committee. In defense of the boat, Celler remarked, "Life without romance is listless and lacks luster."

Garmatz raged. He wrote a letter to his colleagues blasting the maneuver to bypass his committee, and he lobbied furiously to kill the amendment. Just before

the vote, McCulloch had a heart attack, which seemed to end the hope for passage. But Leonor Sullivan and other representatives, including Tom Railsback of Illinois and Bob Mathias of California, came to the rescue and rallied the House. The bill—with the amendment to give the *Queen* an extension to 1973—passed 295 to 73. President Nixon signed the bill on December 31, 1970.

The *Delta Queen* was saved. Again. What a celebration her fans would have for her when she returned to Cincinnati in the spring!

Betty Blake and Capt. Ernest Wagner celebrate the victory.

20

The Incomparable Delta Queen

With a new lease on life, the *Delta Queen* went into drydock for her winter lay-over. She found this interlude more than a routine trip to the beauty parlor. The Greene Line ordered installation of new safety devices, replacement of worn hull plates, and application of fire-retardant paints pioneered by NASA. When maintenance and repairs were complete, the *Queen* headed north from New Orleans to make a much-heralded return to the Ohio.

Arriving at her home port of Cincinnati on April 29, 1971, the historic stern-wheeler was greeted by a joyous celebration. Bands played and people cheered as small pleasure boats escorted the *Queen* to the dock. Traffic on the waterfront stood still, as drivers paused to see her victorious homecoming. Television presented special programs, while newspapers ran feature stories and jubilant editorials. All in all, a celebration befitting a queen.

In September of that year, she won a contract to carry U.S. mail and received her own official postmark: "Delta Queen Steamboat Mail." A postcard or letter dropped into the Cabin Deck mailbox received that unique postmark, making the piece a collector's item for friends and family.

1972 turned out to be a year of discovery for the *Delta Queen*. She plied two rivers for the first time: the Arkansas and the Illinois. In February, her cruise to Little Rock on the Arkansas River was a new one, but it must have seemed like old home week for those aboard. Capt. Fred Way, whom Tom Greene had put in charge of getting the boat from California to the Mississippi in 1947, rode aboard. So did former owner Dick Simonton and calliope virtuoso E. Jay Quinby. Captains C.W. Stoll and Charlie Brasher, both from the *Belle of Louisville* and long

associated with Greene Line, took the trip. Near the end of the cruise, G.F. Steedman Hinckley of Overseas National Airways (parent company of Greene Line), joined Betty Blake, Bill Muster, and Capt. Ernest Wagner on board. In July of that year, the steamboat made history again when she entered the mouth of the Illinois River and steamed up to Peoria. Not only was it the first time the *Queen* had traveled that river, but it was the first time any overnight passenger vessel had plied those waters since the *Golden Eagle* went to Starved Rock Park in the 1940s.

Trips on rivers other than the Mississippi and the Ohio had long been offered by the Greene Line. The *Queen* regularly cruised to Chattanooga via the Tennessee River and Kentucky Lake, where passengers experienced the boat rising 58 feet in a lock. And at Wilson Lock (on the Tennessee at Florence, Alabama) they were treated to a 93-foot lift. Trips also went onto the Cumberland River and Lake Barkley to get to Nashville, Tennessee.

In October of 1972, I had the good fortune to ride the *Delta Queen* downriver on the Mississippi from Muscatine, Iowa, to St. Louis, Missouri, and to witness the riverbank foliage beginning to turn shades of crimson and gold. One evening about 11 o'clock, I was surprised and impressed to see a turnout of small-town citizens, including a father with a young boy on his shoulders, waving and watching as our famous steamboat traveled through a lock at that late hour.

Next day, October 13, we docked at Hannibal, Missouri, the boyhood home of Mark Twain. We arrived in time to join the excitement of the first-day issue of

a commemorative postage stamp. The new stamp depicted Tom Sawyer whitewashing the well-known fence in a scene inspired by a Norman Rockwell painting. In my sightseeing jaunt about town, I gained the dubious distinction of being escorted out of the Mark Twain Museum by the Secret Service to make way for Tricia Nixon Cox, who had come to speak at the day's ceremonies.

The Delta Queen, *by night or by day, an impressive piece of history*

After that cruise, I read Letha Greene's description of typical pilothouse dialogue and was reminded of what I had overheard—conversations between the *Queen*'s pilot and the off-duty pilot, talk between pilot and captain. Mrs. Greene's example: "Say, you think it'll fog tonight, Cap?" Reply: "No, there's a little wind starting up, and that lightning down there on the horizon looks like we might have a little rough weather here before long." That exchange, though not repeating word-for-word what I had heard, was close enough to sound surprisingly famil-iar. Discussions of weather, visibility, and river level; talk of other boats and their crews; the effortless dialogue possessed a timeless quality. As I had listened to those verbal exchanges, I thought to myself: "Aren't these the same conversations heard in steamboat pilothouses in Mark Twain's day?"

On that trip I had the privilege of meeting Capt. Ernest Wagner, master of the *Delta Queen,* in his 11th year on the vessel (in 2004 he was inducted into the National Rivers Hall of Fame). One night, as he came up to the pilothouse, I became fully aware of what a physically big man he was—the hard way. He arrived

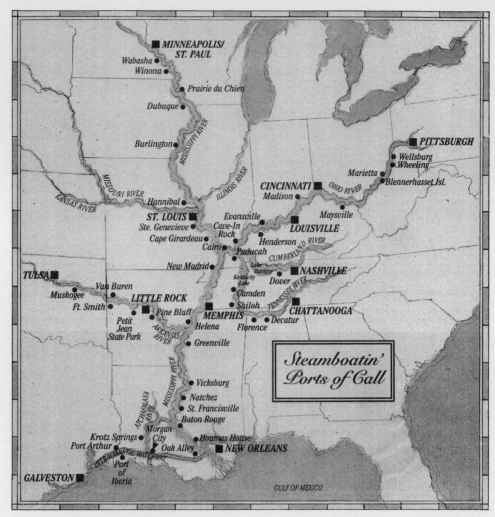

The **Delta Queen** *has cruised most of the above waterways in recent years.*

at the top of the stairs and paused for a few seconds. Then, before his eyes became adjusted to the almost-total darkness, Capt. Wagner sat down, all 6-foot-4, 250 pounds of him, on what's known as the "lazy bench." Unfortunately, he chose the exact spot where I was sitting. Fortunately, there were no casualties.

In 1973, Greene Line Steamers, wanting a more colorful image for the company and recognizing that the Greenes were no longer involved, changed its name to The Delta Queen Steamboat Co. The new name would also help to get instant recognition in the firm's periodic lobbying for an extension. The existing one expired that year, so it was time to try again. But now the challenge had eased. The *Queen*'s arch foe, Congressman Edward Garmatz, no longer headed the House Merchant Marine and Fisheries Committee—he had lost the last election. Muster and Blake went to Washington and lobbied for a permanent exemption, explaining that the company had spent nearly $5 million in repairs and improvements and that the *Queen* carried the very latest in safety equipment. But it was not to be—they had to settle for a five-year extension.

Bill Muster resigned as president in 1974 and returned to California. Steedman Hinckley took over. But financial strains had begun to burden Overseas National Airways, a company hit from several directions at once—the cost of improvements on the *Queen;* expenses, including huge overruns, in building the new not-yet-finished steamboat; and, finally, two charter plane crashes affecting the parent company. It was against that background that ONA sold The Delta Queen Steamboat Co. to the Coca-Cola Bottling Company of New York, and Betty Blake became president.

In 1976, the *Delta Queen* received another extension, this one covering five years from 1978 to 1983. She also took a unique cruise—a trip up the St. Croix to Hudson, Minnesota, her first on that river. But the big news in 1976 was the inaugural service of the company's new all-steel vessel, the *Mississippi Queen*—the first overnight paddle-wheel steamboat built in the United States since the *King* and *Queen* were born in California a half century before. President Gerald Ford called the launching "a tribute to the heritage of America's rivers." The glistening modern craft, built by Jeffboat of Jeffersonville, Indiana, began her maiden voyage on July 27 with Capt. Wagner in command. Decked out in red, white, and blue bunting, the new *Queen* pulled slowly away from Cincinnati's public landing and headed for New Orleans. *Delta Queen* fans asked for and received assurance that the new vessel was *not* a replacement for the older boat but that *both* would be used. They were told the vintage steamer would now assume the role of company flagship.

If there had been a choice, it's likely company management would have preferred to forget all about the great expense of building the new vessel, the cost overruns, and the resulting debt. In 1967 the estimated cost came to $12 million, by 1970 $24 million. The final tab: $27 million. Longer than a football field at 385 feet, with seven decks and capacity for 416 passengers, she dwarfed the *Delta Queen* (285 feet, four decks, 176 passengers). The *Mississippi Queen* was billed as "the largest steamboat the world has ever known."

The new sternwheeler offered all the amenities of an ocean cruise ship: a whirlpool spa, sauna, exercise gym, beauty shop, wide-screen movie theater, passenger elevators, room-to-room telephones, two-deck dining room, and grand saloon. But, in spite of the luxury appointments, the inaugural cruise was not

without trauma. The boat developed boiler trouble the first night out of Cincinnati and broke down completely on the return trip from New Orleans. In a light vein, *Time Magazine* reported on this first voyage of the craft owned by the Coca-Cola Bottling Company: "The sauna was closed, and elevators didn't always work. At the premier playing of the steam calliope, a three-foot column of hot vapor shot from a nearby sink." The article concluded, "Owners notwithstanding, the Coke machines were not working."

Those who traveled on the *Delta Queen* when Capt. Wagner was her master may recall the little Volkswagen "bug" he kept near the bow for running errands at river stops. In later years, the car wasn't there. Where did it go? The short answer is that the little car accidentally went overboard at Memphis. One day someone forgot to set the brakes, and over the side it fell. The long answer is more fun. According to Don Deming—who at various times worked as cruise director, lecturer, and public relations director—the car died a proud mariner's death and received a wake with flowers and a burial at sea. Betty Blake, never one to miss a public relations opportunity, had quickly decided to get some mileage out of the mishap. The VW was posthumously awarded the rank of honorary First Mate. Then crew and passengers gathered for a wake. They mourned the passing of their little friend, sipped champagne, and listened solemnly as Capt. Wagner bid his car a sad farewell.

In 1979 Betty Blake made a personal decision. The new vessel had been oper-

At left, the
Delta Queen
begins the
1992 Great
Steamboat Race
at New Orleans;
that's the
Mississippi
Queen *in back.*
At right, a race
with Belle of
Louisville.

ating for three years, and the extension for the old one still had several years to go. Many of the challenges she had faced were gone now. After 17 years with Greene Line and The Delta Queen Steamboat Co., she decided to leave. She resigned as president and opened her own public relations business, handling many different river clients, including the steamer *Natchez* at New Orleans. Unfortunately, just three years later, she lost a battle with cancer and died at the age of 51. Betty Blake was mourned up and down the river and remembered for her brilliant efforts in saving the *Delta Queen*.

The excitement that reigned along the Mississippi in 1979 when the First Family rode the *Delta Queen* was shared daily with the rest of the country via newspapers, radio, and television. And from August 17, when President Jimmy Carter, his wife Rosalynn, and daughter Amy went aboard at St. Paul until arrival at St. Louis, thousands of Americans lined the riverbank. Secret Service agents had their hands full, checking all bridges en route before the *Queen* was allowed to pass. *Air Force One,* the President's airplane, stood by during the trip—first at St. Paul, then at Moline, Illinois, and finally at St. Louis. Radio code for the *Queen* became "Steamboat One." Don Deming recalls that the President and the First Lady stayed on the Sun Deck, aft near the paddle wheel. "It's a hard room to get to from outside without being seen," he says, "so it was good for the President's security." According to Deming, at mealtime the President and Mrs. Carter ate at different tables so every passenger got to eat at least one meal with the First Family.

President Jimmy Carter and First Lady Rosalynn Carter wave during 1979 cruise down the Mississippi on the Delta Queen.

President Carter wasn't the only celebrity to have traveled on the *Delta Queen* in her years east of the Rockies. Passengers have included Lady Bird Johnson, Supreme Court Justice William O. Douglas, Helen Hayes, Princess Margaret of Great Britain—and Chief Justice of the United States Earl Warren, who, in his California days as state Attorney General, had closed down slot machines on the *King* and *Queen*.

Two notable happenings took place early in the decade following Carter's trip. In the early 1980s, Sam Zell and his partner Bob Lurie, both of Chicago, acquired control of the company's outstanding stock. For the next two decades, a rather complex ownership ensued, involving various companies and trusts controlled by Zell and Lurie's heirs. Soon after these new principals came on the scene, the *Delta Queen* won another extension to operate, this one good until 1988 (later extended to 1993, then 1998, more recently to 2008).

In 1985, the river community was saddened when Letha Greene passed away. Letha, who had shared the early excitement of owning the *Queen* with husband Tom, was buried next to him on a slope near the Ohio. Also in 1985, a big geographic change took place, when the company moved its headquarters from Cincinnati on the Ohio to New Orleans, near the mouth of the Mississippi. But,

THE INAUGURATION OF U. S. MAIL SERVICE
BY AMERICA'S ONLY RIVER PACKET
STEAMER DELTA QUEEN

Tom Sawyer

DELTA QUEEN
STEAMBOAT MAIL

United States 8c

Departing Cincinnati September 27th, 1971
with Mail Stops at St. Louis, Hannibal,
Muscatine, La Crosse, St. Paul, Winona,
Nauvoo, Memphis, Vicksburg, Natchez,
with Arrival in New Orleans Nov. 12th, 1971.

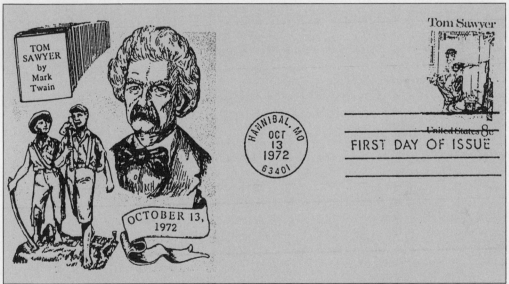

TOM SAWYER by Mark Twain

OCTOBER 13, 1972

Tom Sawyer

United States 8c

FIRST DAY OF ISSUE

HANNIBAL, MO
OCT
13
1972
63401

Delta Queen's U.S. mail service (top)
starts in 1971 and is highlighted a year
later at ceremonies for the first-day issue
of a new stamp in Hannibal, Mo. That
day included a speech by Tricia Nixon
Cox and honors for Capt. Ernest Wagner.
Big 1990 milestone (right): 100 years
of service since the company began as
Greene Line Steamers.

THE DELTA QUEEN STEAMBOAT CO.
1890 100TH 1990
ANNIVERSARY

acknowledging the *Delta Queen*'s long-standing connection with Cincinnati, the inscription over her paddle wheel remained "Port of Cincinnati, Ohio."

Less than a year after the *Delta King* celebrated its 1989 grand opening in California, The Delta Queen Steamboat Co. began celebrating its 100th anniversary on the other side of the Continental Divide. A century had passed since Gordon C. Greene founded Greene Line Steamers. Starting out as a deckhand, he had saved enough money by 1890 to buy his own boat. From that purchase came the most prominent name in passenger and freight service on the Ohio.

Throughout 1990, the company paddlewheelers—the two *Queens*—offered special cruises in a salute to the "Golden Age of Steam." The firm held open houses at New Orleans and at various ports of call. Period costumes, steamboating tall tales, and make-believe riverboat gamblers created an atmosphere of fun and frolic. Mark Twain, portrayed by actor Roger Durrett, charmed passengers and shoreside viewers alike. And to commemorate the centennial, The Delta Queen Steamboat Co. held a rechristening ceremony for its two vessels.

Indeed, from its beginnings a century before, Greene Line Steamers had grown and had become the company bearing the name of a legendary steamboat, the incomparable *Delta Queen*.

21

Irrepressible River Royalty

Following the *Delta Queen*'s 1990 season and celebration of the company's 100th anniversary, the historic steamboat went into drydock for the most drastic structural changes since her original construction in California.

Over the years, as more and more heavy equipment had been loaded onto the *Queen*—air conditioning units, large generators, and refrigeration—she sat lower and lower in the river. The draft of the boat, originally six to seven feet, had increased to nine, causing the paddle wheel to sit too low in the water. The wheel was 24 to 30 inches too deep, and its efficiency suffered. Naval architects came up with a solution: During the annual winter layover, they would install a new, wider and deeper hull to give the craft more buoyancy. But, rather than remove the old hull to install a new one, they decided to leave all but the aft 30 feet of the old one intact and wrap the new wider hull around it. Gulf Coast Fabricators at Pearlington, Mississippi, began the work in December 1990. When the major overhaul, with other minor alterations, was complete the following March, the tab came to $3.4 million.

The *Queen*'s new double hull became a big topic of conversation along the river in 1991. How would the new hull affect the boat? What would it do to her speed and performance? The new hull turned out to have several advantages and only a few minor disadvantages. Not only does it lift the vessel up for more efficient paddle-wheel operation, but it also gives more space for storing bunker C fuel oil for the boilers, diesel oil for the generators, and drinking water for passengers and crew. These larger capacities allow the *Queen* to cruise much longer between stops for water and refueling. Also the double hull gives an extra safety

Passengers enjoy calliope music on Sun Deck. Left photo shows Capt. Gabriel Chengery, Delta Queen master since 1976. In right photo, John Burns stands next to Capt. John Davitt in 1991. It's Burns' first time aboard since serving on King and Queen in California 55 years before.

margin should she strike an underwater object. As another bonus, because she's heavier, the *Queen* is less affected by cross winds.

As for speed, what has been lost due to added weight is almost compensated for by extra buoyancy and more efficient operation. The maximum rpm of the paddle wheel has increased, keeping the *Queen* competitive at race time. A disadvantage of the *Queen*'s new hull is purely aesthetic—she has lost her girlish figure. Instead of a hull that curves inward, it now goes almost straight down from the guard rail. But, as the hull is black, your eye goes first to the white superstructure above. And to borrow a thought from the March 1991 *S & D Reflector*—the quarterly publication of the Sons and Daughters of Pioneer Rivermen—the new below-the-waist broadening of the *Queen* "befits a dignified dowager."

In 1992, a new topic took over conversations along the river. The Delta Queen Steamboat Co. announced plans to build a big new sternwheeler—the company's third overnight passenger steamboat, even larger than the *Mississippi Queen*. In fact, the company touted the new *American Queen* as the largest river steamer in history. It was built at McDermott Shipyard in Amelia, Louisiana, and was ready for the maiden voyage in June 1995. As a new hybrid, the craft sports both a paddle wheel driven by steam and a 360-degree propulsion system powered by diesel-electric motors (known as a Z-drive). Total cost was $65 million.

The *Delta Queen*'s schedule in 1992 included her first cruise on the Tennessee-Tombigbee Waterway between Chattanooga, Tennessee and Mobile, Alabama. In October she participated at Tall Stacks, the second such celebration to be held at Cincinnati (the third came in 1995, the fourth in 1999; the fifth took place in 2003). Tall Stacks brings together a large gathering of riverboats for several days of river fun and races. The highlight of 1992 for many *Delta Queen* fans, however, proved to be an August cruise. It celebrated the venerable steamboat's 65th birthday and included a trip to St. Charles on the Missouri River. Her entrance into the mouth of the Missouri came at dusk and was punctuated by fireworks, heralding the first time she had ever cruised that river.

On that trip I was pleased to see Helen Prater, daughter of the late Jesse P. Hughes, and his granddaughter, Lillian Prater Smith. Capt. Hughes, who began his steamboat career in 1891 and died in 1973 at age 96, worked for the Greene Line longer than any other person. As the *Delta Queen* turned from the Mississippi into the mouth of the Missouri, where the two river currents swirled together, Mrs. Smith wiped away a tear. Later she explained to me that she had been thinking of her beloved grandfather and wondering what his feelings might have been, had he been there to experience the moment.

Following the Missouri River jaunt, luck was with the *Queen,* when she managed to avoid what was called the most destructive natural disaster in U.S. history to that time. Keeping to her scheduled itinerary, she headed north up the Mississippi River, rather than downstream where Hurricane Andrew hit just four days later. By the time the storm reached the lower river, the *Delta Queen,* with her vulnerable wooden superstructure, was cruising far out of harm's way near Dubuque, Iowa. The other company boat, the *Mississippi Queen,* was not so fortunate. Caught on the lower river with high winds and rough water, she was forced to tie up at Baton Rouge. Her passengers disembarked early, ending the trip 130 miles short of their destination at New Orleans. But the all-steel vessel escaped without damage and was back in service as soon as winds subsided.

In addition to avoiding the storm, the *Delta Queen* also missed a small earthquake that shook Missouri after she left. Not surprising, though. Avoiding a hurricane and an earthquake seemed like just another day in the life of the celebrated lady of the waterways, who has proven herself an irrepressible survivor for three-quarters of a century.

Next year came the Great Flood of '93, another major disaster. At St. Louis, the Mississippi River reached a record level of almost 50 feet and a flow of over one million cubic feet per second, a massive deluge of water described by some as a 500-year flood. All navigation on the upper Mississippi came to a standstill. During weeks of high water, the two company boats continued to provide service but in other areas: the Ohio, lower Mississippi, Tennessee, and Cumberland—rivers not at flood stage.

In October 1992, the river community along the Mississippi and the Ohio—and steamboat fans across the nation—were saddened when Frederick Way, Jr., died in Marietta, Ohio, at the age of 91. As legendary patriarch of the river and foremost riverboat historian in the country, Capt. Way drew from his experience as both captain and pilot. He authored several books and edited the *S & D Reflector,* as well as towboat and river-packet directories. Since Capt. Way had been in charge of arrangements for bringing the *Delta Queen* from California to the Mississippi and the Ohio in 1947, he had a strong connection to the boat. After his death, with her flag flying at half-mast, the *Queen* had the solemn duty of picking up his ashes in Marietta and delivering them to Sewickley, Pennsylvania, his hometown. The *Mississippi Queen,* the *Belle of Louisville,* and the *Natchez* also flew their flags at half-mast.

In 1995, two bold new *Delta Queen* cruises were offered. One went from New Orleans, via the Gulf Intracoastal Waterway, to Galveston, Texas. The other went up the Arkansas River to Tulsa, Oklahoma, the farthest west the *Delta Queen* had traveled since leaving California almost half a century before.

The highlight of 1997 was the special Anniversary Cruise from New Orleans to St. Louis, celebrating the *Delta Queen*'s 70th birthday and the 50th anniversary of her arrival on the Mississippi in 1947. On that trip, Huell Howser came aboard to produce an episode for his PBS television show, which would also include the newsreel of a 1930s *Delta Queen* steamboat race in California. 1999 brought two unique trips: a 14-night cruise retracing the 1811 route of the historic *New Orleans,* first steamboat to travel from Pittsburgh to New Orleans—and, a grand finale to the 20th century, the Millennium Cruise that began in late December 1999 and ended in January 2000.

The dawn of the 21st century found Delta Queen Steamboat Company and its parent, American Classic Voyages Co., in the midst of great expansion. By 2001, despite a soft economy and lagging passenger sales, the organization had forged ahead with new sea-going vessels and plans for building more. Then came the tragic events of September 11, 2001—terrorist attacks on the World Trade Center and the Pentagon. Five weeks later, the company filed for Chapter 11.

In the spring of 2002, the *Delta Queen, Mississippi Queen,* and *American Queen* were purchased in a bankruptcy auction for $80 million by the Delaware North Companies of Buffalo, New York. This century-old firm, which operates many travel-related businesses, kept New Orleans as home port and continued the popular cruise plan of on-board lectures and shore tours by day, with entertainment at night—all, as before, without offering gambling on the boats.

Out of service from January to August 2002, the *Delta Queen* experienced her longest layover since coming to the Mississippi 55 years before. On August 26, she resumed service with a cruise from New Orleans, celebrating her new lease on life in her 75th anniversary year. In January 2004, a new honor came to the *Delta Queen* when she was inducted into the 2003 National Maritime Hall of Fame.

Two able captains alternately share the duties of *Delta Queen* master. Capt. Gabriel Chengery began as night watchman in 1968 and worked his way up to chief purser, first mate, and relief pilot—and, in 1976, became master of the *Queen.* "Capt. Gabe" has visited the *Delta King* in Sacramento several times. Two of those visits came in the early 1970s, soon after the "piracy," when he was appalled by the condition of the boat. He was pleasantly surprised, however, when he returned 20 years later to see the restored vessel and stay overnight.

The other master of the *Delta Queen* is Capt. Mike Williams, who began his river career as a teenager working on excursion boats at St. Louis. One day in 1981, he visited the *Queen,* immediately fell in love with the boat, and was hired as a carpenter on a cruise leaving that night. Over the years since then, Capt. Williams became a second mate, first mate, and eventually got his pilot's license. In 1996, he earned his master's license—and, three years later, began working as master on the *Delta Queen.*

Passengers riding on the *Delta Queen* often get hooked on the vintage steamer. Sometimes it takes a few days—sometimes it happens the first time they set eyes on her. Many return for repeat trips; a few come back dozens of times. In the early 1990s, Bobbie Meyer of St. Louis held the record among recent passengers for most cruises taken. But by 2001 it appeared that she had been overtaken by two *Delta Queen* fans with at least one hundred trips each: Pat Sullivan and Ann Zeiger, both from Cincinnati.

People get sentimental about the *Queen,* a survivor from another era. Emotions ran high more than three decades ago when her future looked dismal. During that period, a disembarking passenger wrote an anonymous poem about the trip just completed. The verse described the sights and sounds—unforgettable images of stained-glass windows, teakwood, shiny brass hardware, green shores slipping quietly past the rail—the piercing notes of the calliope, the steam whistle's deep tones, the splash of the paddle wheel. The poem concluded:

> *Too soon our trip had ended,*
> *We had docked at St. Louis.*
> *Time to go down the gangplank*
> *And onto the cobblestones.*
>
> *I felt I was saying goodbye to a loved one*
> *Who, like a favorite aunt getting along in years,*
> *Might not be around for long.*
> *I realized I'd likely not see her again.*
>
> *I started up the levee, then stopped*
> *To look back once more for a final view.*
> *I stood for a moment till I felt the tears begin,*
> *Then turned toward town and the long trip home.*

The *Delta Queen* isn't the only one of the irrepressible twin riverboats to inspire poetry. At Sacramento, the *Delta King*'s restaurant menu for several years carried this verse written by Edmund McKnight Campbell:

> *Welcome aboard the Delta King,*
> *Come spend the hours remembering,*
> *When life moved at a slower pace,*
> *And people valued charm and grace.*
>
> *The days when life was in its prime,*
> *And no one feared the thief called Time,*
> *When every heart was made to feel,*
> *The romance of the paddle wheel.*

When the *Delta King* opened to the public as a floating hotel and conference center in 1989, it quickly became the meeting place for groups with earlier connections to the boat. In July of that year, the "pirates" who had abducted the *King* from Stockton in 1969 held their 20th anniversary reunion aboard the vessel. Geoff Wong and Tom Horton, two of the prime movers in the adventure, attended along with more than a dozen other people who had kept Riverboat's Comin' alive almost four years at Sacramento. Adding spice to the reunion party, guest Rod Shepherd, partner in Melvin Belli's law firm, presented "legal documents" declaring Belli's claim to "ownership and title and right to possession of the vessel *Delta King*" and stating that Belli had been "unlawfully deprived of said vessel through larceny, fraud and deceit." After serving the papers, Shepherd tried to keep a straight face as he made a beeline for the hors d'oeuvres table.

The same month, those intrepid souls who had taken "The Last Voyage" from the Bay Area to Sacramento in 1984 celebrated the fifth anniversary of that trip. On board for the party were Walt and Joanna Harvey, Hal Schell, and a score of helpers from the "work crew." After a buffet dinner, they cut a large cake that had an artist's rendition of the *Delta King* in the frosting.

In October 1989, the Delta Queen-Delta King Plankowners held their 49th anniversary reunion aboard the *King*. Plankowner members are Navy reservists who reported for active duty in 1940 aboard either of the two boats on San Francisco Bay. For many years, the group met at Treasure Island, but now members were able to get together in a new and even more appropriate setting. Not

1989 saw a reunion of men who served on the King or Queen as Navy reservists 1940-41; front left, Carl Heynen. In left photo, observing 20th anniversary of King's 1969 "piracy," are Geoff Wong, Tom Horton, and Dan Clarke.

The McCords honeymoon in '39, return to King in '89. Card honors 50th anniversary.

1939   1989

Annabell and Glen

only was this the first time they held their reunion on the *King*, but it was the first time most had set foot on either vessel since World War II.

It wasn't just groups and organizations that were drawn to the newly-restored *Delta King;* it was also individuals, many of them remembering the twin vessels from bygone days in California. Typical was Betty McFerren, to whom the boats were familiar sights at Sacramento in the 1930s. Soon after the opening, she and her husband Bill enjoyed a weekend at the hotel on the *King*. Then in the years that followed, she fulfilled a half-century's dream by taking Mississippi and Ohio River cruises on the *Delta Queen*. She said, "It felt like coming home."

The historic boat added much new life and excitement to the Old Sacramento waterfront. On the weekend after its grand opening, the *King* served as one of the sites for bands performing at the annual Sacramento Jazz Jubilee—an event that had its beginnings on the decks of the same vessel, at the same city, 20 years before. The jazz festival continues to use the boat as one of its venues each year. A month after the 1989 Jubilee, the craft became one of the main attractions at a weekend celebration and dedication of the city's new riverfront park, a public area that re-created part of the waterfront as it was in the early days of Sacramento.

A mysterious event took place on the *King* in 1989. A little after 5 o'clock on the afternoon of October 17, the boat began a gentle, rocking motion at its moorings. Normally, the vessel sits with no discernible movement. What could it be? The mystery cleared up shortly. Radio and TV news bulletins reported widespread damage in the San Francisco Bay Area from the Loma Prieta earthquake. Seismic shock waves from the epicenter, more than a hundred miles away, had reached the *Delta King*. But they were minor—the quake did no damage in Sacramento.

Soon after the grand opening, the Delta King Theatre began offering entertainment. "An Evening with Mark Twain" came first. Later offerings included "Tune the Grand Up," a review of Broadway tunes by Jerry Herman. Tim Busfield produced and acted in his own show, and Pat Paulsen, the perennial presidential candidate of Smothers Brothers TV fame, made an appearance. In recent years, the Suspects Murder Mystery Theatre has been giving an interactive comedy performance while guests enjoy dinner on the boat.

Since its opening, the *King* has had a number of notable visitors, including California governors Gray Davis, Pete Wilson, George Deukmejian, and Jerry Brown (later, Mayor of Oakland); also former Speaker of the Assembly, Willie Brown (later, Mayor of San Francisco). Attorney Melvin Belli spent the night aboard two decades after his unique battle with the *Delta King* "pirates."

Ownership and management changed in 1989. After the opening, Ed Coyne stepped down as president of Riverboat Delta King, Inc. His brother Charlie took over and, two years later, also became general manager. Mike Coyne continued as vice-president and assistant general manager (later to become general manager in 2004). Then, in the fall of 1989, the Coyne family became sole owners of the *King,* when they bought out the interest of Walter and Joanna Harvey.

To celebrate the 65th anniversary of the original dedication of the *King* and *Queen,* the Coynes hosted a party aboard the sternwheeler on May 20, 1992. It had been 65 years to the day. That date also marked the third anniversary of the *King*'s grand opening, again to the actual day. Guests included people who had traveled on the two boats back in the 1920s and '30s, when the craft ran nightly between San Francisco and Sacramento. They reminisced about their trips.

"Friends had sprinkled rice on our sheets," said Annabell McCord, as she told about her honeymoon on the *Delta King* with husband Glen in July 1939.

Ron Davis told of riding the *King* and *Queen* to the world's fair on Treasure Island: "I was a student at Sacramento JC. Couldn't afford a cabin, so I slept in the lounge—only $1.95 round trip."

Ylene was the bride, Gene the groom, when the McMillans honeymooned on the *King* in 1937. Ylene recalled her fond memories by writing new words to an old tune: She called the song "Sentimental Journey on the Delta King."

Ten years after the above 1992 get-together, the Coynes again hosted a special party aboard. On June 2, 2002, they celebrated the 75th anniversary of the *Delta King*'s arrival at Sacramento on its maiden voyage in 1927. Invited guests had played their individual roles in the *King*'s colorful history: Herb Rummel, the only surviving crew member from the boat's service in the 1920s and 30s; Tony Rigoni, who lived aboard during the *King*'s landlocked years in Canada (1950s); Geoff Wong and Jerry Vorpahl of *Delta King* "piracy" fame (1969–74); and Joanna Harvey, designer of the interiors during the boat's restoration (1980s). Honoring the *Delta King*'s adventurous life after three-quarters of a century, the party was rich with nostalgia and good cheer.

In fall 2002, the *Delta King* passed a milestone: The vessel had been established as a floating hotel at Sacramento longer than it had operated as an overnight boat between San Francisco and the capital city. It seems this historic California steamboat has become an integral part of the Sacramento waterfront.

22

Echoes from the Past

"Last year for the King and Queen?" That leading question headlined an article in the January 1970 issue of *Sunset,* a magazine of western travel and lifestyle. While not definitive, the answer given by the publication implied a future with little hope. The story reported on "the rotting hulk of the *Delta King,* prematurely aged by vandalism and neglect." And it said that, while the *Delta Queen* still operated, her days were numbered: "She will carry passengers until November 2; then . . . she will be retired."

As we know now, such early reports on the deaths of the two sternwheelers—if not "greatly exaggerated"—at least turned out to be premature. Due to the efforts of countless people along the way and a generous helping of luck, both vessels survived against the odds.

Although the boats have led totally different lives since they went their separate ways, they easily could have switched places and nearly did. After World War II, only a twist of fate kept the legendary twins from playing roles opposite the parts they eventually played. Had Capt. Tom Greene been successful with his first bid in 1946—an offer on the *Delta King*—almost certainly the vessels' roles would be reversed today. The *King* would be cruising the Mississippi and the Ohio, while applying for periodic extensions. The *Queen,* meanwhile, undoubtedly would have suffered through hell and high water from California to Canada and back again. By now, she would have been restored and given a new life as a floating hotel at Old Sacramento.

A look at the "last trips" of these boats reminds us again that we never really know the future. When the *King* and *Queen* made their final runs from San

Francisco to Sacramento in 1940, no fanfare marked their departures or arrivals. Passengers and crew looked upon these voyages as merely the last of the season. Because no one knew the two riverboats were making their final appearance as passenger and freight carriers on California waters, no one mourned the loss. On the other hand, the *Queen*'s "Farewell Forever" cruise to New Orleans in 1970, billed as her last trip, caused great excitement and aroused strong emotions. Yet, ironically, it wasn't her last. More than a third of a century later, the *Delta Queen* still reigns on the river.

But most important, both these historic paddle-wheel steamers still exist. In quite different ways, they are available for us to enjoy today. If you are familiar with the history of the boats and feel a fondness for them, interesting things can happen. When conditions are right, it's possible, with the help of your imagination, to go back in time for a glimpse of the vessels' earlier lives.

The feeling of being in touch with a bygone era may come suddenly upon returning to the *Delta Queen* from a shore stop or while walking her decks. Almost anything can trigger the sensation: smoke from her stack, the steam whistle's deep tones, the splash of her paddle wheel. A good time to catch these echoes from the past is late at night or early in the morning, when it's quiet with no one around. When traveling on the *Queen*, try getting up early one day, well before sunrise and before anyone else is out on deck. Observe a timeless scene as the sky lightens and riverbank shapes begin to take form through the early-morning mist.

A similar sense of history can be felt at Sacramento, where the *Delta King* sits proudly at the dock. Experience the ambience. Try walking the decks at midnight. Enjoy the lights from the two bridges and their reflections on the moving water. Or rent a stateroom and, after a night's sleep, rise before the sun. If your timing is right, off the port side you'll see a full moon as it sinks behind the western shore. And if a dense fog is hugging the river, remember this is what pilots of the *Delta* boats had to deal with on many a long night in the 1920s and '30s.

If you're driving home after visiting the *King* or another Sacramento attraction, take a side trip south along the river. You'll be following the route the two sternwheelers traveled each night in their youth; most of the way the road runs atop the levee. Visit a river town or two. Stop at Locke, where rickety two-story wooden structures, built by the Chinese, still stand. Or drive to Ryde, where the old hotel that once operated as a speakeasy still sits behind the levee. Picture, in your mind's eye, how the river might have looked when the boats passed by on their nightly runs.

If it's quiet and you have time, find a spot on the riverbank. Relax. Sit and let your mind wander; allow your imagination and emotions to run free for a moment. Absorb the sights, sounds, and smells around you. Then listen—see if you can hear a steamboat whistle in the distance. And see if you can catch sight of the *Delta King* or the *Delta Queen* coming around the bend.

Credits for Photos

and Other Graphics

Bill Alonzo: 87(M); R. Valentine Atkinson: 196(T); Capt. Robert W. Atthowe Collection: 50 (T); Bank of Stockton Photo Collection: 31(B), 82, 143(T) (B); Bill Bean: 131(BL); John Burns Collection: 30(T) photo taken by (his father) James Burns, 33(B) taken by James Burns, 119(T) taken by John Burns; California State Library: 8(T) (B), 10(T), 20-21, 38-39, 44(B), 45(B), 67(BR), 76((B); Cincinnati Enquirer: 229 "Delta Queen sails..." and "Run aground..."; Cincinnati Historical Society: 220(BL), 228(R), 229(BL); Public Library of Cincinnati & Hamilton County: 222; William T. Cooley Collection: 50(B); Joe Cornyn: 92(BR); Michael Coyne: 200(B), 205 (all), 207(M); Daily Colonist, Victoria, B.C.: 131(T) (BR); Delta Queen Steamboat Co.: 220(BR), 230 James Stanfield, 232-33(R), 234, 239 (logo), 242(BL) Jackson Hill, Southern Lights Photography; Myrtle Duensing Collection: 80(T); George Fay Collection: 31(T); Ray W. Fisher: 63(TL) (TR); Stan Garvey: Author's Collection: 40, 76(TL) (TR), 85(L), 91, 159(M), 170(B), 171 (all), 239 (T) (M); Photos by author: 188-89 (all), 196(M) (B), 197 (all), 200(T), 207(T) (B), 210(TR) (M) (BL) (BR), 216-17 (all), 236, 248(T) (M); Greene Line Steamers: 232(L); Library-Archives Collection, The Haggin Museum, Stockton: 30(B); Stan Haynes Collection: 92(BL); Carl Heynen Collection: 96(T) (BL) (BR); Holt-Atherton, UOP Library: 102(B); Arthur W. Hormel Collection: 109 Oakland Tribune; Gene Johnson Collection: 108, 228(B); Andrew J. Lodder: 123(TR) (B); Robert Lodder: 14(T) (B); Linda Mahrt: 242(T); Annabell and Glen McCord Collection: 248(BL) (BR); Betty McFerren: 242(BR); Modesto Bee: 138(M) (B); Bea Morgan: 176(BR); Murphy Library, University of Wisconsin, La Crosse: 31(M) John Burns Collection, 119(B) Frederick Way, Jr., 123(TL), 220(T) Delta Queen Steamboat Co., 237 Frederick Way, Jr., 238 Delta Queen Steamboat Co.; Robert W. Parkinson Collection: 85(R), 138 (ad); Richard J. Perry Collection: 92(ML); Gordon W. Ridley: 55(BL); Glenn Rudolph Collection: 104(B); Herb J. Rummel: 56(T); Dick Rutter: 182(TR); Sacramento Archives & Museum Collection Center: 33(T), 44(M), 51, 55(T), 63(B), 67(T), 83, 102(T), 153(B) Sacramento Bee, 159(TL) Sac Bee, 162(B) Sac Bee, 176(BL) Sac Bee; Sacramento Bee: 159(TR); Sacramento Public Library: 72(T); Sacramento Union: 153(TL), 158(R) Jerry Rainbolt, 159(B), 162(T), 166(T) (B), 170(T), 210(TL) Bryan Patrick, 229(TR); San Francisco Chronicle: 176(T), 228(TL), 229(TL); San Francisco Maritime National Historical Park: 45(M), 75(T) Proctor Collection, 75(B), 80(B) Associated Press, 87(B) Oakland Tribune, 136(B) San Francisco Chronicle; San Mateo Public Library: 73; Hal Schell Collection: 34 (ticket); Grandon Sherman Seal: 55(BR); Society of California Pioneers: 5(T) Roy Graves Collection; Stockton Record: 34 (cartoon and ad), 182(TL); Bill Stritzel Collection: Front cover photo, 17, 18-19, 44(T), 67 (ticket), 87(TR), 182(B); Dorothy Sweeney Collection: 56(B); Harry Sweet Collection: 35, 45(T); Treasure Island Museum: 92(T), 104(T); Jerry Vorpahl Collection: 158(L); Fred Way Collection: 136(T); Ted Wurm Collection: 5(B).

Location on page: T = top, M = middle, B = bottom, L = left, R = right

Acknowledgments

This book, as it exists today, would never have been possible without the wonderful help I received over the past decade. I'm especially indebted to the following articulate and knowledgeable river historians, journalists, and steamboat enthusiasts who spent many hours of their time reading the manuscript and offering suggestions: Richard E. Brown, Jack Oglesby, Bill Stritzel, Robert W. Parkinson, Dick Rutter, Jim Swift, and Martin Litton. And special thanks to George W. Hilton, Professor Emeritus of Economics, UCLA, for his astute counsel and for writing the foreword to the book.

I owe a debt of gratitude to Karl Kortum, founder of the San Francisco Maritime National Historical Park, for his fine help and encouragement. Many thanks also to the following, whose knowledge of the two boats came from their firsthand experience in the 1920s and '30s: John Burns, who worked as fireman on both steamers and whose father supervised their construction; Capt. Robert W. Atthowe and his mother Marie Atthowe (his father piloted both vessels and his grandfather was captain of the *Delta King);* three former crew members, who worked close to the boats' nerve center as freight clerks and assistant pursers—Ray Fisher, Gordon Ridley, and Herb Rummel; and Eldridge "Jim" Bowie, the *Delta Queen*'s last purser in California.

Special thanks to Herb Caen for excerpts from his columns in the *San Francisco Chronicle.* Thanks also to the following: Stanford University Press for excerpts from *Paddle-Wheel Days in California* by Jerry MacMullen; Richard Reinhardt for excerpts from his book, *Treasure Island;* George Fay, whose father and grandfather were among the founders of River Lines, for supplying background material on that organization; Carl O. Heynen, Jr., for details on the period preceding Pearl Harbor when Navy reservists lived aboard the two boats; Branwell Fanning for excerpts from his book, *The Wartime Adventures of the Delta Queen;* Tony Rigoni for providing a firsthand account of the *Delta King*'s years at Kitimat, B.C.; Melvin Belli, Geoffrey Wong, and Jerry Vorpahl for sharing their memories of the 1969 "piracy" of the *King* and Tom Horton for excerpts, dealing with that episode, from his spirited columns and news stories that ran in the

Sacramento Union; Robert Taylor for relating his experiences with the sunken *Delta King* at Richmond in the early 1980s; the Coyne family and Walter and Joanna Harvey for their cooperation in allowing me full access to the *King* during the restoration years at Sacramento.

To those people who so generously provided missing pieces to the postwar story of the *Delta Queen,* a special "Thank you": Bee and J.W. "Woody" Rutter, Don Deming, Russell Dale Flick, Pat Sullivan, John Weise, Helen Prater, Lillian Prater Smith, Robert Lodder, M'Lissa Kesterman, Ralph DuPae, Tom Greene, Jr., Patti Young, Capt. C.W. Stoll, Capt. Alan L. Bates, Capt. Clarke "Doc" Hawley, Capt. Gabriel Chengery, Jim Way, Fred Way III, and the late Capt. Fred Way, Jr.

I would like to acknowledge the information, photographs, and assistance received from the San Francisco Maritime National Historical Park, the San Francisco Public Library, the Sacramento Archives & Museum Collection Center, the California State Library at Sacramento, The Haggin Museum at Stockton, the National Archives at San Bruno, the Bank of Stockton Photo Collection, the Murphy Library at University of Wisconsin/La Crosse, the Cincinnati Historical Society, and the Public Library of Cincinnati & Hamilton Co.

I'm particularly appreciative of the long hours spent by my friend and former co-worker Sam Connery in editing the manuscript. And in bringing it all together, I'm thankful for the excellent assistance I received from my design consultant Bill Cheney, production manager Fred Sandsmark, illustrator Lucy I. Sargeant, indexing coordinator Pat Atthowe, and printing consultant Chet Grycz. Thanks to Caroline Beverstock, Mary Ann Irvine, and Bobbie Burri for their critical readings and to publishers Hal Schell and Dick Murdock for their help and encouragement. My apologies to any person or organization I may have overlooked from the many that contributed to the creation of this book.

Finally, I want to thank the former passengers who shared their priceless stories from those trips of long ago, tales of life and travel aboard the two historic riverboats.

S. G.

Appendix

A Good Manager

In the shipbuilding world of the 1920s, it was unusual for a company to be involved in the construction of its own boats as the C.T. Co. was with the *Delta King* and *Delta Queen*. It was also uncommon to have such a project supervised by someone whose primary experience was not in shipbuilding. But Jim Burns, born in Ireland in 1863, had a background that served him well—his "hands on" knowledge of iron-ship building from an apprenticeship in Scotland and his engineering experience gained later in this country. He also had highly-professional technicians and shipwrights reporting to him.

Burns was fortunate to have Louie Cinnamond, a skilled woodworker from Scotland, as foreman and lead finish carpenter. Through careful supervision and his own personal craftsmanship, Cinnamond was responsible for all the beautiful wood interiors, including the fine paneling, built-in seating, and grand staircases.

Jim Burns proved himself a good manager and had a minimum of problems building the *King* and *Queen*. According to his son John Burns, although the boats were costly, the C.T. Co. built them for much less than they would have cost at an outside shipyard

Focus on Construction

Scotland to Stockton: It's occasionally said that the *King* and *Queen* were built in Scotland. Some "purists" agree with that premise, since the galvanized-steel hull plates and other steel parts were manufactured by William Denny & Brothers, Ltd. at Dumbarton, Scotland. And they argue that this part of a boat is the *important* part—in other words, the heart and soul of the vessel. Others, who might call themselves "realists," have a different viewpoint. They say the steamers were built in *this* country, because all steel components were shipped to Stockton, California, and were assembled there. Furthermore, they point out, the massive wooden superstructures, four decks high, were built entirely by craftsmen at Stockton. In any case, work on the boats at Stockton began in late 1924 and continued until spring 1927. The shipyard was on the north side of the channel at the foot of Harrison Street.

After steel hull plates and other structural components were fabricated in Scotland, workmen bolted them all together to be sure of correct size and fit. The men then carefully numbered, disassembled, and shipped them by freighter to San Francisco. From the bay, barges carried them up the San Joaquin River to the shipyard at Stockton. There, workmen assembled the frames, bulkheads, and plates "by the numbers" and secured them with rivets.

CN&I Yard: Long before hull plates and other parts arrived at Stockton, Jim Burns, serving as superintendent of hulls and machinery, had the California Navigation and Improvement Company shipyard ready for the major work ahead (building a new wharf, enlarging the launching ways, and installing a 25-ton steam crane for lifting parts and machinery onto the boats).

Occasionally, people referred to the shipyard as the "C.T. Co. yard." While this was not technically correct at the time of the boats' construction, the C.T. Co. had owned the controlling interest in CN&I since 1922. The two companies formally merged in 1927, two months before the vessels began service.

Parts and Machinery: Some accounts suggest that the famous Krupp plant in Germany forged the paddle-wheel shafts and cranks, which were then machined in San Francisco. Steamboat enthusiast Russell Dale Flick reports that a recent search of the Krupp archives in Essen, West Germany, revealed no connection between that firm and the building of the *King* and *Queen*. He says, "Their archives were complete and apparently did not suffer from Allied bombing attacks during World War II."

One important clue points to Denny's in Scotland: A shipping list of March 9, 1925, shows the *Delta Queen*'s wheel shaft, with cranks attached, being sent from Denny's to San Francisco aboard the S.S. *London Importer*. Also listed on the same manifest were one high-pressure cylinder and one low-pressure cylinder for the *Queen*'s steam engine (shipping records for the *King*'s cylinders, shaft, and cranks have not been found). The Charles H. Evans Co. of San Francisco is credited with designing the engines and with installing them after they arrived from Scotland.

According to John Burns (son of Jim Burns), the C.T. Co. bought the boilers in Benicia, California, at a government auction of new-but-surplus machinery from World War I. He recalls that they were originally built for U.S. Navy destroyers. He also says the reason for having hull plates and machinery manufactured in

Scotland was because Denny's offered the best price in competitive bidding and, in addition, had a reputation for quality workmanship.

According to David John Lyon of the National Maritime Museum at Greenwich, England, in the 1870s Denny's built the first of a long series of shallow-draft steamers for tropical rivers. That form of construction rapidly became one of the firm's great specialties. Later, around the turn of the century, Denny's became generally known as the leading builder of cross-channel steamers. The company also achieved renown for its passenger liners, freighters, and destroyers (the latter built for the Dutch, Turkish, and British navies). Karl Kortum, founder of the San Francisco Maritime National Historical Park, describes Denny's clientele over many decades as "worldwide and exotic." As evidence, he cites the following list of the company's customers: Irrawaddy Flotilla Co., Peruvian Corp., the Sudan government, Russian Steam Navigation & Trading Co., United Africa Co., Nigerian Railways, China Navigation Co., and Lower Ganges Bridge & Eastern Bengal State Railway.

Innovations: Virtually all California riverboats had hulls of wood before the C.T. Co. built the *King* and *Queen* with galvanized-steel hulls. And according to naval architect David Seymour, the galvanizing of hull plates was expensive and not the usual practice for such boats in the 1920s. Apparently, Capt. Anderson wanted the very best for his royal pair.

The two new steamboats were designed to hold their shape from the strength of the steel structure in the hull and freight deck. Thus they did not need "hog chains," the utilitarian framework of posts and rods that stuck up above superstructures of boats with wooden hulls (to keep them from sagging at bow and stern).

According to river historian Richard E. Brown, the new riverboats were the first in California to have air-cooled staterooms—probably also the first in the country. Cooling was accomplished by forcing air through wet excelsior pads, a method that worked in the dry climate of interior California; it was called "washed air." Brown says, "While air-cooled staterooms did not come into general use on even the best of ocean liners until after World War II, the *King* and *Queen* offered this comfort in 1927."

Another departure from almost all other California riverboat design: The *King* and *Queen* were built with paddle-wheel covers to protect passengers from spray carried by gusts of wind and to minimize noise for sleepers (such covers were standard in the Pacific Northwest and British Columbia).

Original Specifications and Other Data

Overall length: 285 feet, including paddle wheel.

Hull length alone: 250 feet.

Beam: 58 feet.

Tonnage: 1,837 gross, 1,318 net (both refer to volume, not weight).

Draft: Approx. 6 to 8 feet depending upon load.

Engines: Cross-compound, condensing, double-expansion, horizontal, reciprocating steam engine; 26" high-pressure cylinder, 52" low-pressure cylinder; 10-foot stroke. Rated 2,000 horsepower. At 16 rpm, developed 1,500 horsepower.

Boilers: Two water-tube marine boilers, 225 pounds pressure; each fitted with four burners using bunker C fuel oil.

Smokestack: One stack just aft of pilothouse, divided into two sections (one for each boiler).

Paddle wheel: Stern wheel 26 feet, 4 inches, in diameter; just under 20 feet wide; 28 buckets, 28-inch dip; wood cover (with copper-sheathed sides) over wheel.

Rudders: Four steel rudders, forward of the wheel.

Speed: Rated at 15 mph maximum. Average speed in California service: 10-11 mph. (In 1939 race, both boats averaged under 12, but tide was against them part of distance.)

Hull: Galvanized-steel hull plates fabricated in Scotland; steel reinforcement up through top of freight deck.

Hold: Divided into seven watertight compartments by six steel bulkheads across the boat (see side-view chart on page 27).

Decks: Four—freight deck plus three passenger decks (see side-view chart and deck plans on pages 27-28).

Staterooms: 96 cabins, all with hot and cold running water, electric lights, and call buttons; 28 private or communicating baths plus public rest rooms.

Passengers: Approx. 200 capacity in cabins, plus space in chairs or on built-in seating; 42 men-only berths in hold. Up to 1,000 passengers for races and other day trips.

Freight: Approx. 1,000 tons of cargo (including freight and autos).

Lifeboats: Eight boats total, 3 on each side of Observation Deck (sometimes called Boat Deck) and 2 on bow house.

Schedule: Depart 6:30 p.m., arrive 5:30 a.m. (depart 6 p.m. late 1930s). Daily except Sunday in early years, seven days a week by mid-1930s. For brief period in early '30s, boats made Rio Vista stop but ran non-stop most of service period.

Fares: $1.80 one way, $3 round trip (early years); $1.50 and $1.95 (mid-1930s). Autos extra, $3.50 and $5. Cabins extra, $1 to $5. Men-only berths in hold, 50 cents (no passenger-deck access).

Distance: San Francisco to Sacramento via bay and river: some old records show 125 miles; current records indicate 108.

Construction: Hull and other steel components manufactured in Scotland by William Denny & Brothers, Ltd. Steel parts assembled at Stockton, California, where wooden superstructures were built by California Transportation Company, 1924-27, at the California Navigation and Improvement Company shipyard.

Service: Commercial passenger and freight service on the San Francisco-Sacramento run, June 1927 to September 1940.

Bibliography
and Other Readings

Andrist, Ralph K., *Steamboats on the Mississippi*, American Heritage, 1962

Curry, Jane, *The River's in My Blood*, University of Nebraska Press, 1983

Fanning, Branwell, *The Wartime Adventures of the Delta Queen*, The Delta Queen Steamboat Co., 1976

Flexner, James Thomas, *Steamboats Come True: American Inventors in Action*, The Viking Press, 1944

Gardner, Erle Stanley, *Gypsy Days on the Delta*, William Morrow & Company, Inc., 1967 (one item used in Chapter 12)

Gilliam, Harold, *San Francisco Bay*, Doubleday, 1957

Greene, Letha C., *Long Live the Delta Queen*, Hastings House, 1973

Harlan, George H., *San Francisco Bay Ferryboats*, Howell-North, 1967

Hilton, George W., *The Night Boat*, Howell-North, 1968

Hunter, Louis C., *Steamboats on the Western Rivers*, Harvard University Press, 1949

Keating, Bern, *The Legend of the Delta Queen*, The Delta Queen Steamboat Co., 1986

Kemble, John Haskell, *San Francisco Bay: A Pictorial Maritime History*, Cornell Maritime Press, 1957

Leale, Capt. John, *Recollections of a Tule Sailor*, George Fields, 1939

MacMullen, Jerry, *Paddle-Wheel Days in California*, Stanford University Press, 1944

Marx, Samuel, and Joyce Vanderveen, *Deadly Illusions*, Random House, 1990 (one incident used in Chapter 3)

Newell, Gordon, *Paddlewheel Pirate*, E.P. Dutton, 1959

Reinhardt, Richard, *Treasure Island: San Francisco's Exposition Years*, Scrimshaw Press, 1973

Samish, Arthur H., and Robert Thomas, *The Secret Boss of California*, Crown, 1971 (one incident used in Chapter 4)

Samuel, Ray, Leonard V. Huber, and Warren C. Ogden, *Tales of the Mississippi*, Hastings House, 1955

Schell, Hal, *Cruising California's Delta*, Schell Books, Stockton, CA, 1995

Twain, Mark (Samuel L. Clemens), *Life on the Mississippi*, Osgood & Co., 1883

Way, Frederick, Jr., *The Saga of the Delta Queen*, Young and Klein, Inc., 1951

Wayman, Norbury L., *Life on the River*, Crown Publishers, Inc., 1971

Index

Page numbers in italics indicate illustrations.

See next page for special references to the Delta King and Delta Queen.

Delta Queen